The Restless American

A Middle-aged Man on a Middle-aged Horse

THE
Restless American

A Middle-aged Man on a Middle-aged Horse

BY TOM POWELL

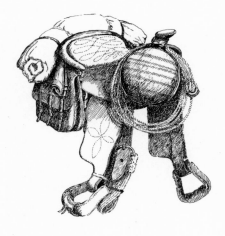

With illustrations by the author

LITTLE, BROWN AND COMPANY   *Boston • Toronto*

To Charles H. Eden —
horse artilleryman, attorney-at-law, father of my wife,
and friend whose proxy rode in my saddlebags
throughout the journey

The Restless American

A Middle-aged Man on a Middle-aged Horse

Introduction

The heavily laden paint mare topped a gradual mile-long rise and stopped. We turned and looked back over the Rhode Island woodlands to the waters of Narragansett Bay, bright where they empty into the Atlantic Ocean. It was a clear, crisp autumn day. The little mare was not to wade again through the salt marshes of the Pettaquamscutt for a long seven months that would take us some three thousand miles from home. We were started down the winding roads and trails to Arizona and the Grand Canyon, a trip that was destined to put us in the midst of a great many varying situations and enable us to meet hundreds of American people. We were to experience wonderful days, and some that were terrible; suffer the cold and the wet, the hot and the dry; become acquainted with the finest people imaginable, and a few that were not; buck drifting snow and gasp our way through the swirling dust. Our sleeping accommodations were to range from the plush guest rooms of a wealthy man's estate with adjoining immaculate stables to a run-down auto court with all the earmarks of a bawdy house, and a nearby hog and cattle barn. Always, the extreme highs and lows were leveled off by pleasant weather, the warm and kindly people who live near all of us, and the great, unspoiled regions of outdoor America.

In looking back and attempting to pinpoint the reason for a horseback trip across a large part of the country in the mid-twentieth century, I find it difficult to indicate any specific catalyst for those who insist on knowing motives. I doubt that there is one, or even that there has to be one. I suspect that there's a restlessness in all of us that we are early trained to subdue in the name of responsibility. Although this is not intended as a "how to do it" book, I found that the trick of indulging the irresponsibility lying latent in most of us is to scheme until you can come up with a "cover" that makes a harebrained escapade appear not only logical but, hopefully, profitable. By combining whatever talents I have as an artist and an ability to spell fairly well, I decided that an illustrated journal was the most convincing cover.

Perhaps the most important phrase is not how to do it, but when to do it. Holding a daydream in abeyance until a time when its realization will be more convenient is like waiting to pay your income taxes or have babies. Delay usually brings with it greater obstacles, not lesser ones.

Already the perceptive reader will have determined the simple truth — at heart I'm an undisciplined bum. Shortly after my return home, a lovely young newspaper lady was sent to my home for an interview. I'm sure she detected that I was just a hobo who happened to like to ride a horse, but her suspicious editor was not to be trapped into calling me what I am. Back she came for a second interview with instructions to dig deeper and get my "Motivation." As no cocktail party can be complete these days without an earnest probe into everyone's Motivation, I realized the importance of her second mission and tried to help her with whatever it was that actually caused me to reach for the stirrup and climb aboard.

My wife Nicky and I went to Providence one evening to see a movie that we'd been looking forward to. On the return home, we got into a newly opened, multilaned stretch of interstate highway. Roaring along three abreast, in a fog of stinking exhausts, nervously straining to discern which lane to choose to avoid being swept into an underpass or up on an overpass, I vented my outrage in a profanely reactionary diatribe on the subject of progress in general and auto travel in particular. Nick agreed with me, and somewhere in the conversation that followed injected the remark that it was almost incredible that less than two hundred years before, George Washington and his escort had traveled through this very territory on horses. It was something to think about.

A short time later, we decided to spend a day on Block Island, a small chunk of land that lies off the southern coast of Rhode Island. I'd lived in Rhode Island for ten years; Nicky was born in the state, but neither of us had ever been to Block Island. As Nick is an excellent watercolorist, we packed up sketching materials, left the car on the mainland and rode the ferry to the island with the intention of doing some painting. Disembarking from the ferry, we rented a couple of bicycles and started to explore, looking for a likely place to stop and paint. After the first ten minutes, painting was forgotten. I don't think either of us mentioned it but we came to an unspoken decision to see as much of the island as we had time for. It was a hot day. We pedaled up juniper-covered hills and coasted down into deep valleys. The scent of bayberries, clean, non-sweet and unbefouled by carbon monoxide, filled the silent air. The combination of fragrance and stillness awoke a nostalgia for an earlier summer when the pace was slower and the air was cleaner — a time when you could walk down the center of a winding country road without thinking about being run over by a speeding automobile.

We paused once on a quiet ridge and looked down on a white-rumped marsh hawk soaring lazily across the valley below. I think that neither of us wanted to leave the island.

Not long after this, I began to think seriously about making a long, solitary trip on a horse to satisfy my curiosity about how much of America remained unaffected by cement blocks and steel girders. A ride of this nature would also satisfy an itchy foot and a desire to escape from daily routine, and if that isn't sufficient Motivation, it will have to do.

The next step was one that took a certain amount of finesse. Because I'm quite happily married with a large family, diplomacy in broaching the subject to my wife would be of utmost importance. Somewhere inside must lurk a salesman; and when I brought up the subject of an inexpensive ride taking not more than three months — it cost a lot and took seven — my wife was easily convinced. That left only a publisher to be sounded out — a comparatively easy obstacle.

Thus it was that after the necessary preparations, a middle-aged man climbed on a middle-aged horse and headed for Arizona. In retrospect, I'm certain that the greatest dividend gained from the long journey was the large number of friendships struck up along the way — many, I'm sure, to be long lasting. A complete and painstaking recital of the daily journal, although a wonderful experience to me, would doubtless be a repetitious bore to the reader; thus some of the more similar situations must suffer editing. This doesn't indicate lack of appreciation for the many hospitalities extended to me, only lack of space. Some of these hospitalities included a sort of horse-hiking, if you will, as when on several occasions rides were offered to us both, I accepted as a part of the experience. But the great bulk of the trip was in fact done on horseback. It was not intended as an endurance test, nor was it in any sense a race. It was only a leisurely tour with a companionable horse across a wonderful, big country filled with fine people that could not fail to make me feel extremely fortunate to be an American.

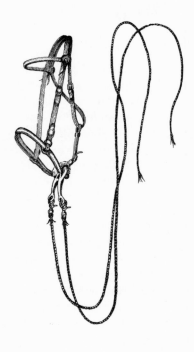

1.

For the reason that both Nicky and I are primarily artists and in addition have five children, three dogs and three cats, our living room is seldom uncluttered. Ordinarily, the huge brick fireplace of the old center-chimney Colonial house is flanked by stacks of canvases, piles of watercolors, a three-wheeled toy truck and a cap pistol. To pass from one end of the house to the other requires a certain navigational skill in order to get around a large easel and over at least two sprawling dogs.

On the night before I departed, the house was a jumble of objects with the center of the floor resembling a combination tack room and sporting goods store. A weatherbeaten sawhorse had been dragged in from outside and served as support for a saddle from which was suspended a formidable array of equipment that ranged from saddlebags and fitted grain pouches to tarps, rain gear and a sleeping bag. The saddlebags bulged with a camera, a Boy Scout mess kit, grooming equipment and anything else that could be wedged into a space that remained unoccupied.

The younger family members were at their usual post in

the rear part of the house glued to the television set while the living room facilities were taken over by the adults, who included a couple of friends from Boston, down for a last-minute consultation. Bob Farnsworth, a friend who had expressed an early interest in the proposed trip, brought down a Volkswagen-load of camping items and supplies rounded up at a Boston store where such equipment was a specialty of the house. With him came Jerry Kelly, whose help as a literary agent and friend had put me in touch with an interested publisher.

We'd already gone over maps and details as fully as possible and now I was opening the parcels with the ill-concealed delight of a newly commissioned Boy Scout the night before leaving for his first camp. On this night I was well into my forty-fourth year, but then or now, or twenty years from now, I doubt that I'll ever become blasé about removing the oiled paper wrapping from a new, shining, stag-handled pocketknife.

The packages that Bob and Jerry brought with them contained a number of items I'd been unable to find locally, primarily due to the suddenness of my decision to go ahead with the project. From the box containing the blanket-insulated canteen, to the packages of freeze-dried foods, with an enthusiastic pause over a small folding candle holder that Bob had been unable to resist, I was no different from any six-year-old on Christmas morning. The problem would be one of weeding out anything not absolutely necessary so that it could all fit on one medium-sized horse who would also be carrying me. With the sawhorse as a substitute, we stowed, packed, unpacked, rejected, experimented and finally wound up with a reasonable approximation of what was to go on the horse the following day. The mare herself, a twelve-year-old named Sioux, was out in her small

9

red stable behind the garage, as yet blissfully unaware of what changes were scheduled for her future.

"I'd like to see the horse that's going to provide the transportation," Jerry mentioned after we'd exhausted all combinations and arrived at what seemed to be a probable arrangement.

Always willing to visit the only family member that didn't actually live in the house, I led the way out to her stable, looking suspiciously at the night sky and wondering how many reasonably comfortable autumn nights were left to the year.

At our approach, Sioux turned in her stall and hung her head over the side looking for the usual apple, ate it with relish, then frisked me with her nose in the hope that I might be concealing more. A chunky bay and white mare with black knees and hocks and a dash of black in her otherwise white mane and tail, Sioux is called a pinto in the East and parts of the West where the Spanish influence is felt. In some of the South and other parts of the West, she's called a paint. Later, in a portion of Texas, I heard her referred to, with no offense intended, as a li'l ol' brush-bred spotty-ass hawse. Regardless of color, she's hardly the noble steed depicted by the usual equestrian statue in the park, having long before abandoned the pose of the wild-eyed, distended-nostriled charger for the more honest, if less impressive, appearance of a bossy, omniscient and self-assured animal who knows exactly what she wants and how best to go about getting it. She hadn't always been quite as frank about her personality.

She became a member of the family several years ago as a purportedly gentle mare suitable for children. I'd been prevailed on by the kids to get a horse because they knew I'd had a number of them long before and had worked with them throughout most of my teens and early twenties. Prior to World War II I'd labored for a period on a ranch in Wyoming, and shortly after Pearl Harbor served a stint on the Texas border with the old 7th Cavalry when it was still horse, which it was until 1943. After the war, I owned a stable in Connecticut until I decided to go to art school. Neither the school years nor the lean period following left me much opportunity for associating with horses, but I never lost interest in them. It took a minimum of coaxing for the kids to convince me that a horse was a necessity, and Sioux was the result.

On the day of her arrival, she backed shyly down the trailer ramp and hesitantly entered her temporary stall in the garage. She seemed timid and I cautioned the kids to restrain themselves until she had a chance to get used to her new home. When I rode her, she seemed willing and lively but well-behaved and dependable enough for children, and for the first several days, she was. Knowing her now, I'm certain that she was sizing us up and arriving at the conclusion that she was surrounded by patsies — an astute observation on her part. I soon found that while she could be utterly fearless when passing anything from a chain saw to a roaring bulldozer, a falling leaf could touch off a sideways spook that would take her from one side of a trail to the other in one jump. At other times, while moseying down a path in a somewhat lethargic mood, she'd suddenly squeal and bolt like a quarter horse for no discernible reason whatever. Again when returning from a lengthy ride, when I'd expect her to be normally tired, I'd ease her gently into the last short lope of the day to discover that a playful whim would have her sashay sideways, duck her head and hit me with two or three mild buck jumps. When she got a little too rough, I usually reacted with a slap on the neck, which invariably brought about a back-slanted ear and a reproachful roll of the eye.

11

Her uneven performance convinced me that she wasn't a horse for beginners and the sensible course would have been to acquire a more dependable horse or to discipline her a little more firmly. The fact that I liked her and was amused by her peccadillos led me to use a well-behaved gray gelding named Walter for the kids, and I retained Sioux for my exclusive use.

Actually, Sioux's personality development came as a surprise to me. As much as I'd been addicted to horses, I'd never thought that they were the most brilliant creatures to emerge from the ark. I'd subscribed to the theory that most of their trained behavior was the result of fear of punishment combined with the use of painful devices in training. Unquestionably, bits, spurs and whips, used with intelligence, are essential to the control of a large, powerful animal that has no inborn wish to cooperate, but this is only one part of their training. Having Sioux living in close proximity to the house caused me to reassess my skeptical views of stories about genuinely affectionate and intelligent horses. It hadn't occurred to me until Sioux came along that since most horses are kept in stables or pastures except while being worked, ridden or groomed, they seldom get a chance to display much real intelligence or capacity for mutual affection. Dogs and cats often do, but I believe this comes about largely because they are raised in an environment which encourages them to do so. In Sioux's case, she readily began to display many of the qualities that we humans seem to feel we have a corner on. She can, as the mood strikes her, be playful, sulky, mischievous, headstrong and fun loving. At other times, she's jealous, curious, affectionate and possessive. I've never noticed any indication of insecurity, perhaps due to the rather high position she's allotted herself in the family pecking order.

Sioux is incurably nosy and an inveterate meddler. A

12

shovel leaning against a building must be knocked down, aluminum lawn chairs tipped over. Wheelbarrows are a source of acute distress to her until they are upside down. The secrets of all containers must be ascertained, the ground-floor windows peered into with the regularity of a watchman on his rounds and all fences periodically breached. Her interest in human foods makes outdoor dining all but impossible.

One day several summers ago, when we entertained the foolish notion of attempting to harbor both a garden and horses, I stormed out and drove her away from the tomatoes with a bull roar and a stout stick. The usual horse, under like circumstances, will cut and run — Sioux prefers not to give you the satisfaction. Tossing her head in annoyance, she wheeled around, spotted one of our luckless tomcats who was sunning himself on a nearby rock and chased him, nipping at his heels until the startled cat made it to the sanctuary of a thick boxwood tree. Having saved face, she then non-chalantly trotted off.

Many zoologists assert that learned behavior is the basis for all animal activities and that what we sometimes imagine to be instinct is merely programmed reaction. I don't deny that all animals, including humans, possess certain behavioral patterns, but I do maintain that the higher animals do a lot more thinking, feeling and reasoning than many scientists are ready to admit. Sioux, for example, quickly learned to open our aluminum storm door with her nose by simultaneously turning the round knob and pulling on it. She continually unfastens the spring-loaded snap on her halter shank and I don't feel unreasonable in my rejection of the idea that this is either an example of learned behavior or instinct.

She's a companionable horse around water as well as on land. Warm summer days often find us headed for nearby

Lake Pettaquamscutt, where a pebbly beach at the edge of the woods makes for pleasant swimming. With the airedale in the lead and the collies bringing up the rear, we trot along the path that cuts through the woods. With the first indication that I plan to cut left to the water, the collies head for home and the airedale circles to a safe vantage point where he can watch without danger of being caught and dragged in. Sioux plows on into the lake with what certainly appears to be relish, and when I slide off at a depth of three or four feet and start swimming, she curls her lip up like a windshield and churns alongside. Regardless of her steel-shod feet that were never designed as paddles, it's impossible for me to keep up with her without grabbing a handful of mane and cheating a little. After circling in to the shore, she enjoys standing withers deep and baffling the flies and mosquitoes. Although she displays much better manners than most children, neither splashing nor shrieking, I notice that most of the other bathers take to the shore while we enjoy a complete absence of aquatic traffic.

The relationship that exists between Britt, the airedale, and Sioux is not cordial. Sioux puts up with his presence on our woodland tours provided that he stays out of reach. When he gets engrossed in squirrel or chipmunk trails, which have an irresistible fascination for him, she's quite apt to come up behind him and nip at his tail. If, on my trips across the backyard, I stop to talk to the old girl and scratch her withers and Britt bounds up to get an equal measure of attention, back go the ears and Britt departs in a hurry or risks Sioux's version of a cavalry charge.

Her relations with me I find difficult to discount as affectionate. When I'm in the kitchen, she frequently stands at the back door peering in. If I transfer to the side porch, it's only a matter of seconds before she appears around the corner of the house seeking me out. When I stand around

14

outdoors talking to a visitor or guest, she'll amble up behind and rest her big bony jaw on my shoulder. Formerly at night when I carried water into the stable she and any other horse that was there scrambled to their feet. She now remains lying down, having identified me by my approaching cigarette cough, and waits for me to deliver her bucket and hold it for her while she drinks like a reclining Roman.

The term horse lover has a curdling effect on whatever I last ate, like the adjective artistic. This li'l ol' spotty-ass hawse is slightly cow-hocked and has an unfashionably long head and tail, but I'm not likely to trade her for a while. I may be presumptuous in believing that she's fond of me — I know how I feel about her.

A certain amount of preliminary planning was necessary as to the general route to follow. I couldn't carry feed for Sioux other than grain and it would be essential to find grass growing along the way. Since we were starting the trip in the fall of the year, as soon as possible we'd have to head south, where I hoped the grazing possibilities would be better. As it turned out, most of the Southern roads that I followed were planted in fescue grass, which remained green and nourishing as I gambled that it would. As for any unforeseen contingencies, I hoped to be able to cope with them as they were encountered.

Several years back, I was pleasantly surprised to find that wide tracts of Rhode Island were still rural. The southern and western areas are heavily wooded and many roads remain unpaved. There would be no difficulty in covering the stretch from Saunderstown to the Connecticut border. Dirt roads wind through woods where once-prosperous farms long ago lost the struggle against the ever-present bull briers and oak and cedar trees. All that remains of these flourishing farms of Colonial times are twisting overgrown stone walls, crumbling foundations and an occasional small family burial ground where lichen-covered, gray slate stones mark the graves of long dead men, women and children whose names time has all but erased. The more legible tell of mothers and babies who died in childbirth, brave patriots who fought in the Revolution and the hardy ones who were more than a match for a seventy-hour week and survived into their eighties and nineties. They lie there undisturbed by the rabbits, the raccoons and the bobwhites, or by a man traveling west on a pinto mare.

Crossing into Connecticut, I planned to head briefly northwest, keeping to the rural areas and avoiding the more populated regions that skirt Long Island Sound. I could then pick up the Appalachian Trail in Pennsylvania and begin a southward curve taking me into a corner of Maryland, a bit of West Virginia and Virginia. From there, I'd follow a loosely decided route, since I felt that being too closely tied to a specific plan would tend to "can" the trip too much. I pretty much expected to get into Texas, either through Tennessee and Arkansas or through Kentucky, Missouri and Oklahoma, according to the weather, and then continue to New Mexico and Arizona.

People, and I'm one of the guilty ones, frequently don't trouble to visit points of interest close to their homes, while out-of-towners come great distances for the express purpose of seeing them. It is a cliche that there are more residents of New York who haven't been up in the Statue of Liberty than there are those who have. Probably the same holds true for the residents of Agra and the Taj Mahal, or the English and their Stonehenge. I'd once worked near both Yellowstone and the Grand Canyon but had never gotten around to seeing either of them. Perhaps that was why the Grand Canyon seemed a likely destination. What may have been a more valid reason for selecting the Grand Canyon was that an old army friend, Walt Drye, was running a cattle ranch near Flagstaff and it had been twenty-odd years since we had gone our separate ways. Through sloppy correspondence, I'd lost track of him but I hoped to be able to find him out there.

Deciding what equipment to take required some thought. I got out everything I felt I'd need and then had to throw half of it back, since Sioux couldn't carry it all. In spite of the weight involved, I felt that a Western stock saddle was required. Not only does the stock saddle have places from which to suspend gear, but its extended skirts and rather long bars give the horse more protection. Saddlebags and a bedroll, if rested directly on a horse's back, can easily cause a sore spot. Saddle skirts act as a buffer and prevent problems of this nature. These are the practical reasons for a stock saddle — there is another. I wouldn't have had the guts to face any of my old cowboy friends on a flat saddle. Most of them take the stand that an English-type saddle is a direct insult to any self-respecting horse. Not surprisingly, the opposite opinion is just as firmly clung to in other circles. Horse people are both partisan and snobbish. Lest this be misinterpreted, no one is more of a snob than a dusty, battered old cowpuncher who, with his hand on the rope rein of a hackamore bridle, snorts in derision at a full double English bridle with its four reins — fully enough, in his snickered opinion, to drive a wagon with a four-horse hitch. I selected a hackamore-type bridle. It has no bit in the mouth, enabling the horse to graze with no interference or change of head gear. Sioux performs as well with a hackamore as with a steel bit, so there was no reason to use the more severe bit.

Lightweight canvas saddlebags seemed sensible in view of the weight limitation. A zippered pouch called a carryall fitted behind the cantle for additional equipment. A mummy-

19

type, goose-down sleeping bag weighing only three or four pounds provides reasonable warmth and a space within for extra clothing. A friend made up a pair of sturdy canvas grain pouches to hang across the saddle horn and a Western-style gallon canteen was guessed at and later proved to be adequate. I attempted to locate as much of the weight as possible over Sioux's shoulders rather than back on her kidneys and this was pretty closely adhered to all the way. As to the loading, better than half of the trip was accomplished before objects were permanently situated.

If I were to repeat the trip or take a lengthy ride in any direction, I'd get a saddle made up to my specifications and it would be more similar to the saddles used in the last century. The modern Cheyenne roll on most cantles interferes with the bedroll, which almost requires being tied on behind, and the old-fashioned slick or A fork would allow the grain bags to ride higher and out of the way of the rider's knees. Full grain bags, hanging too low in front, were the biggest source of annoyance and were the cause of a good many hours of unnecessary cramping. I would also have large leather saddlebags with sheepskin lining where there could be contact with the horse's flanks. The canvas bags were too thin to protect the horse and required very careful packing. They also tore in several places due to the excessive weight of their contents. I wound up replacing them in Virginia with old cavalry saddlebags, which have a larger capacity than most commercially produced bags of today; even these caused some trouble when hair was rubbed off on Sioux's hips.

Horseshoeing was a problem and again, in order to lighten the load, I gave up any plan to carry tools or extra shoes and decided to gamble on locating farriers. I did have an eight-ounce hatchet which could double as an emergency hammer and a few horseshoe nails; fortunately I never had need for them. Howard Lee, horseshoer, horseman and friend, came up with the suggestion of borium-welded shoes. This is a conventional shoe to which a hard alloy is welded. It not only greatly increases the wearing qualities, but also prevents slipping on hard pavements. I lean toward leather pads between the shoe and hoof and used them on several occasions with success. Pine tar or similar packing keeps the hoof soft and pliable in dry country, and the leather prevents stone bruises to the frog, or sole. The other school of thought maintains, doubtless with justification, that gravel can work in under the pad and stay lodged there to cause serious trouble. I had no difficulty while pads were used; on the other hand, Sioux got a stone bruise on two occasions while traveling without pads. This is not a significant argument for pads. It's merely my personal experience.

Service in World War II in the dismounted cavalry, as our outfit was euphemistically designated when they took our horses away and set us afoot, taught me that survival is possible, barring a hostile bullet, with a minimum of personal possessions. When everything you own must be carried on your back, you can accept the Spartan life very readily. Nothing matters but the pure essentials. A poncho doubles as a raincoat and tent fly, so keep it. Extra socks are an acceptable luxury; keep them. A fork with which to eat is, after all, merely an affectation.

Even with what I thought was careful planning, there were to be many changes as things perhaps necessary in one part of the country became excess baggage in another. When we started, the mare was carrying about two hundred and fifty pounds. The saddle weighed thirty-five pounds, the baggage another thirty-five and I weighed a hundred and eighty. My weight was to decrease soon.

2.

There had been so many delays for one reason or another that the actual departure seemed unreal. As expected, the start was late. Nick and Robbie, our youngest, came out. We took a few photographs, shut the dogs up so that they would be unable to follow, kissed goodbye and I headed up the lane which would take me out to the road.

The day was cold but sunny and I hoped that it had rained itself out on the previous day. I expected to get wet many times before the conclusion of the trip but I was hopeful that the first few days would be pleasant.

A high ridge about a mile from home gave us a last look at the Atlantic, so I took a photo over the mare's ears and was done with the sea.

Sioux and I spelled each other throughout the first day. To avoid overworking her and prevent cramping on my part, I got off and led her about every half hour. At this point, I was certain that my gear was confined to absolute minimum necessities. This, of course, proved to be a false assumption. We were both overweight and soft. I was to lose eighteen pounds and she probably a hundred and fifty. With the excess gear and poundage it shortly became obvious that we were not going to reach our first night's objective.

An old unused dirt road curved around by a large field that was bordered by trees and a stream. I guided Sioux in and located a level grassy area near the edge that looked to be a suitable campsite. After unpacking and watering, I led the mare to a large area of grass and clover and while watching her graze, noticed a pattern of car tracks circling the field.

Most deer killed in Rhode Island are the illegal victims of a technique known as jacklighting in which a light is played on a field at night and the reflection of the eyes becomes the target. I suspected a connection between the car tracks and jacklighting and decided that I had no wish to provide some nervous nimrod with the humiliation of a mistake. We moved camp back into the woods behind a ridge.

As I expected, it did not go smoothly the first night. I was too hurried to take time with dinner, so I cooked everything rapidly and tastelessly, and wolfed it. My original fastidious plans for a change of clothing while sleeping were abandoned as a result of the cold and I crawled into the bedroll trousers, socks, shirt and all. One of the first night's mistakes, shortly to be corrected, was that of leaving my boots outside.

The last-minute change of campsite had left me with a slight side hill for my bedroll. Although I knew better than to expect a comfortable night, it was preferable to getting shot at by the deer jackers.

The night that followed proved I was right. It was miserable. Sioux was nervous and started at every sound. Each time I dozed off, she'd awaken me with brush cracklings. I fought a constant battle uphill, which was perhaps a blessing in disguise since it prevented me from freezing to death. There had been absolutely nothing to do after dark fell and it had fallen shortly after five, so for twelve long hours I made rather futile attempts to squirm back onto a downhill air mattress which had, of course, been overinflated to start with. Occupying a sleeping bag on an over-inflated air mattress located on a side hill is like combining the fine points of a potato race and attempting to stay upright on one of those inflated toy rubber horses in the Atlantic surf.

Regardless of the discomfort of the bed, six A.M. found me reluctant to leave it. Frost covered everything in sight including the boots that I had piously left outside to air, and I regarded them for some time with greatly dimmed enthusiasm. There was nothing for it, however, but to get into them. I did so, cursing softly.

I gave Sioux her grain, shiveringly lighted the alcohol stove and thawed the slushy, half-frozen water in my canteen into what passed for a cup of coffee. By then the mare was done with her grain and I led her out into the field to eat the frost-covered grass. In a tall dead tree at the edge of the field, a crow sat warming himself in the early rays of the sun that had not yet reached me. I stood shuffling from one cold foot to the other and cursed him enviously.

A half hour of this and the protesting mare was hauled back into the woods to be saddled and packed. Everything was stiff and frosty including myself, and my only thoughts were about what kind of gibbering idiocy had gotten me into this foolishness.

Not surprisingly, my friend Sioux had an arched neck and a hump in her back. Observing this, I slid up and on her as gently as possible and held a fairly close rein. I was in no mood for a rodeo at that moment and was extremely grateful that she didn't start one.

A half hour on the road and exercise and the sun began to ameliorate my mood. Suddenly, everything was beautiful.

24

Squirrels ran along the old walls and grouse roared out of the brush. The still-frosty dirt road crunched hollowly under Sioux's feet and life was great. There was no plausible reason in the world why I couldn't make Arizona on horseback.

An easy day's ride over dirt roads bordered with woodlands took me to a state park. The trees changed from hardwoods to pines and shortly a lake appeared, surrounded by plenty of grass. The park was officially closed for the winter but the gentleman in charge, who was felling trees with a chain saw, gave me permission to stay one night.

"Just you pull in behind one of them log shelters and don't tell anybody — and I won't even see you."

I explained my plans. He listened, studied them a bit and allowed, "Guess you got spunk." I suspected that he really felt I was some kind of nut but had arrived at the decision that I wasn't dangerous.

Sioux and I backed into the lee side of a small log building and I set up a comfortable camp. It was early for a stop but already I was in need of repairs to my haversack that contained the drawing materials and camera gear. That morning, to add to the cold and discomfort, the shoulder strap had pulled out, and at intervals throughout the day I'd profaned the nameless sewing machine operator who had undershot her target. Some good stout linen thread fixed it — permanently, as it later proved.

Night came on cold and clear. The stars are so brilliant and sharply defined when they're not dimmed by our usual artificial light sources that I wished then and at later moments that I knew something of astronomy. On the other hand ignorance doesn't necessarily prevent enjoyment. I'm reasonably sure that a squirrel doesn't know that a walnut is called a walnut.

Cold as it was, I slept soundly, awakening only a couple

25

of times throughout the night. I eventually found out that it is next to impossible to turn over in a mummy-type sleeping bag without waking. A little practice enables the sleeper to shift sides without rolling off the air mattress and return to the business of sleeping with almost no interruption.

Morning made me aware of the fact that all was again heavily frosted. This time my boots were not included, because I had squirmed them off inside the bedroll and they were lovely and warm. I was to become quite expert at this somewhat neat trick of wriggling out of a pair of tight-fitting riding boots while zipped up in a sleeping bag.

I lighted the stove for a quick cup of coffee after graining the mare and found my canteen to be frozen solid. I made a trip to the lake, where the ice had to be broken, and in a few shivering minutes I had the coffee. I made a mental note that from here on out I'd sleep with the canteen inside the bag as well as the boots. Another refinement of technique is to place the stove and coffee within easy arm's reach of the bed. Coffee can then be managed before rising and the dawn becomes much more cheerful.

While I was packing my gear to leave the lake, a middle-aged man dressed in a red and black buffalo plaid jacket and cap with earflaps strode up. He was a fine healthy-looking robust figure with a canvas backpack and walking stick and he pulled up four square in front of me to compare notes. He mentioned, after a brief and cordial introduction, that when he'd left his home that morning the thermometer had stood at twenty-two degrees, and that when he came down the valley it had become perceptibly colder. I agreed that I doubted the mercury was old enough to vote. His only reaction to my proposed trip was ill-concealed enthusiasm. There was no doubt in my mind that we were kindred souls.

"You can't get kids to do anything like this today," he stated with a touch of sadness.

I suspected that he'd been rebuffed by his own son that morning and I was sorry. He commented that he knew I was anxious to hit the road and with a cheery "Good luck!" strode briskly away, his stick striking out jauntily.

The trail meandered through a piece of country that I confess I hadn't known existed in Rhode Island. I deduced from a few parked cars that hunters were afoot and, because there are those who occasionally mistake horses for rabbits, I whistled as loudly as I could. This might have served only to identify me as a whistling rabbit but I hoped that any hunters encountered would be more perceptive. The tune was rather brisk and timed to the beat of Sioux's hoofs on the frozen dirt. For some reason the title of the tune came to me and I was amused to find that I was rather incongruously rendering Count Basie's version of "April in Paris." It was most certainly neither April nor Paris, but the beat seemed to fit, so I didn't bother to change.

On one stretch of back road, I was asked directions by a young couple in a car with out-of-state plates. In the brief conversation that followed, they mentioned that the forecast was for rain. It seemed hardly likely, for the sky was cloudless. Nevertheless, when I came to a beautiful little valley with a small river spilling its falls over granite ledges, I noted a state-built shelter nearby. I saw no point in risking an unnecessary wetting and so I made camp under the roof. Throwing some leaves on the cement floor for Sioux, I tied her inside behind the wall and took the opposite corner for myself. It was so comfortable and convenient that I set up my gear on the picnic table, shaved and generally cleaned up. In the morning I was careful to remove the leaves and other unmistakable evidence of a horse's overnight presence.

Earlier in the afternoon of the preceding day, while grazing the mare, a great squeaking of tires had attracted my attention. Sliding to a stop beside me was a little red

Mustang containing three teenagers with an old old lady in the front seat. She had the sunken puckered cheeks of the toothless and the three tire squealers were evidently grand- or great grandchildren giving Granny a ride.

They asked how to get down to the falls and I pointed out the trail. They seemed irritated that they were unable to drive the car down the trail and I observed privately that they were behind the steering gear of the wrong kind of Mustang.

Granny said that she'd visited the falls when she was a little girl and had hoped to see them again. Her charming progeny soothed her by promising to bring her again some- day and squealed off with what seemed a deliberate attempt to rip the transmission out of a nice little car. I questioned that Granny would ever get to see the falls.

By now it was becoming apparent that I had better make tracks as rapidly as possible and get South without delay. A few days of travel had acted as a sort of shakedown cruise and the system was falling into place. I had discovered that I had the state and national parks pretty much to myself and this proved true of the Appalachian Trail. A week's time served to get rid of muscular aches and pains and we made rather good time except for some rough areas of foot trails that frequently slowed progress to a crawl.

Plans had been made ahead of time to skip the Hudson River due to traffic and long high bridges. Actually I believe we'd have had no trouble, but at that time I wasn't certain about the mare's reaction to bridges and felt that it wasn't worth the chance of an accident. To avoid the long Hudson bridges would have required a high northern swing and this was ruled out by the rapid approach of winter. A prear- ranged trailer ride got us over the sticky area and back into the rural countryside and trail.

I was not sure that horses were welcome on the Appa-

T. POWELL

lachian Trail, but I encountered no protests from anyone and the rangers I met were, without exception, nothing but cooperative and helpful. The trail itself is an accomplishment and I wound up with great admiration for those who planned and maintain it. Blazes are clearly visible on trees. Mileages to springs and shelters are indicated and the location provides wonderful panoramic views of the country. This is probably more true during the winter months with the foliage gone than at other times. Many parts are extremely difficult to navigate with a horse and at times it's necessary to detour around rock slides. There were steep rocky areas where I was obliged to dismount and haul myself up with the aid of trees, then pull the mare up behind me. She came through like a veteran mountain horse. She never got frantic or excited by the shifting rocky footing, and often, too, it was deceptive walking due to the cover of newly fallen leaves.

As we shed poundage and our lungs got more accustomed to the uphill exertion, our stops became less frequent. The altitude at this point was not sufficient to cause the trouble with breathing that we were later to experience in New Mexico and Arizona.

I found that there was some difficulty in procuring the customary types of horse feed, since it usually is available only in bags containing a minimum of one hundred pounds. This problem was frequently solved by substituting chicken scratch feed, which consists usually of cracked corn, wheat and oats. It was perfectly acceptable to her. Nor did she object to eating regular grocery store oatmeal and cornmeal.

As for me, I found that it was only necessary to carry rations for a day or two at most. I retained some emergency dried foods adequate for a day or so and these stayed in the bottom of the saddlebags unused throughout the entire trip. In most of the rural areas gas stations carry a limited stock of canned goods and I soon gave up attempting to turn out anything even vaguely resembling the backyard barbecue. I ate in camp with the sole purpose of getting filled up and frequently on cold mornings started my engine on nothing more than a cup of coffee. My intentions were to stop later in the day for a fancier breakfast but I found that usually I wasn't sufficiently hungry to bother. This convinced me of the fact that I, in company with most Americans, eat too much at home. I'm sure that if I were expected to put out a much less physically active day at home on nothing but coffee, I would feel much put upon and abused. On this occasion I got a lot of mileage out of coffee and felt healthier than I had for many years.

Camping has become a plush and complicated affair in many circles. My means of transportation precluded the fancier refinements and I'm afraid my camps failed to resemble the illustrations in most handbooks. I never got around to cutting the little forked sticks on which pots are always supposed to be suspended and my fireplaces were usually three rather lumpy, ill-fitting rocks. I frequently perched my frying pan and coffee bucket right on the burning logs and hoped that they wouldn't become dislodged when the props burned out from beneath them. They never did. Neither did I dig little drainage ditches around the sleeping bag. Again I gambled with the weather and won. I would pull up at night, unload and tend to the horse, then kick enough loose rubble away to provide space to accommodate a sleeping bag, throw down a ground sheet followed by the air mattress and the sleeping bag, and cover it all with a poncho. My extra clothes, carried in the bedroll, served as a pillow and my bed was made. I even confess to the use of lighter fluid to speed up the fire-starting process. My only excuse is that instant coffee was my objective — the instanter the better.

Human contacts in this part of the country were surprisingly few. This was also true at the end of the trip, where I again got into national forest areas. There were a number of hunters encountered, forest rangers and Park Service employees. Then the short side trips to small grocery stores allowed a touch of social life. The questions became predictable and the reactions to the answers about the same. I ran into almost no skepticism, very little catcalling, and in most cases only friendly interest.

I don't know who selects the employees of our national and state parks or what the qualifications are. I do know that they are among the finest people anyone could hope to deal with. Perhaps the type of life they lead has a tendency to mold them. At any rate I met more friendly people while following the trail areas than any others and have nothing but kind words for them. I purposely am neglecting to pinpoint locations of camping areas, since most state parks charge a small fee for camping and not one of the people in charge would accept anything from me for use of the facilities. Many of the rangers who lived on the spot invited me in for coffee and use of their personal bathrooms for cleaning up and I certainly have no wish to repay their hospitality by getting them in hot water for not exacting a fee.

One time I made the unavoidable mistake of pulling in at a commercial campsite and found the situation quite different. Not only was I billed for everything at what I felt was a high rate, but the area itself was dirty and litter strewn. It could be that the economic psychology made campers less careful about picking up after themselves. I think that if people are required to pay a little too much, they may expect janitorial service to be provided. Then again maybe a touch of revenge is involved.

On a morning in western Maryland I was cooking breakfast under a heavy leaden sky while the mare grazed on her long tether. I shortly became aware of flakes drifting down against the nearby hemlocks and hoped vainly that it was ash from my fire. It wasn't. By the time I'd eaten and packed up, a light cover of the winter's first snow was beginning to accumulate. We started off up a mountain road that would intersect with the Appalachian Trail some miles ahead and the snow continued to whiten the road.

Most mountain roads are narrow due to the nature of their construction and when they are paved there is very seldom much of a gravel shoulder for horse travel. Blacktop roads when cold have a tendency to be quite slippery for steel horseshoes, and the cold, snow and steep grades made this stretch a bad one.

Deer hunting was in season, as evidenced by shotgun blasts in the distance, and a car with a buck-draped fender eased past me at the halfway point of my ascent. At one of the frequent rest stops, I got out a red, hooded sweatshirt and donned it.

The snow ended abruptly at noon, and shortly after, the mountain crested and we started downhill into a head wind that cooled everything including my enthusiasm. Some miles of sliding and slipping followed and I got directions to a dirt mountain road that supposedly returned us to the Appalachian Trail. The dirt road wound up and up and the hours dragged on. I began to despair of getting to the trail in time to follow it to the camp area before dark. I'd passed a rather pleasant farm at which I'd noticed a couple of horses, so I decided to return and ask permission to camp there. It was a somewhat isolated area and I don't suppose that by that time on the journey I presented a very handsome appearance. At any rate, after hitching Sioux and knocking at the door I received one of the few rebuffs of the trip; a very gentle rebuff at that.

An old man came to the farmhouse door in response to

34

my knock. He peered out at me through the partly opened door and listened to my explanation and request to be permitted to camp due to the lateness of the hour.

"Wal . . ." He hesitated, and then in a rich mountain twang said, "I believe your best bet is to go on up to the ridge, then turn right on daown the maowntain." He scratched his head with embarrassment and added consolingly, "Me and my wife has done 'er afoot lots of times. You just follow her right on daown the maowntain."

I thanked him, walked out and climbed up on the weary mare. As the old man had directed, we came to the familiar blazes placed on the trees by the Appalachian Trail people. It was by now almost dark, but when I got out my flashlight I found that the tree blazes were quite easy to pick up in the beam. I got the impression that they were done with fluorescent paint, since they seemed to have a luminous quality.

The old farmer had been correct in his directions to the trail, but I very soon decided that he was a bit confused as to which way was up. "Daown the maowntain" was a steady, rough ascent all the way. The trail was almost entirely rock strewn and this was further complicated by a cover of newly fallen leaves. By now I had dismounted and was leading Sioux. She followed patiently regardless of the fact that she was fully as tired as I was. I was flashing the light only intermittently in order to conserve the batteries and this was no real aid to night vision. It did, however, enable me to pick up the tree blazes in what was a heavily wooded area. I'd given up my plan to make the campsite indicated on the map and would cheerfully have stopped at any level spot except for the need for grass.

At long last we broke out into a wide grassy clearing. The opening had been made for a power line that ran across the mountain at this point. It was a clear cold night and the view of the silhouetted mountains with the twinkling lights of a village far down in the valley would have been inspiring to one less tired. As it was, I bedded down against a huge old log which provided a small windbreak, hitched the mare in the midst of the grass and built a fire. I was forced to water Sioux from my canteen, selfishly saving enough for my coffee. She wasn't particularly thirsty, because of the cold, and seemed satisfied. We both finished eating at nearly the same time and then, as was her habit, she wandered over and, heaving a big sigh, settled down near my bedroll like a big dog.

I've heard many who should know better stoutly maintain that a horse always sleeps standing. It isn't so. The only time Sioux slept standing was on occasional first nights in a strange place without my company. If my bedroll is close by, she invariably lies down and frequently stretches out full length. It worked both ways. I knew that anything approaching at night brought her to her feet with a snort and I therefore slept much more peacefully with a large "watchdog" at my bedside. Sioux in turn obviously felt the same way and was able to relax if I was near. It was not unflattering to have a means of transportation that was also a trusting friend.

Morning arrived at my clearing, cold and frosty. A chill wind cut across the ridge and we wasted little time eating and packing. Heading back into the wooded trail gave us a little shelter from the wind and almost immediately the trail started to descend. A few hundred yards of easy going took us out into a large grassy park with handsome log shelters, each with a fieldstone fireplace. Had I kept going another fifteen minutes or so the preceding evening, we'd have put in a much more pleasant night.

Hardly had I stopped the mare, near what appeared to be the headquarters building as evidenced by the woodsmoke coming from its stone chimney, when the door opened and a rather sleepy and surprised-looking ranger stuck his uncombed head out.

"What in the everlovin' world you doing out there on a cold morning like this?" He grinned. "Unload that horse and get in here where the coffeepot is!"

I did. Shortly, another ranger appeared in a pickup truck and joined us. As I had come to expect, they were most friendly and I found that we'd covered nearly thirty rough mountain miles the day before. The ball field in the clearing provided good grazing, so I decided to stay over for a day's rest and make use of one of the log cabins. Again, there was no charge.

"I don't like to charge the trail hikers," the first ranger stated. "Why do you know there's one old lady comes through here every year with a pack on her back all alone? Comes all the way up from the Georgia end of the trail and stops here every year."

"Must be a tough old bird," I opined.

"Dam' healthy lookin' anyhow," chimed in the second ranger. "Bet she's fixin' to outlive all of us."

By this time I was in need of a grocery store, and getting directions from the rangers, I rode the mare off the side of the mountain to the valley below. It was extremely rough and I decided to return to camp via the road. The store where I'd shopped was small and old-fashioned and I noticed that the bacon I'd ordered was sliced and wrapped in white paper. I surmised that it was the real thing procured from a local smokehouse instead of the usual commercial product. Now, I thought, I had arrived in backwoods America.

Taking the country road to my mountain camp, I soon got into an old farm area with ancient cabins and rail fences. Approaching one group of sheds, I noticed some people working around a couple of large steaming cauldrons between the ramshackle barn and an equally weathered and dilapidated cabin.

A skinny old man with tobacco-stained whiskers, faded bib overalls and a shapeless felt hat was perched birdlike on a bench near the kitchen door. I pegged him as Grandpaw. Grandmaw was bustling about in a rather voluminous apron, covering what I think was once referred to as a Mother Hubbard, and an old-style bonnet. Maw and Paw were laboring industriously over some benchlike tables near the cauldrons while a gang of shaggy, barefoot kids in patched overalls looking like something out of *Tom Sawyer* ran around underfoot.

Everything meshed at once. I spotted the white hog carcasses on the benches that were being scalded and scraped. The mare smelled the blood from the recent butchering and went into orbit, the kids started leaping up and down yelling with delight at the impromptu rodeo, a scrawny dog strained at his chain yapping and Maw started yelling ineffectually at the kids and the dog. I got the mare back on all fours and tried to get past. She flatly refused. Maw, aware of my predicament, began waving semaphore signals and trying to yell directions to us over the bedlam. Her gestures indicated a route around the other side of the house; however, I didn't want the mare to succeed with her refusal to go on. Grandpaw leaned back against the house, his hands around one cocked-up knee, and grinned widely and toothlessly. The damned dog stood on his hind legs at the end of his chain and nearly choked himself with his attempts to keep up a constant yapping. I've always been fond of dogs but I was hoping that this one would quickly garrott himself into silence, at least for a few minutes.

I remembered that I'd purchased a few apples at the store, so I got one out, halved it and rubbed the juice all over Sioux's nose, then fed it to her. It worked, after a fashion.

T. POWELL

When I got back on and pushed her forward, she skittered by sideways and scuttled up the road, snorting and rolling an eye back over her shoulder.

Back at camp, the bacon proved to be worth the trip. Several eggs had gotten themselves prescrambled during the action that had taken place on the return trip, so bacon and scrambled eggs were recommended by the chef that night.

By this time I was beginning to veer definitely south. I had always entertained a notion that Virginia, being a Southern state, would enjoy a relatively mild winter. For my peace of mind, I was sure that as soon as I got into ol' Virginny things would be warm and comfortable. The Appalachian Trail seems to follow the high ridges with their consequent lower temperatures and my last day on the trail turned out to be in western Maryland. The wind blew unmercifully, it was cold and the trail was rough. It seemed that most of the last twenty miles was like riding a horse along the top of a New England stone wall. I had been led to believe that New England had a corner on rocks. If they once did, then some early Yankee trader sold most of them to western Maryland and West Virginia. The valleys and mountains are beautiful, and as a location for a hiking trail, it's great country; but deliver me from ever riding a horse over those ridges again.

A murderous rock slide, requiring a tough detour, delivered us to the valley of the Potomac River and the temperature suddenly zoomed. I began peeling off the outer layers of clothing, the mare started to sweat, it was like a lovely late summer day and out came the gnats. These gnats don't bite but somehow they manage to make an excellent living by being annoying.

Still following trail markers, I crossed a railroad track and came to the alder-lined banks of the Potomac River. From a short distance, it was a lovely wide stream, moving

41

placidly through wooded hills and mountains. Closer observation of the banks was less enchanting. A collection of old tires and oil drums was scattered along the shallows and the water looked to be nothing I'd allow a horse to drink. There was available water nearby for drinking purposes, so spurning the Potomac created no problem. The warm summerlike evening and the surroundings made for a pleasant campsite. A breeze had come up sufficient to drive away the gnats and later, as dark fell, I was interested in observing a glow in the sky downriver which could only have been made by the city of Washington. It was pleasant to contemplate the peaceful calm of our riverbank campsite with the noise and turmoil of a large city such a short distance away. Up to then, I don't think I'd ever realized how easy it still is for urban Americans to get away from it all.

Next morning's encounter with the bridges across the Potomac and Shenandoah Rivers evolved a system of operating in traffic that I used from that point on. Both spans were fairly high and long and I took them on with a certain amount of trepidation. Dismounting and leading out, I got well over to the side rail. There was a momentary lull in trailer truck and general traffic as we started out and fortunately this situation prevailed for the first half of the bridge. Shortly before getting to the middle, the unexpected happened when a flight of pigeons, probably disturbed by the unaccustomed hollow noise of hoofbeats, zoomed up from under the bridge. The mare spooked violently out into the traffic lane and I learned a lesson on the spot. From that point on, we took the middle of the traffic lane and stayed there. This forced the traffic either to slow down and stay behind us or to swing wide and pass with plenty of clearance.

Shortly after leaving the bridge over the Shenandoah, I was tempted to make a short side trip to Harpers Ferry. For anyone interested in Civil War history, it is well worth a visit, since it has been and is still in the process of being restored. There is no taint of commercialism and the entire village seems to fit into its period. Again, the National Park Service employees were most pleasant and helpful. A railroad trestle parallels the river across from the buildings and it was suggested that I tie Sioux to the trestle, where there was excellent grazing, while I toured the town. I did and regretted it afterward. The day was warm and gnats were out. My spotted friend decided to rub the gnats off against the creosote-coated timbers and on my return I found her generously smeared with black, gummy creosote. She wore a bit of Harpers Ferry for a number of weeks.

The road out of Harpers Ferry took me past a distilling plant with its sign brazenly announcing it to be the only whiskey distillery in the state of West Virginia. I'm sure an old moonshining friend of mine from horse cavalry days would have had some derisive comments to make about such a presumptuous statement. But perhaps they were being facetious.

Sometime after we left Harpers Ferry, rain started. I pulled up under a tree and got out the rain gear. By now, Sioux had trimmed down and seemed to have more pep and energy than at the start. This reflected itself in one way that was not a contribution to peace of mind. Her skill at sudden shying became greater. It appears that horses shy in the East, spook in the South and West, and in some parts of the West booger. Whether you prefer the term shy, spook or booger, Sioux was an expert. This particular day was an exceptionally spooky one, it seems, perhaps due to the rain, traffic and flopping tarp. At one point, while I was leading her on a narrow stretch through a cut in the hills, she slammed into my heel with her shoe, providing me with a limp that lasted a week.

I was approaching Charles Town, West Virginia, and the

proprietor of a rather plush motel was not the least shaken by a half-drowned horseman in search of lodging. He directed me to the barn next door and insisted on my using the hay stored there. I soon discovered that a large racetrack was across the highway and that the barn was used for hay storage.

I gave Sioux a good rubdown and feed, then basked in a hot shower myself. The television set was a temptation after dinner, but I virtuously resisted the lure and spent the evening developing some rough sketches I'd made earlier. I had both watercolor and pen and ink materials in my gear; as yet the watercolors were unused due to the cold. Eventually I tired of packing a box of frozen watercolors and shipped them home.

I left an early call-in for the morning, because I was hoping to make the post office by noon. I was expecting mail at the general delivery window and the timing was such that it was Saturday with a twelve-noon closing hour.

Having tied the mare outside my room, I was engaged in lugging the gear out and packing her when she spotted the racetrack across the highway. As luck would have it, several racehorses were being worked out at dawn and she threw up her head and shattered the early-hours silence with a series of high-pitched whinnys. There was no way to silence her, so I got aboard as rapidly as possible and hightailed out before any irate late sleepers could begin heaving alarm clocks, shoes and unkind remarks in my direction.

The road soon became paralleled by long stretches of apple orchards and this allowed us to lope along on the open turf between the rows of trees. We made the post office connection with about three minutes to spare and slid around to the front of the building where I tossed the reins over a parking meter and leaped up the steps.

3.

Southern hospitality actually came upon us with the crossing of the Shenandoah River. Probably it existed before that point but I'd spent most of the time in the wooded areas away from farms and more populated places. At first I was reluctant to accept it for what it was and felt that I would be imposing on the good nature of those making the offer. Eventually, when it finally dawned that it was a genuine gesture and not merely a polite formality, I learned to receive it with almost as much grace as it was extended to me.

The Virginia town into which I'd made the flying entrance in a successful attempt to get my mail was large enough to have a certain amount of downtown traffic. After catching my breath and reading the mail, I plowed on through town looking for a place to hitch my horse. The firehouse had a suitable-looking backyard and several firemen standing around the door suggested I use their fence as a hitchrack. I did, and walked back a block to eat lunch in a restaurant. Upon returning, I was engaged in conversation by the next-door neighbor, whose wife shortly came out with several apples for the mare and what later proved to be an excellent rabbit sandwich on homemade bread. For some strange inexplicable reason, I was slightly embarrassed by their gesture but there was no way out of accepting the sandwich. Some hours later, when I got around to eating, I was delighted that my inhibitions had not held sway.

The next encounter with hospitality came the same day. I'd ridden a few miles out of town at a somewhat slower pace and gotten into an area of lovely old farms. One particularly attractive place caught my eye at about the time of day to start looking for a campsite. The house was of old brick antebellum architectural style and the barns and pens stretched off to the south with rolling hills and a fringe of trees. It was obviously a stock farm devoted to the raising of white-faced Hereford cattle and I noticed several saddle horses pastured behind the barn. Almost all farms in this part of the country have a rather pleasant fruity, cidery smell due, I guess, to their method of storing silage, and as I approached the barn area, I observed a man forking silage out of one of a number of piles covered by black tarpaulin. The mare, at first frightened by the black tarp, began to relax to the extent that I got within speaking distance, so I asked permission to camp out in back near the woods.

The pitchfork stopped and the farmer, a tall young blond man, assured me that it would be perfectly all right but how about a cup of coffee while my horse was fed and watered. Dismounting, I took Sioux's bridle off and led her into the barn, where there were several large stalls. Paul, the young farmer, loaded the manger with hay and something new to Sioux — whole corn on the ear. This she nosed rather speculatively at first, but caught on to without great delay.

I gave a hand dealing out the silage and we walked up to the big brick house for coffee. Paul's mother was in the kitchen and a tiny old colored woman was herding a vacuum cleaner around the dining room.

By the time the vacuum cleaner had ceased, the coffee was ready and we sat at a lovely old antique table that undoubtedly was contemporary with the house. I never got around to asking, but all indications — furniture, silver and china and the mother and son — made me feel certain that these people were the less affluent descendants of an old Southern family.

I was later to regret my polite refusal to their offer of an overnight stay at the house. Paul rather shyly suggested it twice and I replied nobly that it would be too much of an imposition.

I had run into a newspaperman while in town that day, and had been interviewed and photographed, and some weeks later in a phone conversation with my wife found that Paul's mother had mailed a copy of the paper to my home. She had mentioned in the accompanying note that they were disappointed I hadn't stayed with them. At that moment I resolved to stop acting like a dam' stiff-necked Yankee, since I would very much have enjoyed staying and talking with these people had I been sure that they "really meant it."

Following Paul's directions, I headed out through his pastures to a pleasant hillside with rock ledges, cedars and sycamores. It was a good camp and I spent a comfortable if cold night. I found next morning I'd overshot his boundary line, and on completion of breakfast, I noticed a man walking toward me accompanied by two dogs. I'd been using a red cotton bandana handkerchief as a washcloth for some time due to its quick drying properties and was just completing this routine job when I noticed the approaching farmer.

He stopped some distance away on the adjacent slope and hollered across to me, "Who are you?"

"Tom Powell," I bellowed back.

It was quickly evident that he didn't wish to be rude and

ask what in hell I was doing on his property, so I explained that I'd had the permission of his neighbor and had accidentally strayed over the line.

"Oh," he politely lied, "I saw your horse and something red and I thought you were hurt. Be careful with your fire, please."

I assured him that I would and he headed back to his distant house.

My map indicated that an old road went along the Shenandoah River at this point, so I cut cross-country in an easterly direction until I came out through a gate. I'd gotten an early start and the air retained a cold bite; however, I was warmly dressed and the countryside was pleasant enough to make riding down the road an enjoyable experience.

The farms bordering the river resembled golf courses — rolling and smooth with fenced-in clumps of oak and sycamore trees. The name Shenandoah has always had an appealing ring to it for me, probably because of the tune, and I was not disappointed with what I found.

Stepping briskly along the frosty roadside, we came to a small horse pen containing a Thoroughbred mare, heavy in foal. A fine-looking old gentleman was feeding her and we chatted briefly.

"This old girl won a lot of races in her day," the old man confided with obvious affectionate pride. "Now she's doing a good job makin' colts."

To a horseman, my bedroll and saddlebags were a dead giveaway that I was traveling. He asked no questions, wished me a pleasant ride and headed back to the warmth of his house.

We were by now entering some of the most beautiful horse country I'd seen. Winding gravel drives leading up to handsome houses and stables were bordered by pastures in which Thoroughbreds ran and played. Groups of curious colts came up to inspect us across the fences, then turned and raced away like little kids showing off.

For all the gracious charm, there was an air of cold formality and I saw little sign of life except for the horses. An exception was a man near a small house in a wooded section. He looked miserably cold and had a red runny nose closely topped by a wool cap with earflaps. He was openly curious and when I answered his questions as to where I was headed he took on an expression of sad futility.

"Sure wish I could get outa this goddam' country," he sniffed. "It's hell tryin' to make a livin' around all these rich bastids.

"Cold as hell too," he continued. "I ain't got near enough wood put up yet."

The implication was clear that somehow the rich bastids were at fault for the weather and as I left him, the day was no longer as pleasant. Probably due again to some insidious plot on the part of them rich bastids.

Later that day, coming to another old brick farmhouse surrounded by barns and herds of beef cattle, I rode up to ask if I might camp nearby. I noticed an 1809 date over the door frame and was duly impressed by the excellent condition of the place. No one answered my knock and there seemed a strange air of vacancy in the whole area, belied by the presence of cattle.

After trying several other nearby houses with the same lack of response, I reluctantly pulled into a woodlot and camped. There's an unpleasant feeling that accompanies camping in a populated section without permission, but I had no choice as the hour was late.

A day or so from here took us into cedar country. Back when I was a bloodthirsty little urchin with my first .22 rifle, some cedar-covered hills were my favorite skulking country. While I no longer get any pleasure out of shooting animals

49

unnecessarily — and I might mention that I have no quarrel with those who do — I still retain a nostalgic love for cedar-strewn hills.

The usual check with the owner allowed me to make camp in the midst of a rolling section of my beloved cedar trees. I'd been cautioned by the woman to whom I'd spoken that there was a pony pastured somewhere in the field. So, shortly after dinner, I was not too surprised to hear the mare snort and see her throw up her head.

A squeal of equine delight directed us to the shortest, fattest, happiest pony in Virginia. His delight at finding unexpected horse company was funny to watch and he promptly attached himself to Sioux, following her every move. His interest was solely fixed on the mare until bedtime, when I tied her to a cedar tree fairly close to my sleeping bag. Hardly had I gotten zipped into my bed when he became fascinated by me. It was a clear, cold, moonlit night and it soon grew somewhat disconcerting to look up and find a pony standing at my feet staring at me. Soon mere looking failed to satisfy, so he'd ease up and touch my feet with his nose. I'd yell at him, he'd jump a maximum of six inches and continue staring at me. Finally in spite of the attention I dozed off, only to be rather rudely awakened about midnight by a stout poke in my posterior. This ended the joke and I threw several odds and ends of firewood and gear at him and finally convinced him that I wasn't in the mood for his overtures, friendly or not.

In the morning, he followed us to the gate and whinnied piteously until we were out of sight.

4.

The cold weather had become, while not pleasant, certainly bearable. I'd gotten quite accustomed to it and conscious only of the change when I stepped into heated buildings. Then my face burned and the closeness of the air was suffocating. Chapped and cracked hands were the only continuing misery and although I wore gloves even while cooking and eating, my hands remained sore throughout the winter. I think the process of filling the small alcohol cooking stove that I carried may have contributed to the situation, since I usually spilled some of the alcohol and doubtless it had a drying effect on my hands.

Shaving was an unpleasant chore. I'd never had nerve enough to grow a beard, even some years back when the wearing of a beaver was not connected with torn T-shirts and sandals. To be truthful, I'm reasonably sure my beard would be tricolored anyhow, with mangy-looking spots, and it's either a luxuriant beard or none. The alternative was shaving and I'm partial to an old-fashioned straight razor with good hot water and lather. Outdoor shaving with a cold wind blowing has an unpleasant tendency to dry and cool the lather before completion of the shave, and I was failing to enjoy the prospect. I discovered gas stations. Here, by timing it after the morning rush, I had the men's room to myself. My offers to pay for use of the facilities were invariably brushed off.

One of the old-fashioned gas stations still found occasionally in this area provided me with some local color along with its Dr Pepper soft drink dispensing machine. I'd spotted the building across the road as I topped a hill in a comparatively uninhabited stretch. The jumble of old tires, oil cans and many years' accumulation of odds and ends had failed to conceal the cold drink machine and I was vaguely thirsty. I crossed over and stepped off the mare as two rather paunchy, florid-complexioned, middle-aged men in bib overalls came out of the door. Our brief introductory conversation led me to believe that whatever they'd been drinking had not come from the same machine as my bottle. The mare was in season and had given me a certain amount of trouble for the past several days. Evidently, a large gray jack burro in a pasture across the road had become aware of her condition. The two gas station attendants had been making admiring remarks about Sioux when the burro opened up with what he doubtless believed to be an equally complimentary if ear-shattering series of amplified rusty pump noises.

"She's been horsin'," I apologized as I steadied Sioux with a jerk on the rein. She seemed unashamedly interested in the racket emanating from the jack across the road.

One of the men, obviously the owner of the jack, beamed with delight. He turned and bellowed across the road, "Hey, Jack, holler at this heah mare and tease her up — tease her up, boy!"

The jack galloped back and forth beside the fence, stopping only to bray, and again his mentor turned to me. "Say,

ol' boy, whyn't you stay the night and put that there mare in with ol' Jack? He'll fix her up if she-uns is ready."

"Sheeit." His companion spit a dollop of tobacco juice. "He wants ta breed her to a good-blooded stud, not a damn jackass."

The owner stiffened in half-drunk offense. "Well, by gawd! Jack's good-blooded! Look at them markin's an' the stripes on his gawddam' back an' shoulders. I'm a-tellin' you, buddy, put your mare in that pen overnight an' ol' Jack'll poon her fifteen times afore mornin'."

"That's right," agreed his buddy in an attempt to soothe the feelings of the owner of the jack and the bottle. Then with becoming modesty, "Jack's a better by gawd man than I am."

Not to be outdone in the turn the conversation had taken to self-deprecation, I allowed that Jack had me topped too. I thanked them kindly for the offer but declined with the excuse that I had to push on. I'm sure they were disappointed on Jack's behalf; nevertheless, they insisted on feeding Sioux a generous helping of horse and mule feed from a cardboard box while I drank my soft drink.

The countryside at this point was no less attractive than it had been. Mountains and valleys continued to roll away to the south and the weather began to get considerably warmer. I had no trouble finding people who were willing to allow use of their farms for my nightly stops and many invited me in for the evening. Still I began to feel an uneasy sense of something hard to define. Much of the housing indicated the decaying result of neglect. Others, of a more recent vintage, were somehow depressingly tasteless. One in particular, a cement-block monstrosity, sat proud in its bilious coat of aqua paint astride a well-kept green lawn, the whole surrounded by a cement wall — also painted aqua. It lacked only a group of artificial pink flamingos to complete the effect. On one lawn there was a statuary display which carried its own message: the black and white plaster figures were of a mother skunk, three baby skunks and a Negro child.

Excessive litter, not surprisingly, goes hand in hand with homes that are nothing more than shelter. Here, beer cans studded the roadside at a frequency of one for every three feet. I wondered if some sort of mandatory I.Q. test should accompany the sale of beer. Signs prohibiting dumping seem to have an inspiring effect on certain people. Maybe a four-letter-word-oriented mind is capable of reading only the first four letters of any word — thus "No dumping" registers as "Dump." The deep gorges with small streams at the bottom, called runs in this area, are frequently flanked by picnic tables, a fireplace and what should be a totally unnecessary sign bearing the legend NO DUMPING. Almost invariably, a huge pile of beer cans accompanies the sign. I'm convinced that the persons using these small parks for their dumping grounds are physical midgets as well as mental midgets — otherwise they'd have been unable to fit into their automobiles while transporting such a great quantity of beer cans.

For some reason, Sioux derived perverse pleasure from intentionally booting the cans along the road, much like a small boy playing the old game called Kick the Can. I was worried that she'd do the same thing with the bottles and cut herself, so I attempted to punish her for refusal to avoid them. I didn't win and she continued to play her little beer can polo game whenever the targets were available.

The brief roadside conversations proved frustrating for the reason that I usually wound up answering questions about myself. The occasional evening conversations were more interesting, since in such instances there was sufficient time to get the talk steered around to the interests and views

56

of the locality. There seemed to be much less racial tension than I had expected to find. Some curiosity about the North and how integration worked, particularly in the schools, was expressed, but I was at no time the object of any trace of hostility as a Northerner.

One man with whom I spent an evening seemed more puzzled and troubled by the integration ruling than embittered. He was a combination farmer and factory worker who had three school-age children. He mentioned that the private school to which he sent his children cost four hundred eighty dollars per year for each child, but he seemed to look at it as merely an inevitable expense of the day and age. I later discovered that he was a native Ohioan and not a Virginian.

The number of slack-jawed, not overly bright youths seemed to be increasing. Their chief activity centered, as elsewhere, on old cars with noisy exhausts and their gathering place was the neighborhood gas station.

"Whur ya from?" came the standard query.

"Rhode Island."

"Ruode *Eye*lan!"

"Yeah."

"Whur 'n 'ell is thet?"

"East of here."

"Oh yeah — thet's near two hunnerd mile, ain't it?"

"About."

"Jee-sus!"

Rather late one evening I stopped at a gas station to inquire as to the mileage to a motel that I had been led to understand was ahead. Some time had elapsed since I'd enjoyed the opportunity to take a bath and a motel was the only answer.

Riding into the lighted area near the gas pumps, I was quickly surrounded by an unprepossessing group of young Neanderthals who peered myopically at me through hanks of greasy hair and proceeded to ask me whur I wuz from. I was in no mood to spend much time over the answers to the usual questions, so I asked about the motel.

One particularly unsavory young man leered at me brightly and asked, "How much do hit cost to ride a hawse crost-country?"

"Not a hell of a lot or I wouldn't be doing it," I answered as noncommittally as possible.

"That 'ere *mo*-tel you lookin' to git to — hit's gonna cost you a *lots*-a money."

A low-keyed consultation going on in the rear of the group gave me an increasingly uneasy feeling which was not lessened when one of them stepped forward with a helpful smile. "They a right nice place to camp down the road heah about a mile — y'all kin jes' pull offa the bridge and git undah hit. Ain't nobody gonna mess with yuh 'cuz nobody can't see yuh oncet y'all git undah."

Whur I wuz brung up a double negative means a positive, so his assurance that "ain't nobody gonna mess with yuh" firmed up my decision to keep a-goin'. I expressed my relief that I had only another mile to go, thanked them for their assistance and put on an additional six miles to the motel, even though it necessitated an hour of after-dark travel, something I normally avoided. I had the definite feeling that I had just met some close relatives of the Scragg family in Al Capp's *Li'l Abner*.

Arriving at the motel, I found that it was closed for the season; however, the proprietor lived next door and willingly gave me permission to camp behind the buildings. My camp was on a pleasant hillside overlooking a fine lake and I put in a comfortable night with the restful assurance that I wasn't going to get hit over the head or stomped on. The desire for a bath was by now becoming an obsession and inquiries the next day led me to a town some miles ahead and slightly off my route that was alleged to have a large rooming house with showers and hot water. The town itself had a lovely name and I looked forward to a quaint tree-shaded village bisected by a softly flowing river with possibly even a mockingbird or two.

By midafternoon I'd ridden into the town and found a large segment of the population in the shade, all right. The shade that had been sought out by the inhabitants was provided not by ancient sycamores but by the interior of a string of sleazy barrooms. The thing that bisected the village was a railroad yard with what seemed miles of freight cars loaded with new automobiles and truck trailers.

Following directions, I came to a large peeling frame building, tied Sioux to a tree in the side yard and went up the old wooden steps and into the lobby. A homemade sign tacked to the inner door warned that no whiskey was allowed on the premises. A number of oldsters sat around in equally ancient chairs and one — a small, lively, red-eyed man in an oversized army field jacket — hopped up and escorted me through the maze of overstuffed furniture and spittoons to the desk. He walked with a twitchy briskness that gave the impression of a birdlike hop and his friendly greeting bathed me in gin fumes.

The white-haired man behind the desk stated wearily that a room was available and my cheerful little escort skipped ahead of me up the stairs to the second floor and down the hall, pointing out the location of the shower room and his room en route.

The room was a tiny cubicle with an army cot and folding chair. The blankets were ancient army surplus and a naked bulb was suspended from the ceiling. The lock had been broken out of the door. Nevertheless, the room was clean and I'd have gladly paid the stipulated dollar and a quarter for the bath alone. I dropped such gear as I had with me and went back down to the lobby, after politely refusing a belt of gin from the pint bottle that had been stealthily slipped out of the voluminous jacket and proffered to me by my newfound friend.

While I was registering at the desk, a small group of curious onlookers gathered around. I asked the white-haired man whether there'd be any objection to my leaving the mare tied out in the rear or side yard.

"Hell," one of the crew quickly spoke up, "y'all better shut her up some'res. Some of the mean-uns round here liable to cut on her — jes' fer sport of a Sattidy night."

"That's right," affirmed my host. "Don't leave nuthin' around neither, else they sure as hell liable to steal it."

He thought a moment, then said, "Y'all go next door to the barroom and ask the feller that owns it to put her in his garage shed. He got a high chain link fence around ever'- thing an' a lock fer the garage. That way none of these here drunks can cut on her."

This serious suggestion from the proprietor convinced me that they weren't fooling, so with my little buddy with the gin bottle again leading the way, we walked over to the bar.

It was still quite early in the afternoon but the place was jumping with an assortment of farmers and railroad men. Four rough-looking types, holding a rather blurred conver- sation over a blasting jukebox, were sitting in one of the booths and I eased over to the cash register where the bored- looking proprietor was refilling the beer glasses of a couple of stool occupants.

While making my request to the bartender, my newfound friend eagerly regaled the boys at the bar with the story of my arrival, on horseback.

"I be go to hell," said a huge half-drunk farmer. "Set down with us an' have a beer."

"Well," I hedged, "right now I've gotta go get my laundry done and my horse put away, but if you're gonna be here awhile, I'll be back later."

"Hell, we'll be here all right," he burped. "I want you to know that y'all air in the toughest gahddam' barroom in the toughest gahddam' town in Virginia. You see them four boys sittin' in that 'ere booth?" He gestured with a sloshing glass of beer. "They do about arything in the world fer you — if y'all wuz to ask — but sheeit, even the state police is afeard of 'em."

I was privately wishing that he'd keep his voice down; however, the occupants of the booth grinned an affable acknowledgment to the compliment.

The big farmer continued in a loud beery voice, "Y'all wanna mess around in this here gahddam' tiger pen, you can get you a cut on the head — 'counta these boys is tough."

The bartender rescued me from the conversation by his return with the key to his fenced-in garage.

"F' chrissake," he cautioned me wearily, "be sure you lock the chain to the fence, else the bastards around here'll steal the chain, lock and all."

I gave my assurance that I would and with fingers crossed, promised to return as soon as my chores were done.

"Y'all do that. As a matterafac', this here's a dam' good town. Y'all stay here awhile, we show you the place an' you gonna have you a time."

Somehow I was reminded of a friend from some years back who was forever attempting to get me to attend one of his weekend bashes. He usually arrived for work on Monday mornings looking somewhat shopworn but with an unmistakable inner glow of contentment.

"Jeez chris'," he'd say, "good party this weekend. Drinkin', singin', dance, fight, puke — goddam' good party. You shoulda came."

61

I cheerfully admit to having attended my share of fairly rough bouts with the bottle. I've been in bars where belt buckles and curb chains were the accepted dueling weapons and I once watched with alcoholic detachment while a diminutive friend, with Sennett-comedy timing, plucked a blackjack from the hand of a combatant whom he felt was taking unfair advantage of his opponent, belted the attacker with the same smooth movement, then helped carry the unconscious victim to the stairs where he was thrown to the ground-floor entrance. I never happened to get hit, cut, shot or bashed with furniture, a fact which I attribute to deft footwork coupled with great good luck. Furthermore I no longer intend to get myself into a situation where this sort of activity is likely. When I reached the age at which hangovers triple in length and intensity, I decided that drinking no longer was that much fun and became a zealot for abstention.

In this case, I got out before someone decided to impress me with how tough a bar I was in and gave me a souvenir cut on the head. I unsaddled Sioux and piled the saddle against the tree where she was hitched, then took the more portable gear such as saddlebags up to my room. After shaving and bathing in the shower room, which was clean if not fancy, I gathered everything in the line of clothing that I wasn't wearing and headed for a nearby coin laundry. There was no alternative to leaving my remaining possessions in an unlocked room; however, I did take the precaution to roll my camera and pistol up in my sleeping bag.

My little drunken guide had finished his beer and spotted me passing the bar. He once again skipped happily alongside. We got to the laundry and he proudly showed me to the soap dispensers and machines. With the machine going, I got a couple of Cokes from a dispenser, one of which I handed to him. He didn't seem overjoyed but drank it politely. The situation that existed with the horse and saddle unguarded next to the rooming house, my gear in an unlocked upstairs room and me in a laundry several blocks away left me with something less than a feeling of ease. A sudden squawk from my guide caused me to start and swivel in his direction. He explained that it was his imitation of a crow. With that he did a brief soft-shoe routine, sang or croaked a bit from a vaguely familiar melody, twirled around with arms extended and waited expectantly for my applause for his imitation of James Cagney. I hadn't quite caught on that it was Cagney but I had been reasonably certain that it wasn't Lionel Barrymore and I congratulated him. The performance was interrupted when he suddenly shot to the door to open it for a colored woman with her arms full of laundry. Having assisted her to a machine, he proceeded to cup his hands in front of his mouth and produce odd squeaking noises that I immediately recognized, with his help, as birdcalls.

I decided not to wait for my laundry to dry completely as I was anxious to get back to my room, so I bundled it up still damp and headed back with James Cagney hopping alongside. We got to my room, where I draped the laundry around in a decorative manner. Then I saw to the mare, who had by now filled up on grass.

I led her over to the garage, hitched her to the side of the tractor parked inside, gave her grain and water, and locked the garage and then the gate in the chain link fence that surrounded the whole thing. We headed back and it dawned that I was not likely to get rid of my helper in the near future.

Following me into my room, he looked cautiously back into the hall and warned me in a low voice, "They all talkin' about you."

"Oh?" I said with surprise.

"They all think you an F.B.I.," he confided slyly.

"Why would they think that?" I asked.

" 'Cause they's so much stealin' an' meanness goes on here," he explained with a touch of outraged virtue mingled with pride.

"Oh, I can see why," I agreed, thinking what a disguise a paint horse and cowboy hat made for an undercover agent and reminding myself to forward the suggestion to J. Edgar Hoover at the earliest.

I held up my hand in a silencing gesture, stuck my head cautiously out into the hall, then leaned over to him and confided surreptitiously, "Just between you and me, I'm not."

His pleasure at my taking him into my confidence was clear and he allowed that he'd offer me a drink if he had one. One of my infrequent attacks of brillance came upon me and I reached for my wallet.

"You've been *so* helpful to me," I handed him a dollar bill, "that I wish I had time to go have a beer with you — but I've got some repair work to do, so let me buy you a couple of beers with this."

His red-rimmed little eyes brightened as he turned and skipped happily down the hall, tucking the dollar bill in a pocket with one hand and waving his thanks with the other.

My small contribution to his delinquency didn't amount to much, but I figured a dollar's worth of beer on top of what he was already carrying would ensure me a few hours of solitude in which to catch up on letters and sketches.

Dinner was served, lunch-counter style, in the rear of the building, and the meals were inexpensive, quite palatable and for me far too generous. A ninety-cent dinner served with hot biscuits nearly foundered me. While lingering over my coffee, I was intrigued by the black-haired waitress, who had been worrying continually throughout the meal. The

64

cash register was malfunctioning and it wuz purely worrisome to her. The coffee cups looked dirty, but they wuz clean, they wuz jest wore so's they looked dirty, and it wuz purely worrisome to her. I entertained the mean thought that possibly the impermanence of her dye job was equally worrisome to her but dismissed it and rebuked myself for uncharitable thoughts. At least she was trying and that's a hell of a lot more than can be said for many.

I wandered back to the lobby, where a television set was the center of attention. The evening national news was in progress and a handful of old-timers sat around the set, most of them with a large spittoon handy. At infrequent intervals, an amber jet of tobacco juice was fired with careless accuracy and I wasn't certain that it didn't represent an opinion of one of the newsmen's pronouncements.

One of the national leaders and a couple of well-known newscasters are masters of the prep school accent, no mean trick as it involves speaking in a softly cultured tone with a completely immobilized upper lip. Tobacco juice punctuation was particularly noticeable when these men spoke. As I climbed the stairs heading for my room, I chuckled to myself, wondering how much communication had been taking place below.

A chair propped against the door and the pistol under my pillow allowed me a sound night's sleep broken only once by the unmistakable sounds of violent vomiting coming from the room of one of my neighbors. Early in the morning, I packed Sioux and quietly left the town to nurse its cuts, bruises and hangovers. Regardless of the colder temperature along the ridges of the mountains, I was about ready to head back up to the Appalachian Trail. The next town of any size changed my mind.

It would be difficult to find a neater, cleaner, more friendly village than Elkton, Virginia. Somewhere, we had crossed an invisible barrier to dirt, litter and ignorance and were entering a community whose pride in itself was clearly evident. The very atmosphere was fresher and now the road through the valley complemented and enhanced the mountains that framed it. Even the beer cans vanished and they were not to reappear for many miles. I stopped to make a few purchases in the neat and orderly brick store buildings, then rode on down a pleasant stretch of highway lined with small farms.

A sparklingly clean walled-in spring came up on my left, spilling over its dam and under the fence. I turned Sioux into a sandy area where cattle had obviously watered and climbed down to give her a drink. The water looked inviting enough to cause me to belly down and enjoy it myself. The stuff emanating from the pipes the previous night had been heavily treated with chemicals, so I dumped my canteen and refilled from the spring. Meanwhile, Sioux had finished drinking and was grazing along the edge where the grass appeared to be particularly succulent. A nearby brick house occupied the level area just preceding the foothills where the land started its rise to the mountains. A number of milk cows stood staring at us and a large barnlike building edging the woods proclaimed by its sign that it was the workshop of a cabinetmaker.

As I stood waiting for Sioux to finish grazing, a tall lean man stepped out of the shop followed by a younger dark-haired man. It was early for a stop, but by now I'd learned to settle for a good campsite early rather than to wait too long and wind up in an unpleasant spot. I walked over and introduced myself, then asked about camping up in the edge of the woods. I was glad I had. The two men turned out to be among the finest people I was to meet. Kieffer, the cabinet-maker, and his wife occupied the brick house near the spring. Their nephew John lived just beyond the barn in a similar house.

Hardly had I stated my business when the offer came to stable Sioux in the barn and stay at the house myself. But it was a beautiful warm day and I'd picked up some perishable groceries while passing the town, so I thanked Kieffer for his offer and went on to the edge of the woods to leisurely arrange my camp. I found a large oak tree in a small clearing, plenty of grass, a few cedars and a flat-topped rock that made an excellent table. Having arranged my bed under the oak tree and cooked dinner, I was leaning against the tree doing a sketch of Sioux grazing when John walked over the rise. We had a brief and pleasant conversation, and then he came to the point of his visit.

"You might be smart to keep an eye open at night," he cautioned. "We've had some bear trouble in the last week or so. Now that the tourists have left up on the mountain, some of the tame bears have come down to the valley looking for food. They killed two near here last week. They'd torn up some camps and beehives and killed a calf."

Before leaving home, there'd been some discussion as to the pros and cons of my carrying a gun. In some states a handgun is illegal, in others it isn't under certain conditions. With the hodgepodge of laws that exists, there appeared to be no legal way to transport a handgun across the country, but I decided that I'd rather risk being arrested than hit over the head. My wife was quite vehement in insisting that I should have a pistol and I was easy to convince. I'd carried it unloaded, rolled up in my gear, and had only loaded it at night when my sleeping quarters seemed to warrant doing so. I had had two handguns to choose from, a Ruger .22 revolver and a frontier model Colt in .357 magnum caliber. The .357 had a long, seven-and-a-half-inch barrel and was considerably heavier than the .22, as was the ammunition;

however, it allowed a choice of low-power "wad cutter" cartridges, medium-power .38 special or the high-powered .357 magnum. I'd settled on the more versatile Colt and was glad I had. I now stuffed it full of the .357 cartridges, and the gun and flashlight accompanied me into the sleeping bag.

The evening was clear and warm and I wrote letters for some time by the combination of candle- and firelight. Sioux dozed, standing hipshot until I'd tossed my last cigarette into the embers and zipped myself in for the night. Then, as usual, she grunted, flopped down and made herself comfortable near the foot of my bed.

At four A.M., a loud snort from Sioux brought me up to a sitting position, wide awake. A bright moon clearly illuminated the clearing and Sioux was out at the end of her forty-foot rope, snorting, stamping and looking past me up the mountain, her ears pointed straight up. The warm feel of that walnut-stocked pistol was at that moment worth any inconvenience it might have caused before. I'd have had little fear of a wild bear, since they usually want nothing to do with humans. A tame bear, accustomed to being fed by tourists, is another thing when hungry, and for a long twenty minutes I leaned on my elbows watching the shadows and the patches of moonlight in the direction that Sioux was looking. I'm quite sure a warning shot would have been all that was required, still I was glad I'd elected to carry the heavier caliber.

Sioux was much more nervous than I'd ever seen her, moving back and forth at the end of her rope, stopping, peering mountainward and snorting. Sometime after I lighted a cigarette, a crackling of brush came from up the ridge and presently Sioux calmed down and came over to stretch out again. I took this to mean that all was well, so I uncurled my thumb from the hammer of the Colt and went back to bed. I'm not sure what it was that visited us in the

68

night but I've never seen the mare react that way since, so I am reasonably certain that one of the tourist bears had toyed with the idea of a call, then decided against it.

Shortly after sunrise, while Sioux was going through her customary and persistent routine of poking at my feet in order to convince me that it was time to get up and feed her, Kieffer came into the clearing with an armload of hay. He laid it down and in a shy but insistent manner asked me to come to the house for coffee.

"Thanks, Kieffer." I crawled out and pulled on my boots. "But I certainly don't want to intrude on you folks."

"You come along!" he said in a tone brooking no argument.

"I've got coffee and the works here."

"You come along now."

I fed the mare her grain and went along meekly.

The house was as attractive inside as the outer appearance indicated, and on the table Kieffer's wife had the openers for what was to be a tremendous breakfast.

One of the less genteel habits I've acquired involves the tossing off of orange juice in one thirsty blast. Following the blessing — and I found that any meal in this part of the country without a very sincere word of thanks was the exception — I, as usual, bolted the sizable glass of juice that had been placed before me. My hostess, whose bustling about the table had been only briefly halted for the blessing, immediately refilled my glass. It was evident that in order to avoid endless servings, I would have to indicate immediately that I'd had my fill. When I'd first approached the table, I'd paused standing for an awkward period, waiting for Kieffer's wife to be seated. It was presently obvious that she didn't intend to sit with us, and only later, when we had been completely served, did she unobtrusively join us at the table. As far as I could gather, this is an old custom in the mountains that hasn't changed with emancipation.

I was to enjoy a number of meals with this couple and with their nephew's family and friends next door. The blessings were almost embarrassing, since they included thanks for the privilege of my presence at the table. The sincerity and humility, the deep belief in God, the genuine pleasure derived from helping others — all struck me as a pleasant surprise. Phony sophistication, the blasé attitudes toward simple values were not a part of life here and I didn't miss them at all. I left with regret after a two-day rest, refreshed by my contact with genuine, warm people.

Virginia has a number of caverns and I'd passed several without investigation. Pulling in for a mail pickup in one small town, I made several inquiries about a nearby camp area and all suggestions pointed to a picnic ground adjoining one of the caverns. I rode out, arrived near dusk and got permission to camp overnight. The elderly ladies living in a large stone house on the property suggested only that I make my presence known to the night watchman, who was to go on duty in the early evening.

Shortly after dark, an old car pulled in and stopped near a small wooden building and I walked over to introduce myself. The caretaker was an old mountain type, bent by the years — shy but not necessarily reserved. He had a few chores to tend to and then the cave had to be checked; if I was of a mind to go along, I could. I gave him a brief hand with some firewood for the big house and then we walked up the hill to a large building that housed a gift shop and the cave entrance.

"Been workin' here five years," he commented with satisfaction. "Best job I ever had — used to allus get far'd on accounta whiskey."

I had observed a few telltale traces of strong drink

etched on his face, the most prominent of which was a red puffy nose that doubtless had cost him a fortune to acquire.

"Now," he continued, "I don't tech whiskey no more. Done read the word in the good book an' my life's some changed. Whiskey like to ruint my life for near sixty years till I learnt to live the good life."

I mentioned that I'd quit such foolishness myself a few years back and he continued to inject his comments on the subject with frequent stops brought about by execution of the chores.

"Hell," he said as the mop paused in its tour of the office building floors, "never used to figure they was nothin' to do, only huntin' an' drinkin'. Only worked long enough to buy whiskey an' shotgun shells — then I'd quit or get far'd. Never knowed what the good life was till I got to readin' the good book an' quit the whiskey. Ain't drank in seven years now and wisht I learnt sooner."

I looked into the dark cave opening and decided to stay over for a tour in the morning. The clean-up work finished, we walked back down the hill to the shed, his flashlight picking out points of interest for me. The old building housed the usual clutter of tools, soft drink cases, a table and chairs and an old cast iron potbellied stove that was soon aglow. The night was becoming fairly cold, but my camp was all set up and I turned down his offer to let me sleep inside. I did, however, go get some water and coffee which I brought back and set on the stove to boil.

"Most all my drinkin' friends is dead now." The old man leaned back in his chair, softly reminiscing in the warmth of the room. "Even a ol' nigger gal I use to know. We'd go by her place huntin' an' she'd allus come out an' give us a drink of her own whiskey. Made it herself an' hit was shore good stuff but I reckon hit kilt her anyhow."

His use of the word nigger was in no way intended as an

71

insult and of this I feel positive. It was only an easy contraction of the word Negro. It would have been as difficult for him to say Negro as for me to say nigger. In fact for him, and for others whom I met, to use the word Negro would have been a conscious affectation and somehow it would for that reason have been offensive.

He mused awhile, keeping his thoughts to himself, then went off on a different subject. "Use to do a lotsa huntin'. I don't know — guess I figured rabbits and the like was jes' put on earth to shoot at. Musta kilt a million. Didn't want most of 'em, jes' shot 'em 'cause they was there . . . Don't like to kill nuthin' no more lessen they's need for it . . . I rather watch 'em than kill 'em. You like to hunt?"

"No," I replied. "I like to shoot — you know, targets — but I don't go hunting much any more."

"Me neither." He shook his head. "Seems like I done a lotsa things that I don't know why."

My coffee was ready now, and I offered him coffee and a package of cookies I'd brought along.

"No, thanks," he said, reaching over for his lunch box. "I got my lunch and a bottle of coffee right here."

We ate and drank, and as he finished his first sandwich he took out most of the second, unwrapped it and limped over to the door. He opened it, tossed the sandwich out by the steps and returned to his chair. I said nothing and after a moment he looked around with a twinge of embarrassment.

"Jes' a ol' possum comes around to eat aboot this time . . . He ain't much but — hell, he's some company when you all alone."

I smiled sympathetically and, judging that I wasn't going to ridicule him, he elaborated.

"One night last summer, I like to got in a mess with that ol' possum. He come for his eats an' a big ol' polecat got

72

there afore he did. Ever' time he'd move in on the polecat, the polecat'd raise his tail — then he'd back off. He finally quit tryin' an' I was some happy. I figgered for a while the whole place would get stank up. First chance I got, I shot the ol' polecat, 'fore they had a fight on the steps."

I told him about the raccoons we have at home that nightly pull the tops off the garbage cans and scatter the contents. They wait until the lights go off and the dogs are shut in, then go to work on the cans with a great clanging of lids and frequent squalling over choice items. I confessed that regardless of the mess that they invariably make, we enjoy having them around and do nothing to discourage them. He was obviously pleased with my admission of foolishness and shortly I observed a fragment of cheese sandwich being tossed under the table. I made no effort to conceal the fact that I'd seen him and looked at him questioningly. This time he was really self-conscious.

"Jes' a li'l ol' mouse comes around for some supper," he mumbled sheepishly, scratching his head and evading my eye.

Sure enough, a small gray form popped out from behind the wooden cases and wrestled the sandwich fragment back into the shadows, from whence now came tiny eating noises. I'd almost gotten the impression of impatience on the part of the mouse, as though he'd wondered what the hell had been holding up his share.

"You're as bad as my wife and I are," I laughed. "We fed some deer mice cookies and chocolate one winter and my wife cried when the dam' cat killed them."

"I'll be go to hell." He chuckled with delight. It was clear that he was glad to find that others in the world were as crazy as he.

The early-morning risings and long days in the open usually combined to put me to bed by midevening, particularly in a heated building. Now the heat from the stove began to counteract any stimulation I'd gotten from the coffee and I left the old man to his four-legged buddies.

In the morning, I took a tour of the caves with a personable young guide. I was the only visitor at that hour and our conversation jumped back and forth between the memorized spiel and ad lib comments, so that I had the strange sensation of being escorted by two different people. I'd never been in a cavern before and it turned out to be more interesting than I'd expected it to be, due in part to the bits of extra information our talk unearthed.

This particular cave had been used by Stonewall Jackson to house a large number of troops at one time during the Civil War. The guide spoke of an old man he knew who had been employed to clean out the caverns after the war when he was a young boy. Many of the stalactites and stalagmites had been broken off by the soldiers as souvenirs, then left behind with the rubble that inevitably is linked with the occupancy of some three thousand soldiers. Black patterns on the walls were as fresh looking as though the torches that had caused them had burned only a day or so before. I think I got more of a sense of identification with these men here than at most of the other battlesites, probably because less had changed in the hundred years separating us. I'd wondered at times how these men had felt and what their thoughts had been as I traveled through the same hills and probably slept and ate and traveled in a style and at a speed contemporary with theirs. It's impossible to do more than conjecture. There have been too many visible changes in just the lifetime of one generation to be able to understand much of what might have been thought and felt in 1860. It's a short time in years but an age in change. Traveling by horse couldn't make me unaware of jet plane contrails streaking the skies. Here, deep in a great echoing cave, the

insulation of high stone ceilings and walls allowed a brief contact with an unmechanized and quiet past. I emerged into a rapidly cooling day and departed having experienced a small but intimate contact with history.

The cold prevailed and the blacktop roads were slick going for a horse. Most of the borium welds were worn from the mare's shoes and she began having difficulty keeping her feet when we were forced to cross asphalt stretches. Concrete surfaces provided much better traction than cold asphalt, and for that reason as I was coming into a good-sized town along about here, I cut a corner by crossing over the cement apron of a gas station. It was a windy day, traffic was heavy and noisy and so, when Sioux hesitated halfway across the driveway, I attributed her balkiness to the confusion and the fluttering banners overhead. I pushed her on and had innocently reached the far side of the gas station when the proprietor stuck his head out of the office door.

"Hey, buddy!" The tone was not friendly.

I pulled up and looked back.

"Y'all comin' back an' clean that up?"

There, scattered halfway across his driveway, was unmistakable evidence that some horse had committed a nuisance. There were no other horses about to point the finger at, hence nothing to do but tie my indiscreet mare and attempt to kick the objectionable matter into the gutter. It didn't lend itself to very successful kicking, so I walked up to the office and asked the glowering proprietor for the loan of a broom.

"Gahddammit — leave it alone," he growled, not looking at me. "Y' done jes' scattered ya dam' hawse crap all over mah place as it is."

"I'm sorry," I apologized meekly.

"Mmmmmph," he grunted, and I got out while I was ahead.

79

The town I'd come into was quite large and appeared to be the main shopping center for the surrounding country-side. I was in need of boot repairs and a number of items, so I decided to get a motel room and stay over a day. I found a place on the far side of the business district with the aid of a reporter who had stopped me for an interview, and I had no trouble getting a room with permission to tie Sioux in the rear where there was abundant grass.

Later that evening, while sitting at the counter of a nearby restaurant, I was amused by the conversation that was going on three stools down between the waitress and a short, extremely fat man who sat draped over his stool. The place was nearly empty and the fat man's voice carried clearly.

". . . An' this here guy checked into the cabin with a horse!"

"Whaddayamean — he was ridin' on a horse?" asked the waitress incredulously.

"I ain't kiddin'," the fat man insisted. "He come in on a horse and asked for a room. An' they give him one — right down the street at the auto court!" He jiggled with laughter and pointed down the street in the direction of the motel as if to further convince the waitress.

I rotated my stool toward him and laughed. "You mean some nut checked into a motel — horseback?"

"Yeah." He turned to me chortling, eager to expand his audience.

I joined him in laughter and then said, "That was me."

The trapped victim's eyes traveled quickly down to the rail, took in my boots, returned sheepishly to my face and said sickly, "I didn't say nothin' bad, did I?"

"Course not." I grinned at him. "I was just trying to get you in trouble."

He smiled with relief and began the usual questions

concerning my destination and background. By now the answers came by rote.

He left after getting my reassurance that he hadn't said nothin' bad and was soon replaced by a sour-looking individual who glumly ordered a hamburger and while waiting for his order looked toward me.

"When you through with the salt and pepper," he observed testily, "you should orter move it over to the next man."

Reflex made me obey but immediately I regretted it as I pondered what his reaction would have been had I refused.

"This is my salt and pepper. It came with my dinner and you'll have to buy your own," I should have said with a completely straight face. Lacking the incredible courage of the man on *Candid Camera*, I said nothing, the opportunity was forever lost, and I probably avoided a punch in the nose.

Watching him from the corner of my eye, I was fascinated by the fact that after successfully browbeating me out of the salt and pepper, he totally ignored it and proceeded to devour his hamburger exactly as it was served. Again the troublemaker in me was tempted to suggest that he should orter eat with his mouth closed, but I didn't. At least I'd had a form of entertainment with my meal, and on the way back to my room I decided that the town had provided me with three good laughs: the gas station man, the fat man and the arbiter of salt and pepper social behavior. Two of the laughs, of course, had been silent in the interests of diplomacy.

The morning of my departure was cold and gray, and the forecast was for cold and snow. I'd brought the mare around to the door of my room and had nearly completed packing when a good-natured gentleman came across the street from a large supermarket where I'd made some last-minute purchases. He was the owner of the store and evidently had been filled in as to my doings.

"How far are you planning to go today?" he asked.

"About twenty miles south," I replied.

"Well," he said with a twinkle, "it's going to snow tonight and I don't give a dam' about you but that horse has to get under cover. I've got a farm just about twenty miles down the road with a big barn and plenty of hay and feed. You go down and put your horse up at my place and feed her on me. I guess it's all right if you get under cover with her but the main thing's the horse."

I laughed, thanked him and assured him that I'd take him up on the offer.

"There's a young couple that run the farm for me. I'll phone down and tell 'em you're coming and you be sure to stop there. It's sure as hell going to snow tonight."

I got explicit directions and after some additional conversation, started off. Suspecting that he was right as to the forecast, I didn't particularly want to delay, but hardly had we cleared town when a car cut in front of me and stopped. A young man with pad and camera emerged from the car, and I could foresee another newspaper interview. Most of the reporters I'd encountered were fun to talk with and many on the trip were helpful in ways that had nothing to do with their jobs. This one was looking for an angle.

"Is this ride you're making a protest against the war in Viet Nam?" he asked with pencil poised.

I guess he was disappointed with my honest reply; anyway he soon left me to make up the time that had been lost. I saw relatively few of the articles that were written and I missed this one; in some cases I wished that I'd missed others. The exaggerations often had a tendency to be embarrassing and I ran into direct quotations attributed to me that had never even entered my mind — unfortunately, none

82

of them profound. If I dared mention a half hour flurry of snow it was quite likely to appear in print as a huge drifting blizzard that should have had me trading in my horse for a dog team. I found that it did no good to guard my answers, because they usually were hypo'd up to what the individual reporter wanted anyhow. In a number of cases the writers were completely factual but these men were in the minority. One or two that I met later apologized for what their editors had done with the story they'd turned in, so maybe the fictional touches came from the deskmen.

The delay brought about by this particular newsman was mostly made up for by a brisk trot which was appropriate to the chilly weather; nevertheless, dusk had fallen before we turned in on a dirt road leading to the farm. No sign of human life was around, but being certain that I had the right place, I went ahead and made us at home in the barn, bedding down the mare and spreading my sleeping bag nearby in the deep sawdust that covered the floor. It was warm and out of the wind and sleep came quickly, to be only briefly interrupted by the crunch of tires on the gravel road sometime before midnight. A few minutes later, the approach of footsteps and a questioning hello from outside aroused me enough for a reply and a flashlight greeting from the depths of my bedroll. I politely refused the offer of house hospitality by the good-looking young farmer and he didn't push it other than to hope I'd at least join them for coffee in the morning.

Daylight gave me an opportunity to look around and find that I'd spent the night at a handsome old farm comprised of a large brick antebellum house, smaller outbuildings and the great stout barn where I'd slept in comfort with Sioux. Hills dotted with white-faced Hereford cattle rolled up on either side of the entrance road and horses, chickens, pigs and several milk cows were penned near the barn.

The young farmer appeared almost with the light to feed them and he introduced himself and apologized for awakening me the night before.

"My wife and me would be proud to have you come for breakfast," he continued almost shyly. "We ain't rich but you're sure welcome to share what we got."

A short walk took us to the fenced-in dooryard of the spacious old brick home. Huge high-ceilinged rooms, carved woodwork, the entrance hall with its handsome staircase climbing to the upper floors indicated a past that linoleum floor coverings, faded wallpaper and the basic necessities in furniture couldn't belie.

Kenneth's wife was as attractive as he was and four handsome kids attested to the truth of the old saying that you don't get cocker spaniels out of airedales. She had just returned with the split logs for the kitchen range and, by some magic formula lost to most of today's housewives, promptly produced a great and wonderfully aromatic breakfast of bacon, eggs, sausage, hotcakes, freshly baked hot biscuits with churned butter, and coffee. As I was easily prevailed upon to remain with this family for the day, I ate four wonderful meals in this simple but warm kitchen. Everything we had, and there was much variety, came from the farm with the exception of the flour, salt, sugar and coffee. Somehow this young girl was managing to raise four children, feed the series of wood stoves that heated a large house, tend to her garden, milk the cows, churn the butter, feed the chickens, help with the butchering and preparation of the three hogs (which were a part of the annual remuneration), tend the clothing problems for a family of six, put up preserves for the year and still give every appearance of being fully as happy, fresh and attractive as the girl in a five-color magazine ad plucking some packaged and comparatively dull-tasting food mix from the supermarket shelf.

We sat at this table lingering over our cigarettes and slowly sipping our coffee from our saucers. As I watched healthy, happy kids frolic around, barefooted on a cold linoleum floor, the thought came that regardless of where these kids were destined to go in later life, they'd have a childhood to look back on that I'm certain would have deeper values than the televisioned, overentertained, radiant-heated, air-conditioned, wall-to-wall-comforted existence which seems to bore so many of our children. I'll be surprised if these farm kids get so jaded with life that they're forced to get their kicks from LSD or whatever else is in vogue when their time comes to go out into the world. And later, when the oldest boy, an eight-year-old, skillfully drove the tractor over the hills while his father and I fed out flakes of baled hay to the beef cattle from the wagon, I'd have been willing to bet that any number of urban kids would have thrown in the color television set on a trade.

Here, for the first time, Sioux was turned completely loose in a small fenced-in pasture near the house. She snorted, kicked at the moon and raced around and around, bucking and having a fine time for herself.

"Dam'," said Kenneth, "she shore is rank for a twelve-yar-old."

That night, the temperature dropped to fourteen degrees and I was prevailed upon to stay in one of the huge unheated bedrooms. When I went in to bed, I found an electric blanket in place, already plugged in. All arguments were in vain; they insisted that it had been a gift that they never used — a doubtful statement — and I wound up spending a suffocating night due to their kindness.

Next morning, while I reluctantly packed up to go, the family came out to make their farewells. The young mother handed me a heavy square package of home-cured "side meat" which I gratefully accepted and stowed away. As I untied Sioux and prepared to reach for the stirrup, Kenneth came around to shake hands.

"Where do you reckon you'll be Christmas Day?" he asked with a worried look.

"I'm not sure, but I expect I'll be down around Roanoke," I said after a rough calculation.

"Well," he continued, "you shouldn't spend Christmas alone. Why don't you phone us where you are and I'll bring the truck down and haul you and your mare back here for Christmas, then take you back down the next day, if you have to hurry?"

As Sioux and I topped the last ridge, we paused to wave to the small group still visible in front of their farm home. The air still crackled with the cold but seldom have I felt more of a sense of warmth.

By now I'd come to realize that getting toward southern Virginia wasn't doing much toward leaving the Northern winter behind. I'd been lucky up to this time in getting hit with a minimum of snow, but any dreams I'd been nurturing about the sunny South were rapidly fading. I'd been reassured from time to time by the type of house and barn construction I saw. Houses that were open to the elements underneath and barns that were built with almost slatted side walls should have been proof that it didn't get very cold at this latitude. To judge by the temperatures I was finding, they only proved that Virginians like fresh air better than New Englanders and that their barns are largely built from green oak which shrinks and opens wide seams after curing. I began to feel that I'd better stop dawdling along and make tracks farther south without delay. The problem was that the people were becoming so friendly and the country so interesting, I was reluctant to leave as promptly as I should. I had the sensation of riding with a nervous eye cast over my shoulder. Somewhere in a dim recess of my mind I could remember an illustration of Old Mr. North Wind that had been in one of those wonderful children's books of years ago. He was great and gray and swooping and had his cheeks puffed out like Dizzy Gillespie blowing a trumpet and there was an impression of icicles hanging from his beard. I had something over four hundred miles to go to make the Mississippi and while by now it was easily possible to do two hundred miles a' week, I had been sliding down to the vicinity of little more than a hundred. I knew that if I didn't speed things up, I'd glance over my shoulder one of these days and there would be Old Mr. North Wind sweeping over a mountain ridge.

Nevertheless, the next town was too much of a temptation to pass by without at least a one-day stopover. Lexington is a charming place. I knew little about it except that it was the home of Virginia Military Institute, where many of our more famous military leaders had gotten their start, and of the equally historic Washington and Lee University. I'd been told by the young farmer and the owner of the farm where I'd stopped over the weekend that I should pull in at a dairy farm on the outskirts of town. Again snow was predicted and a guy named Pete owned the dairy where I would be able to take cover. No one told me that he also owned a large and plush motel adjacent to the farm and a number of other enterprises in town. When I arrived at his barn and asked for him, I was told he was at the motel next door. Still innocent as to his ownership, I walked over and asked the man at the desk if Pete was around.

"Mr. Rodes is out back. I'll call him." He stepped out of the room.

He returned leading a stocky, genial man who listened quietly while I explained that I'd been sent by a mutual friend to inquire about barn cover for me and my horse.

"Sure," he grinned. "You take your mare over and put

87

her in the bull barn — it's empty. My son-in-law will show you where the hay is." He turned to the desk and handed me a key. "You take number eight."

Conscious that my funds were down to about five dollars, I was momentarily embarrassed.

"Fine," I said, "if you don't object to waiting till morning, when I can get into town to collect a money order."

"I don't want your money," he replied with attempted gruffness. "This place is empty — no tourists now — and you're welcome to stay."

I stood stupidly with the key in my hand while he busied himself shuffling papers at the desk. Finally I laughed and said, "The farther south I get, the crazier you people get."

With this he laughed delightedly, waved me out and went back to his office.

Later that evening, after a restaurant dinner, I returned to the office through the wet snow that was at last falling. Pete was in the rear playing cards with three friends, and I sat down long enough for a cup of coffee with them.

"You ought to stay over and visit Lexington," he suggested during the lull for a shuffle. "It's a real old historic town, if you're interested in that sort of thing."

"I'd like to," I admitted. "However, if I stay another day, I want to register the usual way. One night on the house is enough."

"Sure," he agreed and went back to the cards.

In the morning, I walked over to town to pick up the money order and was promptly hooked on Lexington. I hadn't realized that it had been the home of Stonewall Jackson prior to the Civil War and Lee's home after. Both had been teachers here and Lee's last days had been spent as president of Washington and Lee. Jackson's tomb, his home, the church where he'd held Sunday school classes for the colored kids; Lee's home and chapel absorbed me so that I

ran out of time and decided to prowl through the grounds of
V.M.I. on horseback the next day. Returning to the motel to
feed and water Sioux, I stopped to pay the motel bill. Pete
just grinned and would have none of it.

A steep path cutting off the highway led me up to the
heights of the campus at V.M.I. next morning. The snow had
disappeared by now and it was one of those lovely clear days
that continually tempted me to take my time. The students
had left for the holidays, so I got pretty well into the
grounds before meeting anyone. The clop of hoofs didn't
pass entirely unnoticed, however, for a handsome, tweedy-
looking gentleman hailed me and insisted that we hitch
Sioux to a high iron gate and go into his office. My greeter
turned out to be Chaplain Bob Wilson of V.M.I. and we had
a fine talk cut short only by an appointment. Before leaving,
he walked over with me to the museum that I'd come to see
and put me in the capable hands of Colonel Heflin and his
wife, who made the tour particularly interesting. I had long
been an admirer of the great Stonewall, and the large
quantity of his personal belongings in addition to the
mounted remains of Little Sorrel, his undistinguished-
looking but highly trained and companionable war-horse,
added greatly to the tour of his home that I'd taken the day
before. Colonel Heflin next escorted me to the Jackson
Memorial Hall and by the time I'd completed the major
points of interest at V.M.I., I'd been made to feel like some
sort of celebrity rather than a denim-clad saddle bum with a
squashed hat.

I'd finished taking some photographs of the campus, in
the best tourist tradition (including one of Sioux hitched to
a wheel of Jackson's famous battery of cannon Matthew,
Mark, Luke and John), when the chaplain reappeared with
a no-nonsense invitation to have dinner with his family and
stay over another night. He'd made arrangements to stable

89

Sioux at a nearby estate and it was obvious that regardless of that dark cloud breathing down my neck, I was to spend another night in Lexington.

An interesting feature of Lee's old home is a breezeway connection with the stable. Lee always maintained that he wanted his famous horse Traveler to stay under the same roof with him; thus the house was designed and has been maintained that way. I stopped in passing and introduced myself to Dr. Fred Cole, the president of Washington and Lee and the present-day occupant of the house, and he very kindly opened up the old stable and allowed me to hitch Sioux to the stall and take some additional photos. It seemed somehow appropriate that one traveler should pay her respects to a more famous one. I understood that Traveler's skeleton had been placed in the Lee Chapel as a follow-up of Lee's wishes; however, if it's still there, it's no longer on display and as I'm an incurable sentimentalist as to my own old mare, I'd be happier to know that it has been replaced. If it hasn't — and when I was there no one seemed to know where it had been put — I hope there are enough admirers of Robert E. Lee, north and south, to raise a noise until Lee's wishes are respected.

The thoroughly enjoyable evening with the Wilson family started off with a New England boiled dinner in my honor. Bob's wife Mimi, who came from Massachusetts, was delightful, as were the kids. Bob had been a widely traveled Navy chaplain before coming to V.M.I. but he was a native of Kentucky, and we spent some time going over a possible change of route that would take me through part of that state. His glowing account of the Kentucky hill country sorely tempted me: but for the big gray cloud with its cheeks puffed out, I'd have probably switched west at that point. As it turned out, my (mistaken) notion that Tennessee would be warmer canceled out the bluegrass country and next day I continued south to Natural Bridge.

By now Sioux was a confirmed tourist and she occasionally aroused my ire by gawking at the passing countryside while I was forced to glue my eyes to the ground to prevent her stumbling into holes and over various obstacles. She was always interested in the many kinds of livestock we passed and her first mule made me wish I'd had the camera out of the saddlebags. I saw the mule a moment before she did and consequently was a witness to her ear motions as she reacted. The head went up as usual, she nickered eagerly, the mule threw up his head and brayed and Sioux stopped cold with an expression of complete incredulity. Her frozen position with ears straight up and high arched neck said plainly, "What in hell *is* that — a horse with a bad cold?" Even after I'd stopped laughing and moved her on, she'd slow down and angle around to look back over her shoulder at old longears. Mules have been largely supplanted by tractors in this day and age, except for specific areas where they've remained unsurpassed; thus they're by no means as common as they once were. Nevertheless, they're still frequently found in logging country, as they fit between trees where a tractor can't, and I later ran into them in the extremely rough, mountainous cattle country where the going is too tough for saddle horses. Sioux eventually accepted them as just another horse. She even became accustomed to pigs, which I think cause a horse to get neurotic as easily as any animal. There's something about the erratic running motion and the squealing and grunting of a gang of young pigs that terrorizes most horses, and Sioux's behavior was about standard until she spent several nights on farms in close proximity to porkers. She took many things in stride and was surprisingly calm over things that startled me. Rabbits almost invariably wait until the last moment to pop up and scoot

91

from under a horse. I jumped; she never did. Perhaps she smelled them in advance. The one item that Sioux refused to accept was a flat object, such as a fallen signboard lying half buried in the grass. She never got over spooking at these and I'm by now resigned to the fact that she never will.

Probably Sioux felt as good as I did as a result of the active life we were leading. My customary headaches, heartburn and even arthritic aches and pains had magically disappeared. I hadn't had a trace of a cold and I had more pep and energy than I'd had in fifteen years. Sioux was in equally good shape. I made it a practice to stop for a fescue grass break every hour, sometimes more often if we came to a particularly lush spot. I felt grateful to the state of Virginia and later to other states for being so considerate as to supply us with fuel of such good quality.

For those who wonder about the degree of rapport between horse and man, it had become considerable. At risk of being personal, I may say that by now we even shared joint "rest stops." At first I thought it was mere coincidence, but it happened with too much frequency for that.

Christmas came at Natural Bridge. I'd arrived at what looked like a vast commercial complex of gift shop, skating rink, cafeteria and motels and realized with some dismay that it would probably be an impersonal sort of holiday. Again I was due for a surprise. The manager of the complex arranged for a motel where I could stake Sioux next to my room and insisted on complimentary tickets for my visit to the bridge. He went out of his way to help me get Sioux down into the creek area where the great natural stone arch is located so that I could photograph her under the bridge. And after my first night's stay at the motel, the family in charge invited me to stay over for the holidays with no additional fee. I readily succumbed and Sioux used the two-day

92

layover to advantage by spending the time grazing in a large field near the tennis court.

On one of the days, I saddled Sioux and rode the short distance to a small country store. The building was ancient and weathered, with a wide veranda along the front that was occupied by a couple of elderly colored men and what looked to be about twenty hounds — all dozing in the warm afternoon sun. Coming out with my groceries, I found the mare dining on carrots that were being fed to her by her audience. I'd like to have had the time to do a painting of the old store; it was somehow a Southern version of the old New England general store painted by Abbott Graves in the early part of the century.

Christmas afternoon was sunny and warm, and I sat on a rock watching Sioux graze and sketching her in her background of field and mountain. I'd brought some apples and grapes with me — the apples intended for Sioux and the grapes for me. She made short work of her Christmas bonus and then proceeded to make enough of a pest out of herself to get the lion's share of the grapes. Not satisfied with that, she next insisted on poking her nose into my sketch pad until I gave up on the half-finished drawing and devoted my full time to ear scratching.

The raucous yapping of a small and beautifully barbered poodle shattered the tranquility as a man, pulled along by his leashed dog, came up to us. The man introduced himself as a visiting vacationer and we struggled to carry on an ineffectual conversation punctuated by a prodigious racket that was amazing in that it came from such a tiny dog.

"Bobo's never seen a horse before," the man remarked pleasantly as Bobo charged at Sioux's nose, yelling imprecations and straining on his jeweled collar. Sioux gave him her filthiest look and I began to worry that Bobo's first horse would be his last.

93

"I wouldn't let him get too close," I murmured gently. "She might nip him." Sioux's ears were flat back; pure hatred glared from her eyes.

"Oh, Bobo only wants to play," the man chuckled, allowing Bobo to dive closer at the lowered and threatening head. He released more slack on the leash, permitting the poodle to shift his attack to her hindquarters.

For a moment I almost succumbed to temptation, but I knew that a lesson in good manners delivered by Sioux might prove to be fatal, so I jerked the mare's lead rope and stepped in between the combatants before Sioux could drop-kick little Bo over into the tennis court. "I really wouldn't allow Bobo to get too close. He might get hurt," I repeated.

"Oh I'm sure she wouldn't hurt Bo. He loves other animals. He just loves to play, don't you, Bobo?" He shook the leash and little Bo increased the vigor of his leaps at the mare.

To anyone with the slightest sensitivity to animal facial expressions it was obvious that this love of Bobo's was completely unrequited. My maneuvering had thus far prevented mayhem but Bo's master wasn't helping with his fond belief that Bobo was as lovable to the world as he was to his master, and I had a question about which end of the leash the master was attached to. In order to head off an impending disaster, I made a vague excuse, coiled up the lead rope and barebacked Sioux out of range. I hope Bobo never gets a chance to crowd his luck with a less patient horse.

About noon of the first day's haul out of Natural Bridge, I reined Sioux over by a fence to allow her to greet a tiny pony that was staked next to the road. As she sniffed noses with the miniature version of herself, the door of a nearby house opened and a man stepped out.

"Had your dinner yet?" he called through cupped hands.

I assured him that I had and again was pleasantly reminded that I was in a country where people offered immediate invitations, in this case without even first having said hello.

By now the need of a horseshoer was becoming pressing and I'd had several names given me. One, who still operated out of a shop, had left for the day by the time I arrived and I went on, since there were said to be several in the Roanoke-Salem area.

Salem turned out to be the place where Sioux got shod and I ran into further delay of my own making. As we approached the outskirts and traffic got heavier, we passed a gas station and paused at a crossing. One of the station customers waiting for his car to be refueled walked over to ask where I was headed and where I was from. I told him and he grinned in satisfaction.

"By dam'," he said in that soft Virginia drawl that to me is pleasantly Southern without being saccharine. "Ah saw that bedroll y'all got rigged an' Ah said to mahself, that ol' rascal's a-goin' somewhere."

A few words established that he was a fellow horseman and I explained that my presence in Salem was due to the need of a horseshoer. He turned and pointed out the road ahead, directing me to a stable on the outskirts of Salem that was owned by a former sheriff named Emmett Waldron.

"Take your next right and head into Salem. You'll find the stable about a mile down. Emmett's a good man – he'll sure run down a horseshoer for you. And if he can't, call me at my home number and I'll shoe her for you myself."

Sioux's worn shoes were slipping so badly on the pavement that I decided to lead her the remaining distance. As directed, I soon came to a sprawl of buildings on the left that obviously housed horses and ponies. The central barn was quite large and a tack room–clubhouse complex just left

95

of the driveway was fronted by a hitchrack where a genial man stood beckoning to me.

I was reminded vaguely of the gruff but kindly actor Charles Bickford. Emmett, for it was he who'd waved me in, was a ruggedly good-looking man who appeared fifty and was actually in his mid-sixties. A neatly barbered, erect and confident man, with crow's-feet about his eyes that appeared to indicate an underlying good humor, he was dressed in corduroys tailored for riding, topped by a small Stetson. Immediately I was made welcome, the clubhouse was put at my disposal and Sioux was bedded down in a box stall just behind the room.

"My regular horseshoer isn't due for a couple of days." Emmett spoke with that soft Virginia accent. "But I'll see if I can get a young fellow near here to fix you up right away."

I explained that I was anxious to get borium welds on the shoes, if possible; also pads. Emmett assured me there'd be no problem.

The man who'd directed me to the stable had preceded me there which accounted for the immediate welcome I'd gotten. Now he offered me a lift into town so I could pick up a telegraphed money order that had been wired ahead of me.

I wasn't long in town but on my return to the stable found a big, powerfully shouldered young man already at work on Sioux's feet. Emmett had wasted no time in making the connections for me. A small group of older men stood around watching the horseshoeing operation. Most of the conversation consisted of insults delivered with straight faces and the easy familiarity of very old and very good friends.

"Which one of you cheap people is taking us all to dinner this evening?" the horseshoer asked as he paused in his labors on Sioux's feet.

"I don't know," said a thin-faced, wiry man in what I guessed to be his mid-fifties, "but I'll bet Mistuh Harry'll have to leave before we're ready to go."

The accused, a heavier-set man in hunting clothes, looked up in feigned wide-eyed shock. "Why, y'all know I'm not as tight as old Mistuh Stovall. I'll even invite him to go along and bring all his money — even if he has sneaked out on the last four checks. You evah notice how he has to go to the men's room just as the check comes?"

It was evident that this small group of men, ranging in age from their fifties to their late sixties, was a close-knit unit that maintained a sort of unofficial headquarters here at the stable. There were a draftsman, a dry cleaning store proprietor, a trucker and a semiretired dealer in saddlery and anything else that interested him. They almost always referred to each other as "Mistuh" with the exception of Emmett, whom they frequently addressed as "Sheriff." In spite of the almost constant flow of kidding invective, I soon became conscious of an absence of profanity that struck me as being an unusual feature to find in the vicinity of a horse barn. Their restraint may have been in deference to the presence of kids who frequented the place, but I think not.

My stopover for horseshoeing extended itself to a five-day visit, and during my stay I found that it was next to impossible to pay for anything from a meal to a haircut. An unwary diner was quite likely to have his attention distracted by one of the crew while several hotcakes vanished from the plate, but the only time I got a serious reaction was when I succeeded in getting the check. When that happened, joking came to an abrupt halt until I gave in and relinquished it.

Emmett, a bachelor, lived in a small house near the entrance to the drive. He certainly suffered no shortage of kids; there were seldom fewer than half a dozen working out the horses and ponies after school hours and it was clear even to a casual observer that they adored the man. It was also clear that he felt the same way about them. I'm sure that a great many parents could learn much about child handling from this horseman. Praise was forthcoming for a thing well done; a quick, blunt rebuke was just as sure for a breach of discipline. And the kids ate it up.

The youngsters, whose parents boarded their horses and ponies here, ranged in age from the very young to the late teens. They habitually said "sir" when replying to an elder and with them it was completely unaffected. Ordinarily I'd prefer not to be sirred. To me it's an unpleasant reminder of my age and most assuredly if it came from my own kids, I could be certain that it would be heavily loaded with sarcasm. Here, the "misters," the "sirs" and the absence of cusswords came as a sort of nostalgic carryover from a more genteel time in the history of our country. I had an ambivalent attitude toward the custom but at least it was different. Neither were the kids Little Lord Fauntleroys. One cute little red-haired girl, who rode like an Indian, was the squirt-gun scourge of Salem. Several times when I glanced around, I'd find her eyeing me speculatively with poised squirt gun — little devils twinkling in her eyes — and I knew that in a very short time I was likely to be added to her list of victims.

My horseshoeing job was excellent. Sioux was now equipped with extra heavy shoes and leather pads all around, since the young horseshoer had found traces of a stone bruise on one of her hind feet that no doubt had been picked up in the rocky Appalachian Trail country. A double load of the "non-skid" borium material had been welded to the toes and heels of the shoes and I tested her on some smooth blacktop pavement nearby. She at once knew that there was no danger of slipping and where before she had slowed down and proceeded only with caution, she now struck out and broke into a brief trot with complete confidence.

There was no further excuse for delay but when morning dawned cold and clear and I'd breakfasted with Emmett, he asked if I wanted to accompany him to the nearby pasture that he maintained for his pony mares and foals. He'd gotten an early phone call from a farm neighbor to the effect that one of the mares was foaling out in the pasture. I was easily tempted to go along. We drove out in the pickup and hadn't much more than gotten through the gate when we spotted Blue Dawn, the pony mare, soaking up the warmth from the sun's early rays as she lay in the frosty grass with a tiny sorrel colt snuggled up against her belly. Standing in a group nearby were the rest of the pony gang, all peering nosily at the new baby, none daring to get too close.

Carrying the tiny colt with Blue Dawn following close behind, we went up to the barn and shortly the new mother and baby were comfortably installed in a clean dry box stall where they could enjoy privacy from the rest of the herd until the little fellow could get his legs under him. As so often happens, I'd neglected to bring the camera with me, so on the return to the stable I made a small watercolor sketch of Blue Dawn and her colt as we'd found them that morning. Emmett immediately installed the sketch on the clubhouse wall.

The riding club that headquartered itself at this stable was planning a New Year's Eve dinner and dance, and a trail ride in the mountains was to take place on New Year's Day. When an invitation to stay over and attend was proffered, I weakened easily. It sounded much too interesting for me to pass up and despite the fact that I was crowding my luck on weather, this sort of contact with people had been one of the major objects of the trip; I stayed.

99

Salem was an experience that I wouldn't have missed. Emmett usually rose before dawn and switched on the yard lights. The resulting reaction from the horses got me going in time to help feed, after which Emmett cooked up an excellent breakfast. Our other meals were eaten at a nearby restaurant with whatever kids or adults happened to be around and willing to go along with us.

I made several trips with Emmett to either deliver or pick up a horse or pony, but for the most part the time was spent lazing around with the gang and making a few changes in gear. My old canvas saddlebags were abandoned here in favor of large army pigskin bags, and I got rid of the breast collar at the same time. I'd started with a breast collar, thinking in terms of a fat round horse and mountains. I knew that uphill grades would have the saddle constantly sliding rearward. By now, however, Sioux had gotten rid of a great deal of her fat and was well muscled. For the first time she had visible withers and hips, and the saddle stayed put as it never had before. Too, as the breast collar had a tendency to rub hair off her shoulders, it was only an extra piece of equipment that was apt to make a sore spot.

New Year's Eve was fun. The dinner and dance covered all ages and here, for the first time, I found in attendance the old-fashioned family unit, a custom I thought had gone entirely out of existence. Several saddle club groups had gotten together for the dance and the hall was jammed with a happy, noisy mob. The building throbbed to the amplified country music band; kids danced with kids, they danced with middle-aged people and they seemed to delight in being swung by the oldsters. Emmett was as eagerly sought out for a partner as anyone there and I was astonished by his energy. I'd never tried square dancing and it looked too bewildering for me to attempt it now; nevertheless, I didn't

100

entirely escape. One of the more heroic ladies there persisted in leading me out on the floor and gamely went through the paces in spite of the two left feet that I was equipped with. I'm certain that I enjoyed it more than she; yet for me it was, and I fully expect it will remain, a spectator sport.

Bright and early New Year's Day, the group planning the trail ride began to appear at the stable. Some of them had stayed with the dance much later than Emmett and I; still here they were, ready to go. I chuckled to myself, without too much sympathy, when the thought occurred of my many old friends who at this moment doubtless were lying in their beds at home, trying vainly to avoid any contact between their dry tongues and the dark brown roofs of their mouths, and hoping nothing would joggle their aching heads.

Some of the best horse trails I'd ever ridden led up into the mountains just west of Emmett's place. Wide dirt Forest Service trails wound upward in gentle stages and as elevation was attained, the view through the trees became ever more impressive. We splashed through streams of clear mountain water and the air was crisp and exhilarating.

Sioux and another mare were the only two horses with standard gaits; the rest were Tennessee Walking Horses. The Walking Horses had a smooth, swinging, effortless running walk that took them over the ground with much more speed than the standard walk. As a result, we brought up the rear and even then were forced to jog trot for most of the seventeen miles that were covered. Fortunately, both Sioux and I were in condition to go along with no particular strain.

The lead horse, a handsome palomino stallion named Sunrise, belonged to Emmett and he was one of the best-mannered stallions I've ever been around. His movements alone were a pleasure to watch and the high-arched neck, the long cream-colored mane and tail and his deep golden color

101

completely rid me of any lack of enthusiasm I'd had in the past for palominos. One of the trail riders, a transplanted West Virginian, commented on Sun's masculinity in a rather graphic manner.

"Dam'," he said one day, "if we'd a had a horse like that back in the mountains where I was raised, we'd a shortened up his front legs and plowed with him."

Many of the riders here used a saddle that was new to me and I think is not widely known elsewhere. It was called a Buena Vista saddle — pronounced "Byoona" — and was perhaps a carryover from the early Colonial saddle. Basically like an English-type, it was much deeper seated with a touch of the Western style in its stirrup leathers and skirts. There was enough skirt to accommodate saddlebags and it looked to be an all-around comfortable and practical saddle.

By now I was the victim of a certain amount of kidding. Getting needled implies acceptance and I was delighted when Mistuh Stovall started calling me "Taixas." It had been carefully explained to me beforehand that a young, rather clumsy and skinny kid from Texas had worked in the area and had of course been called "Taixas." Stovall one day, having rather carefully studied me from several angles, asked if I didn't remind everyone of ol' "Taixas." From then on I was Taixas and I didn't find a way to get revenge until several days later when weather reports told of unusual rain and snow conditions that were prevailing in the part of Arizona which was to be my destination.

Stovall rode a handsome big Walking Horse named Tommy Lee. The horse was beautifully proportioned but had unusually large feet.

"Mr. Stovall," I purred to him, "how'd you like to trade horses with me before I take off?"

He looked at me suspiciously. "Why — do you like

102

Tommy Lee?" (Tommy Lee was probably worth ten times Sioux's actual cash value.)

"Yeah, I guess he's a good enough horse." I shrugged as casually as possible. "But I figure with all that rain, snow and mud in Arizona, those big pie-plate feet would really do the trick."

The poker-faced stare I got for a reply had just enough of a twinkle behind it to let me know that I'd better keep my guard up from then on.

Rain delayed my departure, which had been scheduled for the day after New Year's Day. I was fully prepared to be caught out in rain and other types of rough weather; somehow to start into it unnecessarily from dry quarters was quite another thing. In this case an additional day's layover provided us with an unexpected bonus. I'd been brushing Sioux off during our last afternoon in Salem when Emmett approached.

"I sure don't want a shaggy-lookin' ol' bear like that leavin' my stable." Emmett was looking disapprovingly at the long winter coat that terminated at Sioux's fetlocks in great bushy clumps of hair. "Bring her over next door after you get the dirt off and we'll trim her up."

I gave the lower legs a thorough brushing so that the dirt wouldn't dull the electric clippers and led her over to the adjacent barn where Sunrise and Tommy Lee and several others were housed. In a matter of a few minutes the clippers had trimmed the unnecessary long hair from the lower legs and cleaned up the long chin whiskers, and Sioux was now a much more presentable-looking horse.

I had vaguely noticed that Sunrise had made a little more noise over Sioux's presence in his barn than formerly and she in turn had responded with more enthusiasm than usual. She'd been in season several times on the trip and had acted like an idiot for four or five days each time. I'd accepted this as one of the drawbacks of riding a mare and fully expected it to occur every twenty-one days.

Emmett had observed her reaction to Sunrise while being clipped. Later that evening, while we sat around watching a television program, I got out my earlier notes and checked the dates. The record verified that twenty-one days had indeed elapsed since her last visitation, at which time she'd whirled about and nickered a response to everything from a bellowing cow to a crowing rooster.

"Why not settle her down now and have yourself a good colt next winter?" Emmett suggested.

Why not indeed, I thought, visualizing the handsome Walking Horse stallion next door.

"Wait till this is over," Emmett said, gesturing at the television set, "and we'll bring her up and see if she's ready."

We did, she was, and at this writing Sioux is back home dozing sleepily under her favorite oak tree. Never straying far from her side is a fine long-legged bay stallion colt born in December. Emmett had indicated that the name should include Sun as the line comes down from Midnight Sun, a famous Tennessee Walking Horse. Hence, the little stud bears the name Sundance Comanche and in this case the tribes seem to be living together in peace.

As an amusing sidelight, on the return trip from Arizona by trailer, we stopped overnight at Emmett's stable. Hardly had Sioux stepped from the trailer when a loud and effusive greeting came from the barn. A glance ascertained that Sunrise was the source. His handsome head was thrust as far out of the window as the dimensions permitted and there was no mistaking the recognition. . . .

We left next morning and all through breakfast, Emmett began to worry about the narrow, heavily trafficked highway leading out of Salem.

"I've got to run an errand about twenty-five miles down that way," he lied graciously. "Why don't we load your mare in my truck and I'll drop you off down where the highway's wider and safer."

As it turned out, I'd already traveled more dangerous stretches and was to encounter much worse, but nothing would do but to load Sioux and go along. It *was* a bad stretch, with a steep grade and fast-rolling trailer truck traffic, and we disembarked at the beginning of the new multilaned interstate highway. I wasn't sorry for having accepted the ride. It made it easier for us and gave me a few more minutes of conversation. Something akin to the feeling of leaving a close family member was with me as we shook hands and I climbed on Sioux and waved goodbye to Emmett and Salem.

Most of the interstate highways are flanked by grassy, fifty- to eighty-foot shoulders with an equally wide center strip. I'd been told that horses were barred from these new roads but shortly before arriving in Salem, I'd stayed overnight at the home of a horse-owning deputy sheriff and he'd checked with the authorities to find that while bicycles, hitchhikers and other unorthodox conveyances were in fact illegal, somehow saddle horse travel was not mentioned, probably by oversight. This, technically anyhow, allowed me to use the highways and I found them far safer than the narrow two- or three-laned roads with dangerously narrow shoulders. In my limited use of these new roads, I'd been passed by numerous patrol cars. None had stopped or done more than give me a friendly wave in passing.

The interstate highway was by far the most direct path into Tennessee and except for side trips necessary for food and supplies, I knew I'd better hightail out of Virginia by the straightest, fastest route possible.

105

5.

The rest of the way through Virginia was as rapidly accomplished as is possible on a horse. The cold remained constant and was soon made miserable by steady rains—only slightly above freezing temperature. The parade of days became an unhappy blur of plodding along in the driving rain with wet boots and a soggy hat that water eventually began to seep through, sliding up and down slick gluey clay banks, damp nights in open-faced hay sheds and old sheep barns, a miserable wet camp at a lake and no break in the gray skies.

A trail hiker's cabin had provided shelter for me on one cold and windy night. There were several double-decker bunks on the walls and a reasonably large door. I couldn't have been comfortable with Sioux outside in the wind, so I brought her inside with me. I probably should have felt guilty over this flagrant misuse of a cabin; I was merely overjoyed that the door was large enough. I might mention in Sioux's defense that she almost never commits a liquid nuisance in her stall and the other kind is easily removed.

I'd made a concession to my hat size in Salem and had

gotten a haircut. I had cause to regret it for some time until I grew enough of a thatch to recover the thin spot on top, since the open end of my sleeping bag was at times drafty. The situation caused me to think of a story told by a socially prominent woman I knew in Maine some years back. She'd been the victim of a disease that left her completely devoid of hair and was forced to paint on her eyebrows and wear a red wig. An old Downeaster was the local garbageman and one day, while picking up the trash, he'd paused and eyed her speculatively.

"Say, Miz Peters," he said, "me 'n you must be buth in ah sixties. How is it I'm nigh onto white-headed an' you ain't got a dab a gray in youah hayah?"

"Why, Mr. Perkins," she explained, "didn't you know? I have a wig."

"Well now, deah," Mr. Perkins consoled, "don't you think a thing about it. I expect it keeps you mighty nice and wahm in the wintah."

I figured Mr. Perkin's speculation was probably accurate and resolved to avoid further barbering until the climate improved.

One memorable day, late in the afternoon, the sun suddenly broke through as if to assure us that it was still there. The effect on the countryside was almost startling. Colors jumped from deep purple on the mountains to brilliant yellow in the nearby fields. For the first time I regretted having abandoned my watercolors. Still I'd have been hesitant to paint the effect of the colors and cloud formations. The light, striking through ragged tears in the dark gray sky and illuminating the great patches on the fields below, would have been so dramatic as to have come across as phony in a painting. I have strong convictions about painting such things as fall foliage, waterfalls and unusual effects of nature. Few painters have nature's judgment and

107

taste in handling grays with the brighter colors. Most who try succeed only in transforming a breathtaking view into a garish eyesore. A beloved old German painting instructor once mentioned that grays to a painter should be like gravies to a cook. Unfortunately most of us don't have the restraint in color necessary to implement this admonition. I am one of the many who have fallen into the trap of color and cringed at the results, and in this case I was happy to merely look, marvel at nature's ability to execute bright color with flawless taste and at the same time bask in the warmth of the sun. In the same way that I feel it impossible to appreciate color without gray, I'm convinced that no one can enjoy the almost sensual thrill of being warm without having been cold. This, of course, applies to the reverse of the situation, also to quenching a large thirst, to being dry after having been wet and so on. I wonder if in our striving for a complete and homogenized comfort in our homes, automobiles and offices we are not in truth depriving ourselves of some very basic pleasures.

The brief barrage of winter sun didn't last long enough to spoil us. Our arrival at the last town of any size in Virginia coincided with a sudden dip of the thermometer to the zero area. A strong wind added to the bite and I was directed to a farm on the outskirts where there was said to be a good chance of shelter for Sioux and me.

The farm was a combination dairy and horse farm and I was welcomed to the use of a box stall for Sioux and the tack room for myself. I cheerfully accepted for both of us and we weathered a two-day cold snap in relative comfort.

At this end of Virginia the mountain ranges that had been flanking the Shenandoah Valley join together, so that we'd been traveling along the tops in a considerably higher elevation. This doubtless contributed to the colder climate, which would continue until we dropped off into the lower level of northeastern Tennessee. The farmlands gave the look of long-used and carefully tended fields, rolling and bare with timber growing only on the steeper, rougher slopes. The soft, muted gray-greens, the silhouetted barns and solid houses gave me the sensation of having been deposited in the middle of an Andrew Wyeth painting and I was unable to resist making black and white sketches with color notations for possible later use.

My host was a wiry man in his late sixties who leaped about with the electric energy of a twenty-year-old. He handled his livestock with a great deal of whip cracking and shouting of phrases that were unintelligible to me but were evidently clearly understood by the animals. "Whooee – soock – soock!" and cattle would congregate on the hillside to be fed. "Whooee!" – a crack of the whip and horses would run out of their box stalls down the center aisle of the stable and drink from the trough; then more "Whooee!" – *crack, crack* and back they'd run to their stalls. All this turmoil was further complicated by a small black cow dog who danced about, barking noisily and displayed an uncanny ability to be in the wrong place at the right time. Invariably when a horse would start to run back up the aisle to his stall the dog blocked its way, barking, but somehow, in spite of what seemed to me mass confusion, the animals were successfully watered, fed and handled. Sioux was obviously fascinated by the excitement and peered over the top of her stall door much in the manner of a spectator in the grandstand watching a new and exciting game. When staying in Salem, I'd found Emmett Waldron's way of handling horses interesting. His belief, and I'm sure he's correct, is that a horse has extremely acute hearing. His control over the stallion Sunrise was marvelous to watch, as it was done with soft, almost imperceptible voice commands. While I'm sure that a horse is capable of hearing and being taught to obey a quietly spoken command, I must confess that my patience is not geared for this degree of self-control. My dulcet tones are limited to the times when all goes well — on other occasions, I've been heard roaring like a bull. Horses being the adaptable creatures they are, Sioux seems to understand that when father is vexed, it is well to tread softly; there'll be other times when she can get away with a few transgressions.

The last day of the cold snap, I was invited to go along on a cow trade. The barn was full of idle horses, several of which were quarter horses, very probably trained on cattle. Nevertheless, they remained unused and we went out to the bitterly cold fields with a truck and several farmhands who operated on foot to drive in the two heifers that were to be traded. It took at least an hour to move the heifers into a loading chute, thanks in great part to the questionable help of the "cow" dog. Each time the "Whooee — soock — soock!" and cracking whip would get the cattle started in the desired way, the little dog would charge in and scatter them in the wrong direction, where, heiferlike, they were more than willing to go. By the time the loading was finally accomplished, I'm afraid I'd have been sorely tempted to shoot the dog and the heifers too.

We hauled the heifers by truck to an old farm where they were to be traded for a fresh cow. They unloaded with ease on the rotted-out, flimsy loading chute — getting the cow to leave her warm barn and climb to the back of the truck was another matter. She flatly refused to be hauled or cajoled up the ramp, so I called up an old technique from earlier days and twisted her tail while she was being pulled from the front. It worked smoothly and the cow hustled up the ramp and onto the truck.

By the time we arrived at the home barn, it was dark. Our cow was no more willing to enter her new home than she

110

had been to board the truck, so, flushed with my earlier success at tailing-'er-up the loading chute, I reached out and caught her by the tail again. She immediately moved out as she had before, but this time I experienced a certain difficulty in getting a firm hold on what had now become a very slippery tail. Entering the lighted barn, I released the tail and found out why. Scrutiny of my buckskin riding glove indicated that the cow had been extremely nervous during the ride to her new home and had quite effectively avenged herself on me.

Leaving Virginia had me torn between sincere regret and anxiety to get to a lower, warmer elevation. Without doubt it has some of the most attractive country and the finest people I could hope to have found. If I'd arrived a month or so earlier, I'm sure the temptation to linger would have been greater — even the cold blast that ushered me out failed to dim the soft winter beauty of its hills. My reluctance about leaving was tempered by common sense when a short truck haul was offered by a cattle dealer who was going my way, and eventually Sioux and I wound up being dropped off in eastern Tennessee near a large town with a stretch of superhighway to make our travels less complicated.

A rather unprepossessing motel with a large barn and some cattle in the rear was the first night's stop in Tennessee. We'd pulled in and secured our accommodations after spotting the place from the highway and for the first time, Sioux was stabled next to a mule. She'd seen enough of them by now so that they were perfectly acceptable to her as company for the night, and I went to my room looking forward to the pleasures of a hot bath and change of clothes.

I was returning from my last checkup on Sioux before turning in when I met a white-haired oldster who was finishing up his chores. A wiry, lively man of seventy-odd years, his spiky hair poked out from under a weatherbeaten hat and his leathery face was seamed with the wrinkles of many years of good humor.

"Ah'm Prophet Elijah," he announced by way of an introduction, and rummaging through the pockets of a heavy winter coat, he extricated a card which he handed to me. "If y'all got a few minutes, Ah'd like to talk to you about the evils that beset us today."

The card indicated that he was a hillbilly prophet who was willing to travel anywhere to lecture and gave an address where he could be contacted. We walked up to my room, where we could talk in comfort, and as we walked he continued.

"The evils of the world today are whiskey, whoredom and communism." He pounded his fist into his hand with earnest conviction. "The Lord done come to me with a message to deliver to mah fellow man when Ah were just a young-un an' Ah've spent mah life a-passin' on the word. The growth of communism today is the Lord's punishment on us for whiskey and whoredom."

We had by now gotten comfortably situated in my room and he'd opened his coat to give greater freedom to his gestures.

"Whiskey is a sin an' whoredom is a sin an' we've done sinned ourselves to the point where the Lord has about forsaken us. He's a-lettin' communism take us over as a just retribution for our sinful ways an' the onliest way we're a-goin' to beat communism is to forsake whiskey and whoredom!"

He pointed a gnarled forefinger at me and pierced me with his bright blue eyes. "Do you know why Goldwater didn't win the last election?" he thundered at me.

I jumped, then stuttered weakly for a moment, fishing

112

for the proper answer. "Enough people didn't vote for him?" I suggested.

"That's where you're wrong," he snapped. "The Lord done tol' me in mah vision to stay plumb away from the polls. Votin' ain't gonna help us at all an' that's why Ah never voted in mah life. Goldwater done lost the election 'cuz the Lord wanted him to. He wants us to continue a-sufferin' till we renounce whiskey and whoredom. We're all sinners — steeped in sin — an' the Lord ain't gonna help us till we do somethin' about hit. I been travelin' around gettin' the Lord's message to the people for over fifty years. Do you reckon they'd be a place to speak to people back in New Jersey where you come from?"

"Rhode Island," I corrected him.

"Wherever," he said. "Maybe you'd take some of my cards with you an' give 'em out. Ah got a passel of 'em in mah car."

"Sure," I agreed, seeing no way out. "By the way, would you know where I can get an extra saddle blanket around here? My mare needs some additional padding to keep from wearing hair off her hips."

"Sure," he said. "You come up to the house for breakfast with us in the mornin' an' Ah'll drive you over to town to a saddle shop. Won't take no for an answer."

With that he rose and said good night and I turned in to ponder the connection between whiskey, whoredom and communism.

In the morning, as I walked up from the barn after feeding Sioux, Prophet Elijah spotted me. Forthwith I was ushered in to a huge farm breakfast with the widder woman who owned the place, the prophet and another farmhand. As usual I came close to foundering myself on the quantity of food served, but went ahead and gorged myself on fresh

113

biscuits, home-churned butter and honey complete with comb.

The prophet insisted on taking me to town to a saddle shop, where I was able to acquire an extra saddle blanket, and on the return trip continued his explanation of the reasons for communism's growth. He didn't forget the cards when I was ready to leave, so I put some in my saddlebags.

While at the motel I'd written a letter to my wife and family and had relayed the message about whiskey, whoredom and communism. A week or so later, during a phone call home, the subject came up and I found that my sister, who had been staying with my family in my absence, had digested the message and then turned to my wife.

"What do you suppose is so bad about a little old whiskey?" she asked.

Doubtless Prophet Elijah would be able to explain it to her.

The first snow in Tennessee was a driving wet storm that attacked us from the rear. We'd been traveling for some time on a large interstate highway in an effort to make as much time as possible. I had had a choice of swinging far south down a valley or climbing over the Cumberland Mountains. If the weather held off for a little while longer, the mountain route would be shorter; however, if I got caught on top of the Cumberlands, I was in for it. I had decided to gamble and head straight west over the mountains. The snow made me think that I'd probably made an error in judgment, but there was nothing to do but rig up my tarp arrangement that covered the front and rear of the saddle where my gear was stowed and climb into the rain pants and parka.

The sticky snow piled up rapidly and the going was tough for Sioux. It wasn't cold enough to freeze the gluey clay soil and the covering of wet snow merged to make a

114

clinging mess on her hoofs. Anyone following our tracks would probably have been convinced that he was on the trail of a four-legged abominable snowman. Visibility was all but completely obscured by the driving snow, but after several hours of sliding along, the dim image of a large gray barnlike building showed up off the road. I was straining to see what sort of shelter possibilities might be available when suddenly a wind shift enabled me to see the word STABLE painted in large letters on the slope of the roof. Delighted that fortune was smiling on us, I cut Sioux over to the far bank of the highway and got as close as the mesh fence would permit. Several people standing in the doorway of the barn spotted us and by gesture indicated that if I rode ahead to a nearby exit, I could return on their side of the fence. In a few minutes the maneuver was completed and we entered the large door of a huge horse barn to be greeted by the proprietor and a number of employees.

The proprietor was a heavy, florid man dressed in expensive stockman's trousers and fancy boots. The employees were mostly young men — some white, some colored — and several were engaged in working out Tennessee Walking Horses in the wide runway that divided the barn. Both sides of the barn were lined with excellent box stalls and I was relieved to think that Sioux was in line for warm dry quarters after a cold wet day on the road.

I paid the two-dollar fee for her stall and was directed to a rear section of the barn that adjoined the main building. This, I soon found, was the other side of the tracks. Some twenty-odd skinny old rental horses and ponies were loosely penned near some ramshackle stalls, and Sioux wound up in one of these which I cleaned up as best I could. A number of the old horses had their necks closely shaven and I immediately suspected the presence of lice, so I tied Sioux in the far corner of the stall where no direct communication was

117

possible. As always in these cases, I was careful to feed and water Sioux in her own folding canvas bucket. We'd been around one or two horses with runny noses and I was afraid of distemper.

The owner of the barn had genially told me that I could sleep there as long as I didn't smoke, so I reserved part of Sioux's stall, which at least promised an improvement over the situation outside. My boots were wet and I was thoroughly penetrated by the damp cold, and any glimmer of hope that I might be invited to bed down in the heated office room was extinguished when the owner left for the night after locking up the office.

The help fed out the horses and I made sure that Sioux got well fed on the good-quality feed that was used in the fancier part of the barn. I noticed that the poor old hacks in our section received what looked to be a less nutritious quality of hay. Sometime after five, when I was about to fill up on the cold provisions in my saddlebags, I was approached by one of the young colored boys who had been schooling a horse when I'd first arrived.

"I don't know if you mind or not," he said, "but I got an extra bunk in my room near here and you'd be welcome to stay with me tonight. We're goin' over to have supper in a few minutes. It ain't a fancy place but it's got heat."

"If you don't mind, I *sure* as hell don't," I replied promptly and gratefully.

It didn't take long to get my bedroll and saddlebags, and we headed for the small house that stood across a field from the stable.

"The old blacksmith and I live over here — I do the cookin' and he washes the dishes. Makes a pretty good deal for us," he explained as we approached the small frame building.

It had, of course, occurred to me that I was in the South,

where there could possibly be trouble brewed by a white man sharing quarters with a colored man. I figured this would be a good way of finding out the truth of the matter; still it didn't seem likely that I would have received the invitation if it had been expected to cause a fuss.

Jim, the young colored man, went to the kitchen to start dinner and I unrolled my sleeping bag on the extra bunk and soaked up the warmth from the electric heater. I was damp and cold clear through and had expected to crawl into my sleeping bag in a rat-infested and dirty horse stall; now the luxury of an iron cot and an electric heater was almost too much to believe.

The short, powerfully built old blacksmith and Jim and I made short work of some excellent fried chicken and we were soon sprawled on our bunks in Jim's room with the glowing heater between us. Jim was a highly intelligent young man, not much more than twenty, and I soon found that he was a musician in addition to being an accomplished horseman.

"I'm not sure I know what I want to do." He spoke thoughtfully. "I sure like the horses and this is a good place to work, but sometimes I like to get away from it and blow my horn."

"You play jazz at all?" I asked.

"Some – but not as much as I'd like," he replied. "The kids mostly want their kind of stuff."

We talked of jazz and then as a matter of curiosity, I broached the subject of race relations in this part of Tennessee. As closely as I could observe, Jim was completely honest in his feeling that there was no problem. Later, the white barn boss came over to Jim's room insisting that we go to his room to see his photo collection and a litter of puppies that were in a box under his bed. He was exceedingly drunk and punctuated his conversation with un-

119

shielded coughs and sneezes that had both Jim and me dodging.

The prize photo that I was supposed to see was one taken of our sneezing friend while jumping a horse with a two-inch ash undisturbed on his cigar. While rummaging through the stack of old photos, we were informed that at least fifty thousand dollars worth of pictures had been stolen from him over the years. Sure enough from the depths of the jumble of beer cans, old mismatched socks and discarded dirty shirts, the photo came to light, and I admit to being impressed.

Jim and I got ourselves extricated as soon as possible and Jim made certain that I understood that his boss was a good friend.

"When the old boy's sober, you couldn't want a better guy to work for. Used to be a top rider and still is when he stays off the juice."

The only inference that I could draw from our visit was that Jim had spoken truthfully about his acceptance by his white associates. I saw nothing to indicate otherwise and wondered if at times the various news media don't find little news value in decent behavior.

The treatment we'd been subjected to by the elements was improved for a while now. The sun shone, the air was pleasantly warm and travel was easier except for the slippery red clay banks alongside the highways. The advantage of being able to operate on either side of a road or, when preferable, down the wide center island had its built-in trap. I walked into it one day when nearing the Cumberlands and outsmarted myself.

A large sweeping interchange with exits and entrances swinging out in wide circles looked to be out of my way. With a certain smugness, I shifted to the left side and in shortcutting the interchange, missed some highway signs. Some six miles beyond, I found myself at a tiny crossroads village south of where I'd intended to go. As it turned out, one of those coincidental happenings resulted that makes the error worth mentioning.

I pulled in at the small country general store which was the center of the village and got permission to hole up in a small barn with a comfortable box stall large enough to accommodate us both. Four bales of hay laid on the floor made an excellent bunk for me in my half of the stall; Sioux made herself comfortable in her sector.

The general store, run by a man named Garner (a distant relative of the former Vice President), remained open until nine o'clock, so I went over to pick up a few items and there I got involved in a conversation that lasted the remainder of the evening.

Prior to leaving Rhode Island, I'd had a luncheon conversation with the prospective book publishers in Boston and during the talk, my probable route through El Paso came up. Tom Lea, Western writer and artist, had been published by this same firm and was a personal friend of the editor. The editor's suggestion that I stop in El Paso and look up Tom Lea met with a great deal of enthusiasm from me, since I'd been a long-time admirer of his writing, his masterful line drawings, his World War II combat paintings and his mural work.

Mr. Garner, after some discussion of my plans, began to reminisce about his youth in New Mexico and a cousin who had owned the Jay Cross Ranch in the area where he had worked.

"I don't suppose you ever heard of Tom Lea," he asked midway in the discussion.

I quickly corrected him and described my hope for meeting with Tom in El Paso. Garner walked over behind the counter, beckoning me to follow. I did and he handed me a tiny engraved .22 pistol designed somewhat like the famous frontier model.

"This pistol was given to my cousin by Tom Lea's daddy. He had it when he was mayor of El Paso and he gave it to my cousin a good many years back. I've had it ever since my cousin died. As a matter of fact, they tell me Tom Lea did some sketches up on the old Jay Cross Ranch that went into a mural in Washington."

Certain that Tom Lea would be interested, I got my sketch pad out of the saddlebags next door and made a small drawing with notations as to the pistol's origins. I'd already met several people in horse circles who were friends of people for whom I'd done horse portraits in various parts of the country. The coincidence of finding a man in a tiny crossroads village in the hills of Tennessee with a link to a man I hoped to see in west Texas struck me as more of a surprise, particularly when I'd landed in the town by mistake.

Getting back to my route next day entailed four miles of nerve-wracking travel. A two-lane blacktop road with almost nonexistent red clay shoulders spiraled through steep hills and farm country. The speed limit was an incredible sixty-five miles per hour and it was observed if not exceeded by the cars and trucks. The only solution was to strain my hearing to its limits in an attempt to hear approaching vehicles and then find someplace to get out of the way while the competition whipped around the turns at full speed. It was with a sigh of relief that we finally reached the wide-banked interstate highway and once again got back on our track.

Late afternoon found us picking our way down pine-clad mountains with a network of lakes nestling in the valley. An attractive village was surrounded by recently built homes

122

and the edge of the suburb appeared to merge into wooded parklike country on the rim of the lake. It looked like a logical spot to find a camp area, so I turned Sioux off at the exit and worked out through a residential area toward the woods.

A few inquiries made of residents indicated that permission to camp on the lake would be difficult to obtain; however, I was directed to a farm where horses were boarded. We quickly left the built-up section behind and passed up a winding road flanked on either side by steep hills. A crackling of brush above us to the left attracted Sioux's and my attention almost simultaneously. Sioux's nicker was returned and immediately a black horse with its young rider astride came sliding and jumping down the steep slope to join us.

Sandy Brown, the young lady on the horse, knew the location of the farm that was our destination and graciously offered her guide services. She was in her early teens and reminded me strongly of my daughter, not only in looks but because of her obvious attachment to her horse Sunny. I marveled at her ability to slide up and down the steep hillsides bareback. She was living an experience that I could understand and identify with and one that so many kids dream of. I myself was really cheating the years by means of a gimmick in using the compilation of material for a book as an excuse for being irresponsible and bumming around the country in the companionship of my horse. This girl and her horse were completely natural and simple and required neither excuse nor explanation.

We arrived at the farm in question and the owner, a generous soul, told me to make myself at home anywhere I wished. I hitched Sioux and walked out back to find a likely spot to unload when I found to my dismay that I'd accepted a disaster area for my night's stopping place. Old cars, mud, a grazed-out pasture and an open sewer that my fastidious mare flatly refused to cross greeted us and I began to wonder how I could gracefully get out of what I'd walked into. Sandy had not yet left and I got her aside and wondered aloud what to do.

"Our place isn't very fancy, but I'm sure you can stay there," she said. "At least there's hay."

Her statement about hay gave me a weak excuse, so I got Sioux and went back to explain her offer to the farm owner. I didn't want to hurt his feelings but neither did I want to camp in the mud, so as diplomatically as possible, I backed out and on the pretense of needing hay, followed Sandy and Sunny back the way we'd come.

The trail Sandy took was a close relative of the steeper parts of the Appalachian Trail and again I was impressed with her ability to stick her bareback horse in mountain-goat country. Eventually we broke out in a clearing and approached a handsome natural wood and stone house that clung to the hillside and overlooked the lake. We rode up to the door and Sandy's somewhat surprised parents came out for the introduction.

I'm sure that the Browns were at least moderately startled by their daughter's arrival at dinnertime with an unshaven saddle tramp in tow, but if they were, they masked their reaction with great skill and in a short time, Sioux and Sunny were put up and fed in the lean-to stable and I was shaving and cleaning up in a model bathroom right out of the pages of a magazine ad. The couch in the playroom with a cheerful fire in the fireplace was assigned me for the night and dinner was shortly on the table.

Sandy's comment about her home being not fancy but an improvement over the muddy barnyard from which she'd rescued me was a considerable understatement and I spent a most pleasant evening with a warm family.

124

Oak Ridge was nearby and most of the residents of this town were connected with the installation. The Browns had arrived here from Georgia some years back and Sandy's father Bob had designed the house in such a way that it blended smoothly with its wooded surroundings, while it clung precariously to the steep slope and provided a panoramic view of a sweep of the lake and valley below.

Rain fell again next morning and I was invited to stay over another day. I was sorely tempted but the Cumberland Mountains still lay ahead. I saddled up, got into my rain suit and with tarps covering us fore and aft, bade the Browns and Sunny goodbye.

A long, heavily trafficked bridge crossed a lake not far from the Browns. Each trailer truck sprayed us as it whooshed past, and as before I took the center of the right traffic lane and doggedly stuck to it rather than attempt to hug the rail. As always this technique forced cars to slow down and swing wide to pass us. Doubtless we were cussed by the drivers; nevertheless we made it across in safety.

The superhighway travel came to an end and we began to get into a less attractive part of the country. The steady drizzle of rain coupled with the heavy wet clay footing probably contributed to some extent to the dismal aspects; too, the type of housing began to deteriorate. An industrial section came up and was left behind and we stopped for the night at the jumping-off place for the Cumberlands. With the help of a garage owner, I got shelter for Sioux in a small barn where she had the company of a pair of gregarious burros. I holed up out of the rain in an old motel nearby.

I'd been unable to raise anyone at the motel until the lady proprietor appeared from around the corner where she'd been "a-burning the garbage." Her explanation hadn't been entirely necessary, as a pall of smog held down by the wet air had a strong aroma that permeated the area. Once in

127

my room I placed my wet saddle blanket over the radiator and arranging other articles of saddlery where they could dry. The room was presently filled with a completely delightful smell of leather mingled with horse sweat. There was always the possibility that the next guest might fail to share my enthusiasm for saddle shop redolence, but my concern over this quite likely event failed to cause any loss of sleep.

In the morning, with the weather clear, we headed up the mountain on a road so steep that at times I felt we must be overhanging the point of departure. Switchback led into switchback and in places the narrow highway was literally carved out of the vertical mountainside. There are many parts of the country, as an example Texas, where miles of straight highway with unencumbered visibility encourage fast driving. I never got used to the speed of most drivers in the Tennessee mountains and I continually encountered hair-raising driving throughout the state. On this particular morning, when halfway up the mountain, I heard the whine of a truck speeding downhill toward us. As it whipped around a sharp curve, I was petrified at the sight of a torn and wildly flapping tarp streaming from its ropes.

As there was no place to go, it was fortunate that Sioux was also petrified. A sheer rock wall was on the right side and a guard rail over a steep drop to our left and I could feel Sioux tense and freeze under me. The moment and the careening truck passed and from then on, I had more confidence in the little mare's common sense. If she was willing to stand her ground in the face of an apparition such as had just passed us, I felt sure that very little could shake her in the future.

I'd gotten fully supplied with grain and provisions at our last stop and the weight combined with the steep grade we were climbing made it advisable for me to do considerable walking. The higher we climbed the colder it got until soon I began to be aware of a strange and beautiful effect seemingly caused by the clouds and the cold. The pines and hemlocks along the tops of the ridges were lightly frosted by the combination of weather conditions and in spite of the steep grade and sore feet that I was acquiring, I stopped numerous times to enjoy the view. At one point along the way, there was a timbered glade where the mountain stream made a waterfall that fell into a deep rock gorge far below. Sioux and I turned in for lunch and had it been later in the day, I would have been happy to camp there.

We went on, eventually the mountain crested and leveled off and we were now on the Cumberland Plateau, which would continue at this elevation until it dropped off some days ahead to gradually decline to the Mississippi Valley.

For some reason, many of the houses that we came across in this section were completely out of tune with the natural beauty. A number of what had been fine old log cabins were still in use and when they'd been originally built, they'd been cut and fitted with great care and skill. A clever way of dovetailing the joints had gone into the workmanship. Now, many of the present owners evidenced neither pride nor care. With timber available on all sides for repairs that would have maintained the original charm of the buildings, patches were usually made with misfitting pieces of sheet metal. If a board was nailed on, it was frequently left with its untrimmed stub projecting out beyond a corner. Either the owners found no market for used cars or they had an affectionate regard for the old vehicles and kept them around for decoration. There were often two or three rusted hulks sitting about like centerpieces in an informal garden of long-empty beer cans. Still there was usually a late-model, functional automobile parked in front, and antennae jutting from the patched rooftops indicated that television had found its way into the old cabins.

Evidently soft coal was the fuel and heavy fumes hung close to the ground near each house. One ingenious soul had found a functional as well as a decorative use for one of his old cars. A door had been neatly wrenched off and the former pride of the highway was filled to overflowing with soft coal.

Indiscriminate dumping was close to criminal in the beauty of the surroundings and I was interested in a newspaper diatribe directed at the dumping of garbage and old cars in state parks. It was hard to understand why some people would haul refuse to a state park when others were perfectly content to leave it in their own front yards. Obviously there were those who were more fastidious than others.

I took an old dirt mountain road that led into a good-sized town — Crossville, Tennessee. A freezing rain had fallen from an early hour and icicles formed on everything including Sioux's mane. I was anxious to find cover for her, so I made inquiries in the town as to anything available in the surrounding country.

"There's a motel about four miles out near a big barn where you could put your mare," my informant said with a touch of reticence, "but I don't know if you'd want to stay there or not."

I doubtless presented a pretty rough appearance and I wondered whether he'd meant that the motel was too luxurious for me or the reverse. I was in no position to be particularly fussy in either case, so I headed on out of town.

Arriving, I got permission to stable Sioux in a good clean pen with plenty of hay and a tight roof. She was surrounded by bawling cattle and squealing hogs, but these would serve to keep her entertained if nothing else. After making the arrangements to stable her there, but before actually putting her up, I rode on to the auto court-café-beer joint that was ahead and found out what the man in town had meant. A room was available "but hadn't been cleaned up yet," so I unpacked at the door of the cabin and led Sioux back to the barn while a tight-skirted peroxide blonde with eye shadow straightened up my room.

After feeding, watering and rubbing down my spotted friend, I walked back to the room and found that another room had just been vacated in my absence — this one with a television set — but it too "hadn't been cleaned up yet." While I lugged the wet saddle and other gear over to the new room, a different blonde with similar eye shadow went through the motions of changing the sheets. She asked the proprietor what to do with the powder blue luggage that had been left behind by the "construction man" who had unexpectedly checked out, and it was taken to another room. Her clean-up job completed, I moved in and happily found a complete edition of the Sunday paper which I used to cover the dirty floor. A cursory glance at the bathroom almost caused rejection of the shower, but I decided to relent and thawed myself out in the hot water after lining the entrance with more newspaper.

Later, against my better judgment, I ate dinner at the café, while trying to avoid thinking about what the kitchen probably looked like. I was easily but not pleasantly distracted by a twelve-year-old boy who hung over the counter and stared up into my face while I ate. He wallowed a huge glob of fruity-smelling gum about his mouth and my food took on a strange fruity flavor. After dinner I ordered a cup of coffee which seemed by the taste to have been brewed long before my arrival in a pot used for questionable alternate purposes. After a couple of halfhearted sips, I staggered in the direction of the door only to be stopped by a cattleman who wanted to discuss my activities. He was a refreshing change from the people I had seen but the conversation was interrupted by a tight-skirted damsel who slunk over with an insinuating wiggle to her behind.

"Y'all gon' play the jukebox fo' me, honey?" she inquired in tones that I'm certain she would term irresistible.

The contents of most jukeboxes today would cause me to cheerfully spring for a quarter's worth of silence anytime and the mere thought of anyone activating the pleasantly quiet box in this place was depressing. Being spineless, I pretended I hadn't heard the lady's request. Fortunately in the interest of peace and quiet, the cattleman stared a silent refusal and swivel-hips slunk off. Doubtless she pegged us as a couple of cheap bastids unworthy of her further attentions.

That evening my ingenuity knew no bounds. I'd washed a few things and had arranged them in my room so that they would dry near the gas heater. This arrangement was too hot for my boots, so while lying in bed watching television, I'd parked them on top of the warm TV set. When I decided to fold up for the night, genius struck. By turning the brightness control to dark and tuning out all sound, I was able to leave the set on all night. Adroit placement of boots on top of the set and socks dangling from the rabbit-ear antennae provided me with warm, dry boots and socks in the morning and a certain amount of malice-tinged satisfaction at having gotten some small revenge for the dirty bathroom I'd been provided with.

Here in these mountains probably more than anywhere else the advantage of my slow means of travel was brought home to me with clarity. Had I been traveling by car, and stopped off where I did, I'd have left in haste the next morning with a seemingly justified unflattering opinion of the place. Now I was unable to get away as fast as I'd have liked and my next stop changed my opinion completely and brought home the value of holding judgment in abeyance.

I'd been moving down a road that was beginning to give the appearance of leading into farm country when I came to an unusually attractive, neatly fenced farm. Fine-looking Black Angus cattle and bands of sheep grazed in well-kept, rolling pastures and a number of neat buildings with groves of trees sat back off the road. The driveway entrance bore small gold-leafed signs that informed me that this was the experimental farm of the University of Tennessee and that visitors were welcome. The day was still young and the general look of the farm was so appealing that I turned in the driveway to find out what sort of an operation was going on. The brief stop intended became a five-day visit with people who made me feel I'd known them for years and who treated me like a member of the family.

John and Callie Odom were enjoying a quiet winter Sunday afternoon by the fire when I tied Sioux to the white rail fence and dragged my clay-plastered boots up to their doorway. Protests over my muddy feet were in vain; John insisted that I join them at the fireside.

John had been the superintendent of the farm since its start a number of years before. Their family had grown up and gone their various ways; now Callie had resumed teaching school in a desire to continue a fully active life.

The farm, a large one, was set up for experiments with livestock, trees, fruits and grasses not only to devise better and easier ways for farmers to operate but to introduce different species that might prove practicable in Tennessee.

The fireside conversation led to coffee and as I started to make preparations for my departure, I was easily convinced that there was no reason for my hurry. A large cattle barn was nearby with tons of fine hay and grain, the temperature was rapidly dropping, and a guest room with bath was at my disposal. If I needed any further argument, fortune had led me to the door of a man whose interests ranged from farming to literature, art, theater, politics and history — particularly of this section of Tennessee. Prior to becoming superintendent John had been a county agent and his fund of stories was inexhaustible.

One concerned a call he'd made at a back country farm for a conversation with the owner. John and the farmer, a white-haired man, were having difficulty hearing each other due to constant yelling emanating from an old man who was plowing nearby with his ancient mule. Finally, in mild exasperation, John turned to the farmer and asked who the old man was and what he was yelling about.

"That's jest Granpaw," came the offhand answer. "He's a hunderd an' one an' the mule's twenty-eight an' neither one of 'em can hear it thunder."

Through our talks, which invariably lasted far into the night, and with the aid of books John suggested, I was able to get an idea of the history of this region. Large parts of Tennessee had been settled in early days by Virginians who had drifted over the line. The Cumberland Plateau had been bypassed for the most part and was only permanently occupied in the period around 1880. Many Eastern homesteaders who'd found the golden promises of the Far West to be hollow had been unwilling to return to their original homes and as a last resort had come here. The glowing reports about the fertility of the plateau were true to a certain extent; however, if the settlers had expected to find themselves residents of the sunny South, they were due for disappointment. While I was visiting the Odoms, the mercury hovered around the ten-degree mark and John told me that thirty below zero was not unheard of.

One ancient journal quoted in a book told of the trials and tribulations of a horseback traveler who had come up the same road I had just traversed. His complaints about the necessity of frequent walking were easy for me to sympathize with, since my own heel blisters were still fresh and smarting at the time.

During my stay I rode Sioux into the back country to look over the remains of some pre-Civil War log cabins and barns, and John drove us in his car to some others. One had been used as a hideout during the Civil War and had been the scene of some local action. All had been constructed with great skill and care, with the snugly dovetailed corners that I'd observed before. A highway passed through these parts in the early 1800s and an old inn stood nearby which for years had catered to famous men in the history of our country. The Civil War brought about the near desertion of the plateau and it had lain all but unoccupied until the disillusioned homesteaders had moved in late in the nineteenth century.

Several times the Odoms drove us to points of interest where the traces of various social experiments were to be found. Old graves marked the spot where a religious sect was once located, and monotonously similar houses stood as a reminder of an unsuccessful communal effort of Rex Tugwell's in the 1930s. The coup de grace to my first opinion of the plateau was delivered by a visit to one of the most handsome summer theaters I've seen anywhere, and New England is, or was, the foremost proponent of this form of the arts. Public subscription and a great deal of energy combined to produce a remarkably successful theater in what I would have deemed to be a most unlikely setting.

Prior to the opportunity the Odoms afforded me to see different facets of the country, I'd come up a tough stretch of mountain road in bad weather conditions. The country was as lovely as any to be seen anywhere and this served in its way to point up the appalling condition of many of the houses I'd passed. I'd often seen cabins advertising mountain crafts. A few had fine-looking fox pelts displayed on racks; most had an assortment of hideous throw rugs with repeated garish peacock designs. The colors were such that I'd have forgiven Sioux if she'd shied at them in the dark. It would have been easy for me to have shaken my head in disbelief and hauled on out of there in a hurry had it not been for the slow mode of travel that allowed me to meet the Odoms and stay over for a second glance.

By the time I left, I'd met employees of the farm, citizens of the town I'd passed through, a group of fine people from all over the country who had come here in retirement, the director who had sparked the theater operation — and I'd completely revised the impression that one stretch of through road had given. Surely horse travel has its discomforts and difficulties. As a way of getting a true picture of the country, it is far and away ahead of any other that I've tried.

I'd become assured that the trip, like most other facets of life, would be a series of highs and lows. Knowing that the visit with John and Callie Odom would unquestionably be a high, I was fully aware that I was due for a few lumps, and feeling rested and ready, I was anxious to get going once again.

A moderate day's ride in the direction of the Hermitage, Andrew Jackson's home, north of Nashville, took me through a town where I was happy to pick up some mail from home. As I rode along once more I saw an attractive brick farmhouse off to my right nestled in a series of cedar-strewn hills. I rode in, dismounted and asked permission to camp. The pleasant young housewife who answered my knock said she was certain that it would be all right but would I check with her husband, who was up at the barn milking.

I walked up a steep hill to the barn and found her hus-

136

band just finishing up with his herd of Holsteins. He was an agreeable-looking young man, clad in the usual denims, mackinaw coat and rubber boots.

"I'm Tom Powell," I introduced myself, with my standard approach. "I'm traveling cross-country by horse from Rhode Island to Arizona and I'd like to ask your permission to camp for the night up back in the cedars."

This straightforward introduction, delivered with what I fancied to be hearty cheerfulness, had rarely failed me up to now and I waited for the usual wide-eyed awakening of interest on the part of the young farmer. His eyes were riveted to a frozen heap of cow manure near his foot and there they remained for a long time without so much as a flicker of reaction. The awkward silence continued while he contemplated the dung and his face began to register a puzzled frown. I waited with fascination to see whether or not he'd kick it. Just as I was about to clear my throat and try again, he grunted something unintelligible and tentatively toed the manure.

"If you'd rather I didn't," I mumbled, a little discomfitted by the manure-kicking experiment, "I'll go on and try another place."

"No," he said rather cholerically, still frowning at the manure, "I guess it's all right — but we had us some trouble with drifters around here."

"Well, look." I started to back away. "I don't want to impose on you. It just seemed like a good spot to camp. I'll go on ahead."

"No, you go on up there in the cedars an' it'll be all right. Just be sure you stay out of the barn!"

As his barn looked to be well equipped with manure this was a small sacrifice to make. For a minute I toyed with the thought of backing out as gracefully as possible; however, his wife had been so affable that I decided to accept the grudging invitation and go ahead on up into the cedars. I walked down, got Sioux and returned leading her. As I passed the barn, the young farmer stuck his head out of the door and grunted something. I stopped and looked back questioningly.

"Just remember," he called ominously, "I'll be watchin' you like a hawk."

Smiling weakly, I proceeded with a wave. Just as I reached the gate leading into the cedar lots, he reappeared from the barn.

"Get your horse an armload of hay outa the barn," he called with slightly diminished hostility.

I waved my thanks and went on up to locate my campsite for the night. I found a suitably level spot for my bedroll under a large cedar tree and staked out Sioux on a similar tree next to it. The next pasture was inhabited by a mule who wandered up to the fence every now and again to bray his greetings to Sioux. She studiously ignored the overtures and munched the hay I'd accepted for her.

Dinner over, I watched the embers of my clean-burning cedarwood fire for a time, then bedded down for the night. Talk sessions with John Odom had been so difficult to break off that neither of us had gotten much sleep on the preceding nights; now I figured to catch up a little.

At about nine that evening, after having been asleep for a couple of hours, I was awakened by a shout coming from the woods below. It was young hawkeye and he was stumbling through the brush evidently trying to locate my camp. Maliciously I let him stumble about for a while, then relented and shouted a reply. I'd left my flashlight on the dresser at the Odoms and so had been using a small folding candle box for illumination. Now I lighted my cigarette lighter to guide him to my camp and he arrived a little winded to introduce a brother whom he had in tow.

138

"It's up to you what you want to do," he said with a considerably friendlier attitude, "but the television says they's a big ol' snowstorm due an' it's gonna hit here about midnight. If you want, I'll carry you back to town an' you can get a mo-tel an' we can put your horse in the barn."

"Well," I hesitated, "I'm all set up with a tarp over me. I'd have a hell of a time gathering up my stuff in the dark and then there'd be the problem of getting back out in the morning. I'll stay put, I guess, and let it snow."

"O.K.," he said solemnly. "I just wanted to warn you."

We talked awhile and I mentioned that I thought some-day he should visit the Odoms' place, that as a farmer he'd find their experiments of interest. I also told him that I'd stayed with them nearly a week and that they'd been great people. He repeated his offer to carry me back to a mo-tel and at last, shaking his head in disapproval of my idiocy, he left for the house.

The forecast had been accurate for once and at midnight snow began to spatter down through the cedar tree and onto my covering tarp. I burrowed down and slept soundly. Morning light filtered through snow that was falling heavily and I knew by the weight on my tarp that I was well blanketed. Kicking my way out, I plowed over to the next tree to feed Sioux and found that her tree had leaked too. Her heavy winter coat was covered with the snow that was falling with increasing intensity.

Ordinarily I have little trouble starting a fire. The method that I find successful with dry cedar is to simply gather some tiny branches and light them. On this snow-bound morning, it did not work. Three times I started my fire and three times it sputtered out. I had some emergency fire-starting cubes but had no idea where they'd been packed, so with a small amount of profanity and copious drafts of lighter fluid, I at length got my fire going. I had the small alcohol stove for coffee water but felt that a good wood fire would make the situation more pleasant. Breakfast out of the way for Sioux and me, I was faced with the unpleasant chore of rolling up my bed in the deep snow and packing up the gear on my saddle.

The neighborly mule was dimly visible over by the fence and now Sioux decided to acknowledge him. I tied her close to her tree and commenced brushing, saddling and packing her. Each time the mule trotted down the fence line and brayed, Sioux swung around, jerked on her rope and nickered at him. Each time she jerked on the rope, I was deluged with snow from the cedar tree. Each time the snow cascaded down on me, I cursed. By the time I was saddled and packed, it's surprising that the snow for miles around wasn't melted completely away. I damned her ancestors, I included all horses, also their half-breed brethren in the mule branch of the family, and I began to look upon the horse as an animal whose existence could only be justified by its being ground fine and packaged as dog food.

The job of getting under way was completed at approximately the same time that I ran out of invective and would have been forced into repetition with slight variations. We emerged from the woods and plowed our way to the barn to find young hawkeye again completing his milking. This time he was considerably more cordial.

"I'm a-goin' up to my daddy's house for breakfast. You come along and have some."

I started to refuse; then I thought, what the hell, the guy's trying to be friendly — let him.

"I've had breakfast," I said, "but I'll go for another cup of coffee anytime."

"You know," he said as we waded over the hill to his parents' home, "I'll tell you the truth, I was some leery of you — I got a wife and family to think about — so I called the

140

Odoms last night. Miz Odom give you a pretty fair recommendation."

We reached the house, where I hitched Sioux under the roof of a breezeway. Climbing out of my rubberized parka, I followed my host into the warm kitchen. There I introduced myself to the elderly parents. Father said nothing and Mother eyed me with disapproval.

"I been fixin' to give you a piece of my mind for campin' out in this kind of weather," she said as she set a steaming cup of coffee before me. Whatever she had in mind she decided to drop, and after coffee and a stiff conversation that was mostly a monologue on my part, I thanked them and left.

The road out was deep in snow and there was no sign of plowing. Going was easy due to the lack of traffic and Sioux and I constituted the bulk of what traffic there was. Most cars that we passed were either stalled and snowed under or moving very slowly. My means of travel seemed to be the most efficient of any. This situation continued until the roads were finally cleared, and then I found myself in trouble. When the plows removed the snow from the traffic lanes, the shoulders on which I'd been riding were covered with heavily packed frozen snow and I no longer had any refuge from the automobiles, which immediately renewed their customary full speed. I found a motel with adjacent barn on my next stop and remained there for a day until a certain amount of melting took place.

A comparatively short ride on the first day of renewed travel took us to the Hermitage, where I took in the sights. It's a handsome place and certainly interesting, but the method of caging off the doorway to each room was upsetting. I must confess that I don't know how else the contents could be protected; nevertheless, I had the feeling that I was being held at arm's length. The entrance is obtained

141

through a turnstile device that can't possibly do justice to what must have been an impressive approach from the original front gate and tree-lined drive. It also prevented Sioux from entering the premises for photographic purposes.

I was fortunate in locating a commercial stable for haven when the next snow arrived, and the remainder of my tour of Tennessee involved snow and cold with periodic letups that were too short to allow me to get as much out of the state as I'm sure I would have at a more pleasant time of year. When a closed truck ride became available I snapped at it, and Sioux was sneaked aboard a furniture van. The ride was to take us clear across Arkansas to Texas, and when I saw the lower part of Arkansas with its dreary flatland and endless procession of what must have been prefabricated houses, monotonously identical, I groaned my relief at not having ridden the stretch. The country began to improve around Little Rock and soon the pine-clad hills tempted me to disembark. But by now I was so anxious to get to Texas that I swallowed the temptation and I guess it was well that I did as seven inches of snow fell on Little Rock the following day.

6.

My truck delivered me directly to the stockyard at Texarkana. The storm that had deposited snow all over the country I'd just left had smeared only an inch or so of ice on east Texas. This ice was enough to make even foot travel hazardous, so I stayed over the weekend in an unpretentious motel near the stockyard and parked Sioux in a covered pen with three or four quarter horses as her neighbors.

According to local comments this was the worst storm of the winter, which was certainly good news to me. Compared to what I'd been in, this was the Riviera. Then, too, being in Texas at last after twenty-two years was a definite pleasure. My hat and boots were no longer the objects of curious stares, except for the fact that my hat was smaller than those worn by Texans.

When I checked in at the stockyard, a young cowboy filled out the slip and assigned a pen to Sioux. He registered no surprise when I gave my address as Rhode Island but merely handed me the carbon copy. I was amused later when I noticed that it was filled out for one paint mare owned by Tom Powell of Rodilan, Texas.

Our arrival coincided with a cattle auction and the large barns and pens were in a turmoil of activity. The bawling of cattle was punctuated by whip cracks and high falsetto yips, and Sioux's high-pricked ears moved constantly as an indication of her interest. The center of activity was the "doghouse." This was a small room in the middle of the loading chutes, occupied to the overflowing point by cowboys, cattle buyers and the crew that moved the stock through the chutes to the sale arena. It was heated by an old oil drum that had been converted to a natural gas stove — this being the prime reason for its popularity. Court was being held by a bearded, middle-aged Negro named Willie. Willie sat on an overturned box next to the stove with his back against the shelf on which I'd piled my saddle and other gear. He was dressed in the usual cowboy attire with a battered black sombrero and run-over riding boots, and nestled between his knees and shielded by his gnarled hands was a pint bottle containing a clear liquid that bore no relationship to its bourbon label. He was quite drunk, as evidenced by his bloodshot, murky eyes and his swaying motions as he perched on the box, but he was completely capable of holding up his end of the banter that was directed at him. Most of the kidding came from a young tobacco-chewing cowboy who grinned affectionately at Willie while heaping invective on Willie's parsimonious ways.

"Whaddaya say, Willie, how about a li'l ol' drink for y' friends on a cold dam' day?"

Willie shook his head and sipped gently at his bottle.

His tormenter grinned. "Willie, y'all are a no-good tight-ass black sunuvabitch who don't even remember his friends."

Willie remained adamant and clutched his bottle protectively. "Ah ain' givin' you young mothahs none of this stuff. It ain' good fo' yuh."

144

"Ah bet a dollah y'all cain't put the rest of thet pint away 'thout puttin' the bottle down," the young cowboy challenged Willie, winking at the man next to him.

"Sheeit," one of the audience cut in, "he can do it 'thout holdin' the goddam' bottle in his hands!"

Willie looked up, suddenly interested. "You gimme anuthah dollah fo' anuthah pint, Ah do it jes' holdin' the bottle in mah teeth."

Another spoke up. "Goddam', man, you gonna lose you a dollah, 'cause I done seen him do it!"

"Ah don't believe you can do it, Willie," said a smiling rancher as he fished a dollar bill out of his pocket and handed it to Willie.

Willie blinked drunkenly at the dollar, stuffed it in his pocket, then put the bottle to his mouth. Remaining seated, he clenched the neck of the bottle in strong teeth, and with hands on hips, slowly tilted his head back while the remaining contents of the bottle gurgled down his throat. The empty bottle was lowered and Willie nodded graciously in acceptance of the applause. He then reached behind and under my saddle where he'd stowed a new pint and gravely uncapped it.

Now he stared at the young cowboy who had been needling him. "The reason Ah din' give you no drink is 'cause it'd a-got you far'd fo' drinkin' on duty — an' that wouldn'ta been frien'ly."

"What the hell you got *in* that pint, Willie?" another rancher cut in.

Without a reply Willie passed the bottle to him. The man sniffed it, wrinkled his nose and passed it to the next man, who did the same. It soon made the rounds and returned to Willie unsampled, whereupon he sipped a bit and carefully screwed the top back in place. He seemed to maintain the same steady level of inebriation, getting neither more nor less drunk, and when I returned to the doghouse later in the day Willie, now alone, still sat by the stove clutching a pint bottle with no appearance of a change for the worse.

"How you doin', Willie?" I asked, chiefly to find out whether the man could still talk.

"Jes' fine — jes' fine," he replied to my question, not moving on his perch. . . .

Evidently I was faded and weatherbeaten enough to blend into my surroundings, for the first of several similar occurrences took place at this auction barn when a rancher with a trailerload of cattle approached me and asked where I wanted them unloaded. It was a refreshing change from feeling conspicuous, and I never felt out of place on the remainder of the trip except for a brief journey by automobile into Dallas, where cowboy attire is not standard.

The weather was such that I stayed over a day in Texarkana. The second morning, after feeding Sioux, I dropped in at the doghouse to check the activity. Willie had gone by now; however, the regular crew was at the stove warming their hands and feet in between chores out in the stock pens. They were a friendly and amiable group and kept up a constant flow of the same inoffensive profane heckling that had been directed at Willie the day before.

A quiet, older rancher came to get three horses that had been penned overnight. He backed his stock trailer up to the loading chute, then drove the horses up the lanes to the loading pen. They didn't load well and the procedure took some time. The old man came close to getting seriously kicked by one of the horses; still he handled them patiently and slowly without resorting to the electric prod poles or stock whips commonly used. Although it was obvious that the younger employees of the barn were itching to touch up the recalcitrant horse with a hotshot electric prod, they didn't, nor did they suggest it. The same cowboy who would address

146

another with the blackest of obscenities would be shocked by
the bad manners involved in telling another man how to
handle his horse.

Back in the doghouse the subject was discussed, and one
of the men told of a horse ranch where he'd worked. The
owner, a wealthy man, had paid an unusually high price for
a stallion that soon became the ranch tyrant. He was such an
expensive horse that most of the hands hesitated to discipline him for fear of damage. A new man was hired who
shortly ran afoul of the high-priced stud. In the corral one
day the stud bit and mauled him until he managed to escape
by rolling under the corral rails. He soon returned, roped the
horse and started working him over with a bullwhip. The
owner, appearing on the scene, ran up hollering.

"My God, lookout — you'll knock his eye out!" he yelled.

"Hell," came the unruffled reply, "thet's what I've been a-
tryin' to do for five minutes, but the sunuvabitch keeps a-
dodgin'!"

Another story told to me years ago points up the inde-
pendent nature of the average ranch employee perhaps more
clearly than it could be explained otherwise.

An Eastern business tycoon bought out a large ranching
operation and when first introduced to the grizzled old foreman took it upon himself to set things straight immediately.

"I'm a man of few words and I don't like to waste them,"
he said firmly. "So if at any time you hear me whistle at you,
don't stand there and ask what I want, just drop whatever
you're doing and come running."

The old foreman studied this for a minute, then looking
squarely at the tycoon said, "Ah shore do agree with you —
Ah'm a man of few words mahself. So anytime you whistle
an' you see me shake mah haid, it means Ah ain't a-comin'."

It was with a light heart and a great feeling of freedom
that next day I started out into the eight or nine hundred

147

miles of Texas. The road was wide and green. The country surrounding me was covered with a mixture of clover and Bermuda grass and studded with pine. Except for the beef cattle grazing along the way and the Bermuda grass, it could have been Maine. One of the most pleasant changes was the refreshingly clean highway. I rode for miles the first day without encountering a beer can or a bottle and the roadside parks were clean, attractively laid out and inviting. Texans get kidded in many parts for their pride. If this pride has as one of its results the state's clean wide highways and well-kept parks, then perhaps it's in reality a virtue that more of us would do well to have. Contrary to being intimidated by the eight hundred miles from Texarkana to El Paso, I looked forward to it with delight and renewed interest.

The weather was still quite frosty and I had been fighting off the only head cold I'd been plagued with on the trip. When I came upon a small auto court with an attached garage some twenty miles west of Texarkana, I pulled in and had no trouble getting a room for me and the garage for Sioux. Before riding out the following day, I added my thermal sweatshirt to my usual attire and as a result was considerably warmer. Normally I used this as a sort of pajama top for sleeping in the bedroll.

The east Texas country continued to charm me. The hills rolled on and on with clumps of pine and groups of grazing cattle, the sky was clear and clean, and best of all there was room to move with a horse. The roadway was only two-lane but there was a paved shoulder on each side the same width as the traffic lane and then the grass right-of-way reached at least fifty yards out in either direction. Prior to this, every time I'd gotten off trails and ridden roads, I'd been nervous over Sioux's tendency to spook. Now, however, she could shy, booger or spook to her heart's content and still have room to spare. Of course, with female perverseness, she didn't. It had

148

been a long time since I'd ridden a horse in such wide, spacious and open country and for the first time I felt free and unfettered. I wondered what it must have been like for the first horsemen who entered this great wide country in the early part of the last century. Maybe the high-pitched Texas yell is an involuntary expression of the sheer exuberance that open country makes you feel.

I stopped in at one of the small gas station-grocery stores that speckle this part of the country and got a can of beans and one of Vienna sausages. These sausages are always referred to as just plain Vie-*een*-ees and until I learned the pronunciation I was forced to point and mumble, "An' a can of them." While on the subject of pronunciation, I might mention another small dividend accrued from slow-moving horse travel. It was always possible to ascertain the correct pronunciation of the name of the next town in advance by means of adroit questioning and I never disgraced myself as I'd once done in Maine. At that time, I'd given Calais, Maine, its French sound and gotten a disgusted reply from the native who advised me that it was called Callous, as on the palm of your hand.

The proprietor of the roadside store where I got my Vie-*een*-ees suggested a stop eight or ten miles ahead at a café with buildings in the rear where he was certain I'd be welcomed to the facilities for Sioux and me, so I rode on with the café in mind.

I'd begun to pass a weatherbeaten farmhouse or two and was barely able to discern my destination ahead when a man stepped out of his dooryard to greet me. Tall and thin, with his complexion weathered by many years of wind and sun, he walked out with the stiff hobble of an old horseman and introduced himself.

"Mah friends call me W.C. The others call me a sunuva-

149

bitch." He grinned through missing teeth. "Ah reckon by the looks of your rig you must be travelin'."

I agreed that I was and without further small talk, he opened his gate and beckoned me to follow.

"Mah house is yours," he said, "an' you sure as hell not sleepin' outside while ol' W.C. has got a roof an' a extry bed."

With Sioux following us, W.C. led the way through the yard and around back between the outhouse and the wood-pile to where a gate admitted us to the pasture next to the house. The pasture was occupied by a small herd of white-faced cows, two buckskin ponies and one of the biggest Brahma bulls I've ever seen. We followed over to a series of sheds leading a procession of curious animals, the most attentive of which was the huge, white, hump-backed Brahma. He was approximately the size of a boxcar. Each time he came up to Sioux, snuffing loudly, W.C. would cuff him on his long pendulous ears and chase him away. He'd back off about ten feet, pause a second, then approach again. I've never been wildly enthusiastic about being on foot around bulls, particularly Brahmas, and in this case I unsaddled Sioux without tying her first. I wanted her to be able to get out of the way just in case the bull suddenly forgot his pet status.

With Sioux finally fed, watered and pastured, I shoul-dered such luggage as I wanted and we returned to the house to be effusively greeted by W.C.'s wife. She was a tiny, warm, cheerful woman whose crinkly smile made me feel immediately welcome. The four-room frame house had been built by W.C. years ago when the family was at home; now his sons were all away in the air force and Viet Nam. The kitchen had the mellow quality that can only be found when a wood-burning range is the centerpiece. My room, sepa-rated from the kitchen by a drape, was in the rear. I unrolled my bedding on the iron bed, hung my saddlebags on the chair and returned to the comfort of the living room. An old man who lived with the family appeared to be incapacitated to some extent and moved only between his easy chair and a bed that was set up for him in the living room. I think he was not related but an old family friend. A couch and several chairs circled the wood stove and a large colored map of Viet Nam dominated the wall next to a television set.

We watched the news with particular attention to Viet Nam while W.C.'s wife got supper in the kitchen.

"I ain't sure where the boys are these days," W.C. said, trying to trace his way around the map with a work-worn finger, "an' if I was, I couldn't say them dam' names – but we get letters ever' now and again. Hope they're still all right."

Three framed studio photographs of good-looking young boys in military uniforms stood atop the television set. I wondered how many times this scene was being repeated across the country: a framed photograph, a colored wall map filled with bewildering names, a few well-read letters and quietly worried but proud parents.

Retiring to the kitchen for supper, I filled up on bologna, hot biscuits, potato dumplings, coffee and snow ice cream – something I hadn't tried since childhood days in Maine. The water in the coffee was tasteless enough so that I commented on it, to find that the reason was that it was not from the well, in which their pet squirrel had recently "drownded hisself." Instead, it was rainwater from the barrel outside the kitchen. Drinking water in Texarkana had been such that the first day there I'd poured a bottle of Coca-Cola into Sioux's water to tempt her into drinking. After a day or so, we both got used to it and had no further trouble.

After supper W.C.'s grandson, young Billy, came to visit with his mother. He was a rugged-looking, bright youngster

151

— all cowboy. His idol was the rodeo rider Jim Shoulders and his dream was to be a bronc rider when he grew up. Now he confided that in addition, he planned to ride a horse around the world. I made a small sketch of Sioux for him and after helping me shut Sioux up in one of the sheds, he left with his mother. He was the owner of the buckskin ponies and W.C. told me of the time when he'd owned his first jack burro. His grandparents had been lecturing him about his behavior when he turned to his grandfather in final irritation.

"Granpaw," he snapped, "if you don't quit a-fussin' at me, Ah'll take mah jack outa your pasture."

The evening's discussion led into the old days in these parts.

"Used to, this was a tough town," W.C. reminisced. "The people was tough an' the times was tough. I remember one ol' boy lived with us when he was in his seventies — every mornin' he had to th'ow his hoss to get him saddled. He'd get astraddle of him layin' down, then turn him a-loose an' find his stirrups on the way up."

An old man that I later met, deeper in Texas, spoke similarly of the type of Texas pony used in an earlier day. As he put it: "We never gentled them ponies much. In the mornin' we'd run 'em into the corral, rope one, climb on an' turn him a-loose. When he'd finished buckin' and tearin' up the countryside, your circulation was goin' good, your bowels had moved an' you was ready for a big ol' breakfast an' a day's work."

W.C. continued. "Up till a few years ago, there used to be a shootin' around here about every year to sorta keep things in line. Ol' Poker Jackson was the meanest, fightin'est man in town. He done kilt him three men an' done time in the penitentiary for the last one — the other two was self-defense. Why ol' Poker'd fight you over a song an' sing it hisself!"

His wife cut in. "Poker was good with us, Paw. He never give us no trouble an', shucks, he'd never even cuss in front of me."

"That's right, Maw," W.C. agreed. "I like ol' Poker — he don't bother nobody these days. Reckon that ten-year stretch in the penitentiary slowed him up some. You see, he'd been a-fussin' some with a neighbor, so he went over one day to call him out. The neighbor hid behind a ol' man an' tried to draw his gun. He got the hammer caught in his coat an' whilst he was a-fightin' to git her a-loose, ol' Poker rech up an' stuck his shotgun over the old man's shoulder an' shot that neighbor right down plumb into his heart. He didn't last too awful long an' Poker got ten years. He don't fight none no more but he'll sure pull his pistol on you if you was to walk up on his house after dark. Still — years ago, I remember Poker got drunk one day an' his hoss th'owed him an' busted his laig. I heard his gun a-goin' *pow! pow!*, so I went over an' fetched him to the house. He give up his pistol right peaceable an' later when his laig was fixed up, come to fetch it. He asked if he'd done anything wrong an' if so he was sorry."

The remnants of my head cold were still with me and I commented that possibly if I smoked less, it might help the situation. W.C. agreed and said that he'd given up smoking some years ago and believed that chewing tobacco was much better for a man. His wife Maudie said that she too would like to give up tobacco but felt that it eased her some. I'd noticed that she carried a small can about from room to room with her, much in the manner another might carry an ashtray. In many parts of Texas chewing tobacco and the spit can are more common than the cigarette and the ashtray, and after a few weeks at this time of year I developed my own theory why. A strong, steady wind prevails much of the time and I discovered that while riding a horse on the windward side of the road, one can spit with ease clear across a four-lane highway. It results in such a sense of accomplishment that I was tempted to take up tobacco chewing myself. I probably would have but for an unfortunate incident that took place during my youth in Wyoming when I accidentally swallowed a jolt while saddling an uncooperative horse. The emetic results were so instantaneous and devastating that I'm still a little "head shy" about eatin' tobacco.

"I'll tell you what," Maudie said while I was complaining of my cold. "An' I wisht we had some handy. But the best cure for a cold, sinus, croup or asthma is polecat oil. You take an' render you out some polecat fat to an oil and swaller a spoonful an' it'll guaranteed cure you. Might not taste too good for a while, but it'll sure do 'er."

"Dunno but what I'm glad you haven't got any," I laughed, "but I'll sure write your suggestion to my mother. She's tried about every other kind of medicine."

"You tell her," W.C. injected. "It'll shore work."

These people were animal lovers of the worst kind, and Maudie had refused to disturb a spider that had appeared next to her while we talked. I mentioned that my wife felt the same way about spiders and that I had to be sneaky if I wanted to step on one at home. I told them about the old caretaker in Virginia and his possum and mouse friends. Maudie allowed that when you're lonesome, company's company. They were still saddened over the death of their pet squirrel who'd fallen into the well. The only house pet now was a small devilish kitten that caused a certain disturbance in the middle of the night.

We'd gone to bed and I'd been sound asleep for some time when I heard the old man in the living room calling rather plaintively for help. Evidently it was not possible for him to use the outhouse and he was forced to resort to a chamber pot.

154

"Maudie," he called, "I can't find my roll."

The creak of a bed in the front room and a light switched on indicated that help was on the way and after a muttered consultation and some searching, I heard Maudie laughingly announce that she'd found it.

"That little ol' devil of a kitten's been a-playin' with it and rolled 'er plumb under your bed."

"Reckon I'd better tie the daggone thing down," the old man muttered a trifle testily, and the household returned to silence broken only by the night wind.

Increasingly now the landscape was filled by long stretches of grass, trees and cattle with only infrequent glimpses of farm and ranch houses. I had gotten the impression that this had been farm country a few years ago; however, as with the small produce farms in all localities, these had faded out and here the land was returned to cattle grazing. Each town of any size had a sale barn and the livestock auctions were a weekly event. Ranchers from the surrounding countryside brought in a trailerload or two of cattle to be sold, others came with an empty pickup and trailer looking for a few calves, and always the front row of seats at the auction barn was occupied by a group of buyers from the meat-packing houses. The buyers were mostly old-time cattlemen who had the ability to judge the weight, condition and quality of a steer or pen full of steers in the blink of an eye. With thousands of dollars changing hands, the cattle sales had a lighthearted picnic atmosphere that infected everyone from the auctioneer to the buyers. This was no serious, flannel-suited business transaction with the participants choked into stiff formality by their neckties. Boots, big hats and unfettered, leathery, sun-wrinkled necks were the costume; good-natured insults and jibes replaced polite conversation.

155

Cattle in bunches of from two to twenty or more were prodded through a gate into a small enclosure in front of the auctioneer's stand and kept circulating by a couple of men with electric prod poles or cracking whips. Tiers of seats started at the front rail and rose up to form a small amphitheater, and the only protocol observed was a loose arrangement whereby the front seats were usually but not necessarily held by the serious buyers.

A man in the pen would open the gate with a certain amount of caution to determine whether a pair of calves was coming through or whether the entrant was to be a belligerent Brahma bull looking for a fight and perfectly willing to take on all comers. In the case of "a ol' anteater of a bull" — one that entered pawing, snorting and hooking at the ground — the men in the pen usually made a deft leap for the rail and operated from a lofty perch. The auctioneer, after a few comments to the effect that the particular animal had obviously been fed and was "fat in the back," started the standard rapid-fire chant that is completely unintelligible to the novice. A buyer, sitting back with boot heels cocked up on the rail, hat pulled down obscuring his eyes and to all appearances completely unconcerned with what went on, would tap one forefinger on his knee. Immediately the chanted price went up and was directed to another man sitting nearby, who perhaps indicated his willingness by shifting a chew of tobacco from one cheek to the other.

With the conclusion of each sale and while the stock were being driven out of the exit gate to make room for the next entrants, the successful buyer usually attempted to appear disgruntled by the abusive treatment he'd been afforded.

"Dam'," was a typical growl, "you people done everything else to me in this hyar place. Whur do Ah go to get kissed?"

To a traveling horseman, the sale barn is a custom-made

place of refuge. I was invariably invited to put my horse up in a pen with plenty of feed, the office was mine for the duration of my stay and attempts to pay were brushed off with a laugh. The proprietor of one sale barn sent me on to the next with explicit directions and usually there was a request added that I deliver an unflattering message to the next man.

Hospitality in Texas, at least to a passing horseman, is a guaranteed fact of life. Whether I symbolized something to the average Texan I can't say, but my reception all along the way was such that it was all but impossible to camp out. Almost without exception, until I got into uninhabited country, my request to be permitted to camp was met with insistence that I stay at the house and eat with the family. A friendly wave became a reflex action with each passing car or pickup truck.

A chance meeting with Rory Calhoun in one east Texas town considerably deflated my ego and provided delight to my kids at home, who frequently make it a point to remind me of my thinning hair and doddering old age. Rory, on a personal appearance tour, seemed a most pleasant and friendly man and while questioning me about my project, our respective ages came up. He was forty-five, I forty-four, and when I mentioned that I had lost fifteen pounds mostly from my belt region, he laughed and wished that he could go along with me at least fifteen pounds worth. He readily consented to being photographed with Sioux and I left shortly after, while Rory went in to do an autograph stint at a large store.

He had ridden a paint horse in his television series *The Texans*, and when I got two or three blocks from the store on my paint mare, I was approached by two colored girls walking toward town. As they got within easy earshot, one looked up and jabbed the other with her elbow.

157

"Is that Ro'y Calhoun?" she asked, pointing my way.

"Naw," the other replied disgustedly, after an all too brief glance, "that looks mo' like his daddy!"

That afternoon, I came to a small gas station-grocery store and stopped for a cold drink. The proprietors, Bill King and his wife, almost immediately asked me to stay over with them and although the hour was early, I did. Bill had a few head of cattle and a roping horse named Shorty, and Sioux was promptly turned out to roam the pastures with her newfound friend. Here again I was exposed to the hospitality of Texans, when Bill asked me to accompany him back to town in his pickup. We wound up in a café and I discovered that his sole reason for the trip was to buy dinner for me, since they'd already eaten theirs earlier.

A day or so after this, I rode into a small town and cut left a block or so to avoid the center of the town. Passing a barber shop, I observed a beautiful quarter horse being held by a couple of boys. While cutting through a parking area behind the stores, I was hailed by two ranchers sitting in a parked car. They were both engaged in lowering the contents of a bottle and appeared already to have spent considerable time in the same pursuit.

"Whar you headed on thet ol' paint?" came the usual question.

I explained briefly and the rancher sitting next to the driver held the bottle out to me.

"Y'all better have a big ol' drink with us or you never gonna make *Ah*rizona."

I turned down the bottle somewhat apologetically and he shook his head sadly.

"If you won't have a li'l ol' drink," he decided, "then Ah'l tell you what Ah'm a-goin' to do. Y'all see that sorrel quarter hawse back by the barber shop?"

"I did," I admitted. "A fine-looking hunk of horse."

"Bet yore boots," he agreed. "Ah'm just a-fixin' to trade hawses with you here an' now with no boot. What do ya say to that?"

"No, I guess not." I attempted to sound regretful. "Your horse is worth twenty of mine but I'm sort of friendly with this old girl."

"You're just plain crazy," he replied. "Here you are a-ridin' from God knows whar to a hell of a ways from hyar an' you won't take a drink an' you won't trade hawses. If I cain't talk sense to you, Ah'm a-fixin' to give you some money."

He pulled out a fat roll of money with a rubber band surrounding it and started to extricate some bills. His partner behind the wheel pulled some loose bills out and tried to hand them through the window.

"Whoa now," I laughed, "I don't want your money. Just tell me a good place to hole up tonight."

"You the craziest dam' man Ah evah met." He looked at me with astonishment. "You won't take a drink, you won't take a good hawse, you won't take mah money — Dam', if y'all were headin' back the other way, you'd dam' sure stay at mah ranch. Anyhow, you go down the road a couple of miles and stop at mah brother's place. You jus' tell him to put you up an' I sent you."

I exited as soon as possible, followed his instructions and stopped overnight with his brother. When I mentioned the horse-trade offer that had been made, his brother looked at me with a grin.

"Was he drinkin'?"

"I guess he'd had a few," I confessed.

"I guess he had," said the brother. "When he rides his hawse to town he's drunk, an' Ah'll guarantee when he's ready to go home he'll need the hawse to carry him there.

159

Hell, you shoulda taken his money. He meant for you to have it."

The land was rapidly leveling out from the hilly pine country to flatter land with mesquite trees. It was more sparsely settled these days than it had been and timber wolves, once a rarity, had reappeared in large numbers. Sioux snorted at several dead wolves that we encountered in the bar ditch, which is a Texas term for the grass shoulders along a highway. We began to have problems with gophers at about this point; they were to remain a constant danger for several hundred miles to come. The only warning of a series of gopher holes was loose dirt in scattered piles along the bar ditches. The holes themselves were so small as to pass unnoticed; however, the tunnels ran for some distance under the surface, and our first mishap took place when Sioux suddenly broke through up to her knees in what looked like solid ground. Fortunately she'd been walking at the time and was unhurt. The same thing happened three times again in the month that followed. Each time luck was with us and no damage resulted.

Wolf hunting with hounds was a popular sport with many of the local ranchers. However, some were giving it up as a result of the government campaign being waged to eradicate the wolves. Baited cyanide gas bombs had been put out and posters in English and Spanish were prominently displayed. This warning device failed to prevent the hounds from getting into baited bombs and the instant death was decimating the hounds as well as the wolves.

Armadillos were probably the biggest surprise to me, for I had thought they were located much farther south than northeastern Texas. I was told that they'd moved this far north only in the past twenty years or so. Regardless, they were thick and considering their poor vision and apparent stupidity, I wondered how they survive at all. The first time

160

we approached an armadillo, I stopped Sioux and got the camera out of the saddlebags with the utmost stealth. Expecting the peculiar shell-backed animal to hit for the hills at any moment, I eased Sioux forward as quietly as possible with my knees, holding the camera poised for an instant shot. We got six or eight feet from where it was busily rooting in the ground and I stopped Sioux and clicked the shutter. There was utterly no reaction from the curious-looking creature, so I advanced the film and moved closer. This time the click of the camera warned him that something was around and he peered stupidly at us with his rabbit ears straight up, then did a sort of double take, jumped straight up in the air and landed running. He rapidly scurried all of twenty feet from us, then apparently forgot all about what he was running from and stopped to continue rooting in the ground.

Our next meeting with an armadillo almost resulted in his demise. I spotted one in the grass along the road and for no particular reason pushed Sioux into a gallop thinking to chase him. He, as usual, leaped straight up, landed in a tight run and just as we started to catch up on him, stopped short and started to root again. Only a quick turn by Sioux avoided his being run down, but he seemed completely unconcerned by his close brush and we left him happily digging away with his odd-looking claws and snout.

Roadrunners began to make their appearance, tearing along in their purposeful manner — always intent on some far distant place and always in a rush to get there with no time for detours or tarrying. Something about a roadrunner always makes me chuckle with amusement, probably their similarity to the animated cartoon version. Too, their intentness of purpose reminds me of a commuter making the sprint from the subway to the 5:05 in New York's Grand Central Station.

Just out of Sulphur Springs, I was put up for the night

161

by a retired but still youthful army man named Joe Hooks and his wife. They juggled their four kids around in order to provide a bed for me. I enjoyed an excellent dinner while Sioux grazed happily on the lawn in the rear of the house. Shortly after leaving next morning, a mobile radio car intercepted me, having been tipped off by Joe. The interview was live from the roadside and must have been heard in every vehicle on the road. The announcer had suggested I be given a big Texas welcome and his suggestion was followed up so thoroughly that I was scarcely able to make any progress for the remainder of the day.

Although it was now mid-February, there began to be a feel of spring in the air. A softer but steady wind from the south carried a faint sweet smell similar to sweet grass found in parts of New England. I never had it identified for me but guessed it to be a close relative. At about this time, we entered the blackland country. A deep and fertile soil covers this section, so rich as to appear almost black. Doubtless it grows great cotton and other crops, but to a horseman it's pure misery. The heavy consistency of the earth makes mud that would be the envy of the old Hollywood comedy producers. For over a hundred miles, Sioux carried nearly five pounds of the blacklands on each foot and every time I dismounted, I became all but mired. It was impossible to remove before remounting; scraping and stamping were in vain. Consequently my boots and stirrups were always well plastered. One comment heard was that if you'll stick with the blacklands, they'll stick with you. The most apt remark was that in the blacklands you don't leave any tracks — you take 'em with you.

The numerous kindnesses extended to us throughout this country are impossible to chronicle. Glistening, wet, black furrows extended to the distant horizon and camping would have been an unpleasant affair. The constant invitations to sleep in a house, on a bed, were gratefully accepted. Had I not by now pretty well succeeded in a mental gear change, the wide expanses of this country would have caused great frustration. Mile upon mile was ticked off by Sioux's hoofs, and oftentimes a look back at day's end enabled us to see a landmark from which we'd started that very morning.

A combination of business establishments, on the highway near Cumby, brought about a stop a little earlier than usual one afternoon. Some new motel units across from a coin laundry and adjacent to a café provided all my needs in one stop. With Sioux tied in some deep grass next to my end room, I stewed myself in the luxury of a long, hot shower and followed up with a trip to the laundry with everything I owned except a wool shirt and corduroy pants, which I'd held out in the interests of decency. A short jog into Cumby for a small bag of grain completed the chores and the final stop was in the café next door.

Good steaks are the general rule in most of Texas and I was busily surrounding a particularly tasty one when I became conscious of being under the surveillance of an old gentleman at the next table. He toyed with a cup of coffee while eyeing me with an increasingly disconcerting directness. I sneaked enough casual glances his way to determine that he was a man who looked to be in his seventies – he proved to be eighty-one. He had long, almost white hair and wore a clean white Stetson, polished black boots and a Western-style suit with white shirt and string tie. His face was vaguely reminiscent of Burl Ives and his piercing, squinted eyes were taking me in from one end to the other as he leaned back in his chair.

When I got to my coffee I looked at him to find the same level stare directed at me, so I nodded to him. With that he beckoned me to join him at his table, and I picked up my coffee cup and walked over.

Dr. Ben K. Green, a semiretired veterinarian, old-time cowboy and horseman, already knew who I was and what I was up to, and before long I'd gathered enough from our conversation to know that he'd left his home in Cumby in his early teens and had ridden to west Texas, where he'd cowboyed most of his younger years. Cumby, now his home again, had been the scene of his boyhood when it was one of the toughest towns around and was called Black Jack Grove. Almost every weekend had been sparked by knifings, shootings or both until a group of local mothers got fed up and jumped the gun on Carrie Nation by arming themselves with hatchets and obliterating the town's two saloons. Ben, a schoolboy at the time, had jumped out of the schoolhouse window with several of his friends and run to witness the carnage.

While the first of the saloons was having its bottles, mirrors and furniture disassembled by the axe-wielding women, the proprietor of the second hurriedly hired a rig from the livery stable and loaded his liquor aboard for a fast gallop out of town only a jump or so ahead of the marching mothers, who were forced to content themselves with the destruction of the furbishings left behind. One brave citizen is said to have grabbed a jug on the run and headed out of town. His salvage efforts were in vain, however, for one of the ladies, with deadly accuracy, threw a hatchet which shattered the jug. The jug bearer, lightened of his burden, merely increased his speed.

Black Jack Grove, its image somewhat altered, took on the name of Cumby and young Ben, all his worldly goods behind the cantle of his saddle, left for west Texas soon after. He didn't indicate that the closing of the saloons had been more than coincidental in the timing and I didn't ask.

One of his early business ventures left Ben and his companions stuck with a large number of heavy draft horses

164

that proved harder to get rid of than they had been to acquire. The two boys had joined a large cattle drive to Kansas, where the steers were sold to be fattened. Tractors were making their first appearance about this time and large unwanted horses were being taken in trade by the dealers. Ben decided, in true Horatio Alger tradition, that a herd of these big horses could be cheaply purchased, driven back to Texas and sold for a profit there. Unfortunately, west Texas cattlemen were not waiting with bated breath for large draft horses and the bulk of the animals wound up being traded off for a chili parlor that Ben's partner ran with rapidly decreasing enthusiasm. Over the years, Ben covered most of the Southwest on the back of a horse, bought a ranch in the Big Bend country, ran the horse and mule sale barn in Dallas, became a practicing veterinarian and was instrumental in forming a quarter horse registry service in which he was currently active. He's also been the author of several books on horses and when I ran into him later in Greenville, he let me read the manuscript of a delightfully funny short story with an O. Henry twist relating his experiences in Vermont with an Indian buddy and a carload of Texas cow ponies that they'd hoped to sell at a good profit. Vermont Yankees being notoriously good businessmen, they returned to Texas with their business acumen increased — if not their wealth.

At the conclusion of our coffee session, Ben walked out with me to take a look at Sioux, who was now full and standing contentedly hipshot next to my room. He walked slowly around her, eyeing her without great enthusiasm.

"Well now, I'm gonna tell you something about this mare," he said at length, "an' you're not gonna like me for it."

"Don't worry, Ben," I laughed. "I never claimed she was

any equine Venus de Milo. I just like her. Aside from having a long head and cow hocks, what else is wrong?"

Ben punctured me with his squinted eyes. "I'll tell you why you're not making more distance than you are an' that's the way her shoulders are built. Her back's too long an' her neck's too short. The slope of her shoulders from here to here" — he gestured with a sweep of his hand — "is angled so's she can't take a long enough stride to cover the ground. She's a little bit cow-hocked an' her head is long, but she's got a good eye an' she looks like she's got some brains — more than most paints. Oh, she's rugged enough an' you'll get where you're goin' on her, no question about it. It's just gonna take you a whole lot longer than it should."

"I don't doubt but what you're right, Ben," I agreed, "but this ol' girl and I have a sort of understanding. I wouldn't part with her for all the tea in China. Anyhow, I never figured I was running a race."

Ben grunted and then looked at me with a hint of a grin. "I guess maybe I've had a few that had some quality that was more important than their conformation at that. An' if you was to get rid of her after all these miles you been together, I wouldn't like you much for it."

We parted with a friendly handshake and Ben's faint smile left me with the strong conviction that he was secretly pleased that my faith in the "old spotty mare" hadn't been diminished by his criticism. Nor had it. After all Sioux has never kicked sand in my face because I'm not built like Charles Atlas.

Leaving Cumby, gusty winds and threatened showers — some of which drove me into my rainproof parka — caused me to think of the Greenville sale barn, which had been suggested to me as a stopping place. The low-flying, dark clouds scudding along had the look of wet weather ahead and at midafternoon I pulled into the midst of a grove of trees that was inhabited by a number of busy squirrels. They gave the impression of being in a hurry to get their outside chores done before the deluge and I took the hint from them and climbed into all my foul weather gear, including the rubberized pants that were always a last resort.

The squirrels were right, as they usually are, and a squally rainstorm lashed at us soon after we left the grove. The welcome sight of the sale barn brought on a fast splashing trot, and in short order I'd introduced myself to Harold Coker, delivered the greetings of Maurice Evans, manager of the Sulphur Springs barn, and arranged for a tight roof for Sioux and me for the night. As the weather turned out, it proved to be a good move.

Harold, a personable man in his late thirties, was busy finishing up the supervision of a sale that had been in progress that afternoon and the office area and sale room were filled with cattlemen, buyers, numerous children and onlookers. He had a handsome quarter horse stud in one of the pens under the huge roof of the barn and suggested I select an empty one nearby for Sioux.

With the end of the sale, the small local ranchers backed their stock trailers up to the loading chutes and headed home with their purchases, leaving the bulk of the bawling animals for the larger-quantity meat buyers from the packing houses in Fort Worth and Dallas. Harold and his chief assistant, a huge, quietly capable colored man, were then free to eat dinner and I gladly joined them for a trip to a downtown café.

The large doubledecked trailer trucks were due in during the night and it was necessary for Harold to be there for the loading. Rain had continued unabated; the pens were getting to be ankle deep in mud and manure, particularly in the west end of the barn from whence the wind was pushing.

167

Several loads of cattle were picked up by midevening and each was more recalcitrant than the last. The cattle were reluctant to go up the mud-slick chutes to the trucks and were more contrary than usual. A steer, balking at entering the trailer, skidded on the wet ramp, jammed himself sideways and was followed by a pileup. About then one of the steers in the rear of the procession wheeled and bolted and then fell down in the slick mud, and cattle piled up in both directions. Somehow Harold managed to free the bovine log jam by hanging precariously from his perch on the top rail and deftly touching up the source of the trouble with his electric prod pole. I was driving the stock up the alley from their pens – a comparatively simple, if sloppy, chore – and had little trouble except for one large white Brahma cow. She took one look at the chute and quickly decided that I presented much less threat. Doubling back, she headed my way with a businesslike approach which indicated that she was not going to be even slightly intimidated by my arm wavings and war whoops. There was no contest. She treed me on the nearest rail and trotted back to her pen. It remained for Harold and his prod pole to convince her to leave.

Wet and mud-caked, we sprawled out on the long bench in the heated office and I slept so soundly that I failed to hear the last truck pull in sometime after midnight. I'd asked Harold to awaken me when it arrived, but he and the truck driver completed the job alone. When I registered a protest in the morning he grinned.

"You were snorin' too pretty," he said.

The rain held out, having caused severe flooding and wind damage in the Dallas–Fort Worth area; it had been the cause of the late arrival of the cattle trucks. Sioux was located on the east end of the barn and remained dry except for one corner of her pen where the water was creeping in. I decided to stay over for the day and when the skies broke and cleared in midafternoon, I got a ride into town to mail some material and make a few purchases.

Walking past a saddle shop, I looked in and was greeted by Ben Green, who was just inside the door. This time he was dressed in a battered hat and ranch clothes so that momentarily I failed to recognize him.

"You wait a minute while I go up to my office. I'll haul you back to the sale barn," he said.

We rode the elevator up to an office that he maintained in a bank building and in short order we were nose deep in some handsome books of Charles Russell's paintings.

"That old boy's been there," Ben said, pointing to one of the prints. The painting showed an old-time cowpuncher in what is today commonly called a "wreck." A longhorned steer was on one end of the rope heading for the brush, the horse was in the process of being jerked down and the rider was high and to one side in his saddle.

"See the way the rider's throwin' his weight in his left stirrup tryin' to balance the horse? Old Charley knew what he was paintin' about."

I mentioned the fact that I'd long been an admirer of both Remington's and Russell's paintings.

"Hell," said Ben, "you better not miss the collection in Fort Worth. The Amon Carter Museum has the largest collection in the country. It's right next door to where they hold the stock show."

Ben went on to explain the route to me — avoiding Dallas by way of Grapevine — then began to sketch out a swing to the south that would take me to El Paso by way of a more attractive stretch of country.

"It's a couple of hundred miles further than goin'

169

straight through would be," he warned, "but if you're interested in scenery it'd be worth it to you."

Walking out to Ben's pickup truck, he turned to me with mock severity. "If you ride in my pickup, be dam' sure you don't mess it up!"

The front seat of the truck was filled just short of the overflow point with odds and ends of all manner of ranch gear from buckets to rope. Ben tossed several of the bulkier items in the back so that I could squirm in and we were off. The junk-stuffed condition of the average ranch pickup is a sort of in-type standing joke in these parts. Most of them are equipped with a rack in the rear window that contains a rifle or two and a stock whip; a lariat generally lies coiled behind the seat. The floor is so strewn with such a large variety of items that anyone dropping an object would entertain much the same problem in frustration as the small boy who supposedly lost his chewing gum while cleaning the hen house floor.

Ben dropped me off at the sale barn along with the manuscript of his short story that he'd agreed to let me read. I arranged to leave it at his office next day on the way through town; this stop proved unnecessary when Ben pulled in next morning just as I was reaching for my stirrup.

Going in to Greenville, I cut off a block to the right of the main street shortly after crossing the railroad tracks and avoided the combined hazards of parked cars and traffic. I wanted to mail some additional notes along with a sketch and figured to approach the post office from the rear, where the parking lot afforded a place to hitch Sioux. As I entered the lot, I observed that the local newspaper office was located next door to the post office.

A small green sports car eased in just as I approached a handy tree and as I climbed down a young man got out of

170

the car with a camera in his hand. He looked over at me and I resigned myself to another half hour of interrogation. At first newspaper interviews had been fun, probably because being asked to talk about yourself is always flattering to the ego. It doesn't take too many of them to begin to pall and I had reached this point by now. I found that small-town weeklies have a tendency to be much more accurate in their reporting than the big-town papers, maybe because of the interpretive abilities of the big-town rewrite men. For some strange reason, the more nationwide the coverage the more inane the questioning becomes. Someday I want to have a television set tuned in when an astronaut returns from a successful trip to the moon. Then when a newsman, while interviewing his parents, asks the typical moronic question about how the father feels now that his son has returned safely, I hope the father scratches his head, spits and says something like: "Well, my son was always a snotty kid and we *did* have ten thousand bucks' worth of insurance riding on him. Truthfully, I was sort of hoping the lousy kid wouldn't make it." I'm resigned to the fact that it won't ever happen, because people have an unfortunate tendency to be polite to those who ask stupid questions.

This reporter stared at me. I busied myself adjusting the flank cinch and he turned and walked into the office. I got rid of my mail in a hurry and slid out of town before I could get caught up in another interview, the results of which were more apt to be embarrassing than anything else.

The blacklands stretched on interminably and at this season of the year, with nothing growing in the plowed expanses, it seemed to me like mile upon mile of mud. Arriving at Farmersville, a small oasis of trees and buildings in the vast sea of blackland, I began casting about for a place to stop with a horse where neither of us would become

171

mired. I was directed to a small gas station-grocery store a mile or so ahead where the owner, one Gilbert Nix, was said to be a horseman. He was, and he made me welcome immediately. His palomino horse Charlie was glad to have Sioux staked out in the grass next to his pasture and galloped back and forth for her benefit like a show-off kid. Nick, as my host was known, made a small shed with a couch in it available and his wife and son insisted on fixing a steak sandwich for me, although I'd eaten earlier at the café in town.

Farmersville was the hometown of Audie Murphy and I gathered that Nick, while not related, had played the role of big brother while young Audie was growing up under rather difficult circumstances. Audie had spent most of his spare time as a youth rabbit hunting with a .22 rifle. When this slight youngster suddenly burst into national prominence as World War II's most decorated soldier, it had put Farmersville on the map.

Audie had not been one to forget old friends and we spent the evening perusing studio-type photographs of Nick and Audie in Hollywood and at some of the larger Texas rodeos. Nick told of having been invited to Hollywood for a visit with the young actor. They'd gone to a rather formal dinner one night and Nick had been wondering why Audie was grinning – until he sat down at his place and found that Audie'd had little identifying tags attached to all the articles in the formidable array of silverware.

Next day I rode on to McKinney, a good-sized town north of Dallas. The blacklands were not conducive to camping, so I stopped at the sale barn just out of town and made arrangements to park Sioux. For myself I felt that the time for a motel with shower had come and I'd seen several signs advertising Brown's Motel. On each sign was the statement that children and pets were welcome. I decided to ride Sioux to the motel, drop my gear, then bareback her on the return to the sale barn. Hitching Sioux outside the entrance, I walked into the office and registered for a room.

Intending only to kid the proprietor a bit I said, "Your sign says that children and pets are welcome. What are the size limitations on pets?"

"What have you got?" asked the man at the desk as he looked up.

"A horse," I said.

"Hell," he laughed, "tie her next to your room. You need any grain, I'll bring you a sack when I come back after supper."

I hadn't intended to be taken seriously, since Brown's Motel was located in the built-up part of town and had attractive lawns around the units, but I certainly preferred to keep Sioux close at hand and I knew that she'd rather eat grass than hay. It didn't take long for me to agree to the arrangement and I phoned the sale barn to let them know I'd made other plans. True to his word, the man in the motel office returned from supper with a sack of oats for Sioux.

Colonel Tom Emerson of the *McKinney Courier-Gazette* came to my equipment-strewn room next morning for an interview. A dignified white-haired man whose consummate taste was easily discernible in his choice of riding boots identical to mine, Tom had traveled widely and returned to his true love, Texas. His excitement and enthusiasm for the state was a sort of electric thing that I observed in a large number of Texans. This was no narrow, provincial man who had never been east of the Red River. On the contrary, a large part of his life had been spent away from Texas: now he had returned and he gave every evidence of being a completely happy man in this land which is his way of life. Before I was through with Texas, I covered over nine hundred miles of a vast and varied land. I met hundreds of people in the course of my many stops and nowhere else have I found so high a percentage of downright kindly, likable people. It is true that there is a type that several of my Texas friends referred to as the "professional Texan." I was fortunate in meeting only one or two of these. One man clapped me on the back and suggested that if I went out snake hunting with him, "Ah could tell them folks back in Nyew Yawk how us Taixis boys stomp them big ol' rattle-bugs!"

Colonel Tom made several helpful suggestions. One for the immediate future was a short side trip to the Phillips quarter horse ranch in Frisco, a small town just above Dallas. He had recently done a newspaper article on the ranch and was insistent that I shouldn't miss seeing it.

With the Phillips Ranch in mind, I cut south after leaving town and soon edged my way into some solid cattle country. I camped one night in a lush green pasture belonging to a dairy farmer, and Sioux was knee-deep in horse heaven. In talking with the old farmer before turning in for the night, the subject of my interest in the Phillips Ranch came up.

"A li'l ol' oil well or two shore does he'p run a ranch," he commented.

I was to see the proof of this statement numerous times as we traveled further into Texas and I don't doubt that it applies equally to ranches in Oklahoma and other oil areas.

The ability to see long distances can lead a stranger into a trap under certain circumstances. The road leading to Frisco proved to be one of them. Usually the town water tower breaks the horizon first in these small Texas towns; then a twinkling miragelike view of a cluster of buildings begins to take form. This day I could see Frisco in the far distance and I knew the ranch to be several miles off to the right. A ranch road headed straight west, and again in the

174

far distance I could see a row of telegraph poles cutting
south, doubtless lining a road heading right where I wanted
to go. Without hesitation I reined Sioux off on the ranch
road and struck up a swinging trot that ate into the miles in
short order. The road was surfaced with a whitish clay that
made for pleasant riding, the day was clear and brisk, and
clusters of cattle grazed peacefully on all sides. Gradually
the tops of the telegraph poles rose higher and became more
distinct until finally, climbing a small rise, I saw to my
dismay that they followed, not a road, but a railroad track.
The road I had been following continued on into what looked
to be infinity and it would have been a long way back, so I
decided to try the railroad right of way, which appeared to
be fenced off with plenty of room on either side and did, in
fact, head straight toward my destination.

All was going well, the distant cluster of buildings that
was Frisco drew closer and closer, and we were forced to
ride the crushed-rock railroad bed only a few times when
brush closed in on us. Just as I was congratulating myself
on the success of my maneuver, we came to a wide, deep and
treacherous-looking creek. The bottom looked to be deep clay
mud and not knowing the country, I was leery of quicksand.
Above us the railroad proceeded serenely across a wooden
trestle and continued its march cross-country to where I
wanted to go. Sioux flatly refused to go on into the mud on
the banks of the stream and I decided against forcing her
into something that could prove to be a bad mistake. It was
now a long, long way back around, so the only alternative
was the trestle. I had no idea whether Sioux would take
kindly to crossing on the ties, but I decided to find out. I led
her up the steep bank to the grade level some distance back
from the trestle, climbed on and guided her in between the
tracks. The wooden ties were square and placed close together with probably not more than three inches between

them. Slowly, carefully and steadily she moved out onto the trestle, her head low, her nose almost touching the ties. Halfway across, I began to think about my idiocy. Visions of her slipping, catching a foot between ties, an oncoming train had my heart in my mouth and when we reached the other side, I slid off and could have kissed the old mare on the spot. Had anyone suggested that I should have had a better horse at that moment, I think I'd have been tempted to take a shot at him.

We soon crossed another ranch road and were able to leave the railroad. An old colored man in a rattling Chevy gave me directions for cutting across some large pastures with careful instructions as to the gate locations, and we had no further trouble. Many pastures could have been entered and crossed in this country, the only snag being that a stranger might be forced to ride miles out of his way in search of an exit gate. In this respect the United States Geological Survey maps would be excellent. I had started with a few of these and for a short trip they'd be ideal, since they not only give all the roads and trails that are not on the standard maps, they also include fences, gates and even elevations, so that to a practiced eye they become very much like a relief map. In my case I'd have needed a pack horse to carry a full set, and even then my route was too indefinite. I had given up these fine maps by mid-Virginia and now was relying on standard road maps, which are a poor thing when the traveler is trying for rural routes.

B. F. Phillips, Jr., a wealthy rancher and oil man, like others in this country appeared to view the wealth-producing oil as merely a means to improve upon his original way of life. Cattle and horses were not tossed aside as an old and no longer necessary means of making a living from a rugged land. Oil money, in the case of such men, only enables them to continue their ranching with handsome ranch houses and

176

efficient and attractive stables, barns and facilities. Money, added to the bred-in knowhow, is put to use in producing some of the finest livestock to be found anywhere.

The entrance to the Lazy P (⊔) leads the visitor over a cattle guard — in my case through the ornamental iron gate — and up a gently curving drive lined with bands of quarter horses. About a mile in, at the top of a gentle hill, stands a soft-hued, brick ranch house trimmed with a pale moss green. I don't know where the bricks come from but their color reminded me instantly of the mellow, faded, two-hundred-year-old ballast bricks from which our old New England Colonial fireplaces were built. Several other similarly constructed brick buildings, the white stables and fences and the handsome mares and colts that followed me along the roadside gave me the feeling that a great deal of money had been put to very tasteful and intelligent use.

Halfway up the drive, I was met by a pickup truck with a sun-bleached, smiling man at the wheel. I explained that I was interested in seeing the ranch, having had it described to me by Colonel Tom Emerson, and wondered if Billy Joe Bryson was around.

"You're talking to him," he said, and then introduced his wife who sat next to him. "I've got to go into town for a minute but you go ahead on up and I'll be right back. We'll put your horse up and you stay at the bunkhouse."

Billy Joe, whose name had been given me by Tom Emerson, was the manager. The closer I rode to the ranch buildings, the more impressed I was by the efficiency and attractiveness of the layout. I hadn't much more than dismounted when Billy Joe returned and helped me haul my dusty gear into a handsome tack room. My shabby old hull was parked on a rack in the middle of a room lined with beautiful roping and cutting saddles, and I was tempted to cover it with the

179

saddle blanket to prevent it from being embarrassed by its surroundings.

Sioux was led to her individual stall and paddock and if she wasn't impressed, she should have been. Her white-painted apartment was floored with hard-packed, reddish-colored sand, her individual water trough was spotlessly clean, and, as in each of the other stalls, a large tractor tire was placed as a feed container. This novel practice prevents hay from being scattered and also guards against possible injury to the horse. It goes along with the sensible theory that a horse should be fed from ground level, as it would feed in its natural state. Sioux's stall was arranged to give complete protection from weather, still allowing her free choice as to whether she wanted to wander in or out.

When Billy Joe mentioned the bunkhouse, I'd visualized a rudimentary building such as I'd occupied in Wyoming as a youngster. This one, built of the same warm-toned brick as the main house, featured a modern kitchen, wall-to-wall carpeting, tile baths adjoining the rooms and a large tele-vision set in a central living room that was equipped with comfortable furniture.

The Brysons invited me to join them for dinner at the café and there I finally got around to trying catfish for the first time. I'd always been fond of fish, but somehow the word catfish conjured up something that tempered my appe-tite. This is true no more, since once past the name I enjoyed it without reservations.

An invitation to stay over next day gave me the chance to see more of the ranch and I gladly took advantage of it. Mart McMillan, an example of the present-day college-bred cowboy, planned to move some cattle from one side of the creek to the other, and I saddled Sioux and rode out with him. I took the camera along and was glad that I had, for Mart made an excellent subject dressed in his fringed

180

leggins astride a handsome quarter horse with the rolling hills and white-faced cattle in the background.

At one point on our ride, we ran into one of the Mexican employees of the ranch on a big black mud-spattered stallion. Under his muddy exterior the horse was a handsomely built animal and I commented on him as we left.

"That's Steel Bars," Mart explained, "a grand champion stallion and cutting horse."

I'd heard of Steel Bars — most recently in a story told me by the storekeeper in a place where I'd stopped for cigarettes. A man had come in the store, having just left the Phillips Ranch.

"I just saw two crazy men that are running loose near here," he said. "One of them offered Phillips a hundred and ninety thousand bucks for Steel Bars — and Phillips turned it down."

After we'd returned and hosed the mud off our horses' legs in a washroom designed for the purpose, we put the horses away. Gin Echols, a filly sired by the famous old Ed Echols, was standing saddled along with another horse. Shortly B. F. Phillips drove in with a Buick to which was attached a tandem, two-horse trailer. A rugged, square-jawed man with a bone-crushing handshake, he'd have been hard to pick from his employees had it not been for Billy Joe's introduction. Certainly his Levi's were more worn and faded than theirs. My impression was that here was a man who was much more interested in his steer roping and in the betterment of the quarter horse than he was in his oil interests.

The Brysons invited me to their home for dinner that evening. Here again was the same muted brick construction that I found so well suited to the soft green of the surrounding grasslands. One of the finest Charley Russell reproductions I'd ever seen caught and held my eye throughout the evening and further whetted my appetite for the Fort Worth collection.

During the dinner, Billy Joe's lovely wife laughed and asked, "Have they ever found out about Dr Pepper up in your country?"

"I doubt it," I said, trying to recall whether I'd ever seen that particular carbonated drink in any of the stands.

"I visited in New York a few years ago," she said, "and asked a girl at a drugstore counter for a Dr Pepper. The way she looked, I thought she figured I ought to check the yellow pages under physicians and surgeons."

"She probably did," I laughed. "Dr Pepper doesn't seem to practice much north of the Mason-Dixon."

Another custom that stops short of the line is the free coffee refills at cafés. My first brush with the "on the house" second or third cup of coffee came in mid-Virginia and continued from there.

Before leaving the Phillips Ranch, I rode Sioux around to pay homage to the twenty-six-year-old Ed Echols, high-point roping and reining horse in the nation. The still handsome old stud was comfortably ensconced in his private quarters and looked little the worse for his years. He certainly had much in his past to be proud of and from all appearances, little to worry about in the future.

I cut across the Garza–Little Elm Lake area on the way to Denton. Water was still running high from recent rains and at one point the paved road was under water up to Sioux's knees. We reached Denton and the sale barn and I stayed over for the sale in order to make some sketches. Denton, like many other county seats in Texas, is a strange mixture of the new and old. The main part of town surrounds an old-fashioned courthouse square with all the cut-stone charm of an older period, while on the outskirts are modern stores, supermarkets and other buildings which characterize the neon age.

The haversack arrangement I'd had up to now had been a sore point. It had seemed necessary as a container for the overflow; my main complaint was that whether it was full or empty, it remained the same size. The decision was finally rendered for me as I rode out of Denton and passed between an excavation along the roadside and a barbed-wire fence. Sioux glanced down into the hole, saw a terrifying pile of black tar paper and spooked violently up against the barbed wire. Fortunately for my knee, the damned haversack was hanging awkwardly in its usual place in front of my leg and the barbs ripped it lengthwise in three places. From then on I settled for a burlap feed bag. When full of such things as extra groceries it was as much of a nuisance as the haversack had been, but when empty it could be wadded up and tied snugly to the saddle horn. If it lacked the good looks of the haversack, its comparative efficiency was more than compensation.

Changes in terrain came more rapidly now and the live oak and limestone began to appear. The footing was no longer muddy and it was a pleasure to divest ourselves of the caked clay that we'd acquired in the last hundred or so miles. The country still wore its winter browns and grays, and the contrast made the live oaks particularly noticeable. These trees have a rather flat-bottomed, almost oriental look due to the fact that livestock reach up and browse off the lower branches. Evidently a stratum of limestone prevents the rainwaters from sinking in, because several times we crossed arroyos or gulches containing fast-flowing water while up on a level with the tops of the banks a sizable pool sat quietly aloof from the action below. From here on west these pools or ponds are referred to as tanks, whether they're man-made or part of the natural contour. The country swept away on all sides to the distant horizons, broken only by an occasional mesa or a distant stark and lonely building.

There was an almost total lack of traffic, so that my attention was readily drawn to a dusty Chevrolet that passed me a few miles out of Decatur, the next town ahead. When I observed it returning sometime later, I recognized it by its cover of Texas topsoil. I didn't suspect at that moment that before I got through associating with the little car it was to be additionally well coated on the *inside* with horsehair, hayseed and manure.

The car slowed to a stop across the highway and a smiling, dark-haired young man slid from behind the wheel and walked across to where I was dismounting. He wore a dark red silk handkerchief around his neck and I pegged him immediately and with considerable accuracy as some kind of eccentric artist.

"I know it's none of my business," he greeeted me with a modulated Texas drawl, "but you look to be headed someplace with all that gear."

"Probably Decatur tonight," I replied, falsely lulled by his disarming manner. "Eventually Arizona and the Grand Canyon."

"My name's Hurshel Farrow" — he pronounced it Farrah — "and I'm a photographer. I wondered if I might take a couple of pictures."

Closer observation allowed me to spot a few lines around his eyes that added a few hard years to my original estimate of his age. Having associated with a number of photographers in the past and having found them almost invariably to be dissolute types, I probably should have climbed back on Sioux and ridden rapidly away. I didn't, and the next few weeks were considerably altered by this chance meeting.

We talked there on the high bank over the road for some time and I garnered the facts that he was married, lived on the outskirts of Dallas and had been cruising around in the hinterlands looking for photographic material. He was due back in Dallas later in the afternoon, but suggested that if I could park Sioux in Decatur, he'd return with his wife Patsy and take me home with him that night. I took his card and a rain check, since I was by then in need of laundering and hoped to find a motel and laundry in Decatur.

I rode in, stopped at a motel and, fortunately, before registering checked the office of the telegraph company. I quickly discovered that it was situated in the railroad depot where there were no check forms, that it operated through the local bank and that the bank was scheduled to close within the hour. To add to the problem, it was a Friday afternoon and nothing could be accomplished before the following Monday. Having become by this time something of an opportunist, I decided that if the Farrows would have me in my unwashed state, I'd take Hurshel up on his offer. I called Pat to firm up the reservation in Dallas, then called my home to ask my wife to wire money to Dallas, where I doubted that things shut down for the weekend. A trip back to the Decatur sale barn, which I'd passed entering town, found an available pen for Sioux and I was safely out of my dilemma.

I'd unpacked Sioux in front of the sale barn and was allowing her to graze when a big, rugged-looking Texan pulled up in his pickup truck. He introduced himself and said he'd heard I was in town on a cross-country ride and he had a proposition for me.

"I've got a big fat quarter horse stud that needs exercise worse than anything in the world," he explained. "About two weeks of good hard roadwork would put him in shape just about right. How about leaving your mare in my corral for a two-week rest? I'll feed and take care of her, then I'll trailer her down and meet you wherever you are in two weeks. Your mare could have a rest and my horse would have a good workout."

It wasn't a bad-sounding proposition, since Sioux certainly could have used a good rest; however, if Hurshel decided to take any serious number of photographs, I wanted Sioux to be in them. I left the deal pending with a promise to get in touch and he departed leaving me a large bucket of oats for Sioux. Unfortunately I lost the man's address and was never able to let him know the decision I'd arrived at.

Presently Hurshel and Pat arrived, bringing with them a friend who was an art teacher from Dallas, Dan Goodwin. Dan, a slim dark man with a great black moustache, said that he'd be glad to drive into Fort Worth the next day if I wanted to see the Amon Carter collection of Western paintings. When I mentioned that I'd have to get back to Decatur to care for Sioux, he cheerfully offered to make that trip as well, which was no short drive.

All four of us piled into the Chevy and headed for Dallas. As Sioux had recently commenced shedding, I was well covered and the poor little car received its first baptism of horsehair. I think that there are many wives who would have reacted to my appearance with scant enthusiasm. I decided that Pat was either an extremely good-natured woman or thoroughly inured to her husband bringing home dirty, unkempt and, in my case, horsy-smelling characters.

We stopped in a small town short of Dallas and Hurshel hosted us to a superb steak at a rustic and crowded steak house that he'd ferreted out in his travels. Arriving at the Farrows' suburban house, I leaped for the shower and attempted to civilize myself as much as possible, and the remainder of the evening was spent in formulating a plan

186

whereby Hurshel could accompany me with his car and camping gear for the purpose of getting a series of photographs. It took no great powers of observation to determine that much of the literature in the house of Farrow pertained to camping and outdoor activities. A simple gadget such as my folding candle box, although unlighted, set off an immediate sparkle in his eye. My compass-sun watch device hooked him with the flashing speed of a rainbow trout rising to a dry fly. The symptoms of my own incurable disease could be diagnosed at a glance. The carefully arranged facade that attempted to convince the casual passerby that H. Farrow was a serious businessman and an asset to his community was a complete hoax. Anyone who starts to perspire over a waterproof matchbox is as much of a hobo at heart as I confess to being and I knew that the merest wave of a lumpy sleeping bag would have this pseudo-solid citizen hunkered down happily eating beans in front of a smoking fire.

A day's commercial camera work was to occupy Hurshel before he could follow through with our plans, and Dan Goodwin took me in tow for that day. We left early for a trip to Western Union for the money order, then drove the long haul back to Decatur to see that Sioux was taken care of. A return trip down the endless highway took us to Dallas and then to Fort Worth, where we located the home of the Amon Carter collection of paintings.

As so often happens, I'd arrived at Fort Worth just in time for the bulk of the Remingtons and Russells to have been put away in the vaults. In their place was the personal collection of firearms put together by Colonel Samuel Colt. As an affirmed gun nut I'd have been delighted with the display, had it not been for the fact that a short trip from my home in Rhode Island to Hartford, Connecticut, where the collection is permanently housed, would have made the same display easily available. Now, I had to content myself with the few paintings that were still in place and the fact that I'd decided against riding a horse into the Dallas–Fort Worth complex. Had I done so, for the purpose of seeing the paintings, and found them gone, I'd have been reduced to some incoherent mumbling. The Dallas and Fort Worth I'd passed through twenty-five years ago were hard to reconcile with the cities that exist there today. High-speed overpasses and underpasses swirl through tall buildings and I quickly became a bewildered, thoroughly disoriented country cousin.

That evening, Patsy's living room was a mess of scattered camping gear reminiscent of my own that previous autumn. Folding cooking gear, hatchets, a gasoline lantern, cans of foodstuffs and an air mattress cluttered the place. Though the air mattress was to provide me with a certain amount of amusement the following evening, at this moment it looked innocuous enough.

Sioux seemed happy to see us in the morning. Hurshel's car was stuffed fore and aft with his camp equipment, to which mine had been added. The front luggage compartment also contained a bag of horse feed and a bale of alfalfa. My usual inability to carry hay had always forced me to pick only campsites with good grazing facilities, but now, with a "motorized pack horse," I could enjoy a campsite chosen solely for its comfort and appearance.

The plan was roughly arranged that Hurshel would drive on ahead for twenty or twenty-five miles and locate an attractive campsite, then return to meet me with instructions on where to find the campsite. He was to waylay me at various points for photographs, and toward the day's end go on ahead to the rendezvous point and get the camp set up for the night.

This made everything considerably more simple for both Sioux and me, since there were no worries about where to find a campsite and Sioux was relieved of all the heavy extras.

Our first day on the road was warm and springlike. The sun was such that I was soon down to a light cotton shirt and already I started formulating plans to rid myself permanently of my winter clothes. We'd gotten some photographs while passing through Decatur early in the day. The old Victorian Waggoner mansion jutted up to the south and a similarly Victorian county courthouse occupied the middle of the square. On the road out of town, Sioux occasionally arched her neck and pointed her ears. Each time I looked up to see what it was that was attracting her attention I found a body sprawled in the bar ditch sniping away at me with his new Leica. Like most people I'd always become uncomfortably self-conscious around a camera. By the time Hurshel had finished with me, I'd gotten so accustomed to it that it was no longer painful. Too, the Leica is so quiet and unobtrusive as to be hardly noticeable and much of the time I was unaware that pictures were being taken at all. In Texas all cameras are usually referred to as Kodaks in the same way that hats are Stetsons and rifles, Winchesters. It's become a sort of photographer's in-joke, so that when a man at the camera store in Dallas phoned to let Hurshel know his "Kodak" was in, he referred to the new Leica that had been on order. A photography trip is generally spoken of as "goin' Kodakin'."

During the latter part of the afternoon, Hurshel returned to advise me of the location of the camp he'd planned. He had run up against the hospitality of the country that in this case, had posed a problem. Spotting a photographic-looking dry wash with an old abandoned wagon lying with its wheels half buried next to a growth of post oaks, he'd driven ahead to the ranch house to ask permission to camp. The rancher was nothing if not genial but insisted that it would be better if we stayed at his house, since it was due to turn cold that night. Hurshel was forced to do a sales job to convince the man that he wanted campfire photographs and therefore needed to spend the night outside.

By the time I arrived the camp was all set up in the lee of the old wagon and there was nothing for me to do other than take care of Sioux and get at the business of eating. Fill-in lights, wired to the camera, and the tripods which were necessary as a result made maneuvering a bit hazardous, but eventually we completed shooting a considerable number of pictures with Sioux tied to the old wagon wheel as a background for the fire.

We arranged our sleeping bags near the fire and went through the motions of inflating the air mattresses. In the interests of keeping weight and bulk to a minimum, my mattress was a short forty-four inches — just enough to cover from the shoulders to the knees. It required only a few lungfuls of air to inflate and I was all set in a short time. Hurshel, on the other hand, was some time in getting his much larger, full-length mattress to the required degree of turgidity and finally stumbled weakly back to the fire, gasping for breath. Reluctant to give up and quit for the night, we added to the fire and talked on for some while. Spending as much time with a horse for companionship as I had, I discovered through my rare inward glances that I was becoming loquacious to the degree that I ran at the mouth when the opportunity presented itself. We finally decided to crawl into our sleeping bags. I was no more than halfway inside mine when I heard Hurshel utter a loud obscenity.

"Troubles?" I inquired solicitously as I snugged down in my bag.

"This sunuvabitch is leakin'," came the ill-tempered reply.

"No!" I said sympathetically. It was dark, and Hurshel

was unable to see my facial expression in the dying flickers of the fire.

I wriggled out of my boots and pulled the zipper up under my chin, then tightened the drawstring that made a hood out of the top of the sleeping bag. It had become cold and the wind had freshened, but my down-filled bag was already cozy.

"How're you doin'?" I asked, aware that my companion was out of his bag and struggling to reinflate his flaccid air mattress.

"This — *puff* — sunuva — *puff* — bitch — *puff* — got a — *puff* — slow leak — *puff!*" he repeated with what I felt was little originality.

"Can you find it?" I asked helpfully.

"If I could, goddammit, I'd plug it up and it wouldn't leak," he responded with unnecessary rudeness.

I realized that the circumstance made him justifiably testy and that no doubt he'd be happier after a good night's rest under the stars, so I resolved to let him alone and go to sleep. I dropped off warm and secure in the knowledge that he'd be his old cheerful self in the morning.

He was neither his old nor his new cheerful self in the morning. The gray, pre-dawn light enabled me to be dimly aware of a pitiful hunched-over figure breaking kindling and striking matches. I wondered idly at his early rising habits and decided that they were admirable but not for me, so I hitched deeper in my bed and returned to a dreamless sleep.

Something nudged me, not too gently, in the shoulder — I think it was a foot — and a grim voice cut through the fog. "Goddammit, I can't sleep on that dam' hard ground anymore. It's cold as hell out here an' I'm out of cigarettes. You could at least get your ass out of the sack and give me a cigarette!"

"Sure," I said obligingly and handed him a mashed

191

package of cigarettes, hastily returning my arm to the warmth of the sleeping bag. "Is the coffee ready yet?"

"No," he snapped curtly as he stomped back to the fire which was beginning to crackle under the coffeepot. Soon he seemed to be talking to someone, probably Sioux, who was munching her hay nearby. "Hell of a note. Camp with a sunuvabitch that won't get outa the sack in the mornin' — have to build a big fire and chase away the buzzards — layin' there like he's dead — doesn't smell too good either — no wonder the buzzards are hangin' around — probably have to wave my arms and holler to keep 'em off him."

"Call me when the coffee's ready, will you, Hursh?" I mumbled from the depths, thinking to cheer him with the knowledge that I was not, indeed, dead.

The reply sounded like a vulgarism but I decided to pay no heed to it, since I knew that many awake to the morn in a cranky mood, for one reason or another. Soon the sun began to rise and that, coupled with the smell of Hurshel's cigarette and the bubbling coffeepot, succeeded in getting me out of my sleeping bag. By means of adroit questioning after a diplomatic wait while the sun, the fire and the coffee had time for a mellowing effect, I found that the slow leak had not been located and that Hurshel had been obliged to get up several times to reinflate his mattress. Too, the knowledge that the mattress was leaking and the anticipation of hard ground sneaking up to dig into him had greatly inhibited restful sleep. To add to his misery, the wind had changed and perversely blown into the large open end of his sleeping bag. Complete this picture by having a person nearby contentedly snoring and I decided that his waspish attitude was justified and that I would refrain from further mention of air mattresses for at least an hour or so.

The sun did a less than efficient job of warming the air, and the wind became gusty and raw. Far from the thoughts

I'd had of ridding myself of heavier clothing, I got out the windproof parka by noontime. Hurshel had gone on ahead to locate a campsite near a large lake and had then returned to Dallas to seek a solution to the leaky air mattress. He caught up with me by late afternoon when I was three or four miles from our destination and by then a strong wind was blowing with what looked like the makings of snow.

A mile from the camp, I passed the entrance of a large ranch and noticed some new corrugated barn buildings near the ranch house. Seven or eight saddle horses came up to the gate on the highway, then followed us along until we arrived at the lake and took to the bridge. The wind, sweeping across the lake, came from the north. By the time I was halfway across the bridge, I began to think we were going to be blown off and almost wished we would be. The right side of my face felt numb. I stuffed my gloved right hand under my parka and tried to hide my rein hand behind the fork of the saddle. Snow was starting to spit by now and during the rare times when I peered out from under my hat brim, I caught glimpses of Hurshel's car parked in the lee of a sloping bank near the lake.

I turned Sioux off and rode her around behind the bank to where Hurshel was making camp. He'd succeeded in starting a fire, but the wind was blowing it around erratically and what was by now a full-fledged norther was swooping over the bank and down on us as though we were completely unshielded. There was no better place in sight and it began to look as though we were in for a thoroughly miserable night.

"You're about the sorriest pathfinder I ever saw," I chattered at Hurshel through my teeth. "You passed up the best campsite about ten miles back."

"What was that?" Hurshel shivered back.

"It was on the outskirts of Bridgeport. It had gas heat,

193

hot and cold running water and television. It was a thing called a motel."

"Why hell, boy," Hurshell boomed with false heartiness, trying to make himself audible against the bitter wind, "you supposed to be roughin' it. The rugged life — takin' on the weather the way it comes. You're not supposed to be holin' up in civilized comforts, featherbeddin' it!"

"Nuts!" I said. "I bet I could put Sioux in that barn back about a mile and we could shag back to Dallas. Maybe Pat hasn't changed the sheets on my bed yet."

"I certainly am surprised and disillusioned," said Hurshel piously, following me with unseemly haste into the warmth of the automobile, which stood with motor running and the heater on, so that we could continue the debate I was certain he hoped to lose. "Why you'd practically be cheatin' the public, runnin' out on a little ol' breeze like this." He wiped the tears from his eyes.

I made an obscene suggestion to him and with that he gave in. "All right, if you want to perpetrate a fraud, far be it from me to keep you honest. Let's go back and see if we can park the horse."

Leaving Sioux in charge of camp, we drove back across the bridge to where I'd passed the ranch. As we arrived, a tall weatherbeaten man came out to quiet a gang of hounds that was threatening to tree us. Bob Evans said that we'd be welcome to put Sioux in the barn and that he'd feed her in the morning or until we got back, depending on the outcome of the storm.

It was a matter of a very few minutes before we drove back, saddled Sioux and threw our camp gear back into the Chevy. Heaving myself aboard, I headed back across the bridge and found out about Texas weather. The old saying is that there's nothing between Texas and the North Pole but a barbed-wire fence, and when a norther starts to blow, somebody has let down the wires. I can attest to the truth of the saying, since I can't recall ever having been any colder than I was while crossing the bridge, heading back to the ranch. I'm sure that I've been subjected to much lower temperatures and certainly that past winter I'd been in more snow, but the wind pushing a norther seems to grope its way into every part of you.

Bob had a large pen ready for Sioux by the time we arrived and she was left contentedly munching alfalfa in the company of Evans's horses, safely out of the biting wind. Halfway to Dallas we ran out of the snow and were hard put to explain our return to Pat and Hurshel's parents, with whom she was staying. Northers customarily stop as rapidly as they begin and next day the weather was nearly spring-like again.

Returning to pick up Sioux, we met Bob Evans riding in toward the corrals paced by the ever present hounds. His work-scarred chaps and saddle made him the picture of the working cowboy. As usual, my offer to pay for Sioux's board and shelter was brushed away.

We made camp at a point farther down the lake shore and this time it was considerably more pleasant. Trees and large boulders edged the shore, and the broad lake that had only the day before been whipped to a boiling froth by the norther now placidly reflected the opposite shores and the tall, lonely mesa that broke the horizon.

I'd sprung myself to a new lariat before returning to the lake and that night spent several hours trying to backsplice a spring snap into the end of it. The lariat was intended primarily as a picket rope and the snap on the end made it more convenient for fastening Sioux. New lariats are tight and hard and I had a rough time trying to backsplice the end. To add to my difficulties, Hurshel had kept up a running flow of skeptical comments about my abilities at splicing to which he'd added vulgar descriptions of what the result looked like. In truth it was a miserable-looking job, and anyway I felt that he should be allowed a chance to regain face after losing the battle to the air mattress.

This night Hurshel had no mattress problem; however, I succeeded in outwaiting him in the morning, chiefly for the pleasure to be had in listening to him carry on his monologue about camping companions who looked, acted and smelled dead and the fact that once again he was forced to build a fire and frighten off the buzzards to keep them from carrying off his photographic subject.

7.

Hurshel and I breakfasted early, broke camp and headed out in the direction of Jacksboro. Hurshel, as planned, drove on ahead. He returned a couple of hours later to suggest that I turn off on a little-used road that would reach Jacksboro by way of a small village called Wizard Wells. He then left to go check out a likely spot to stop off in the vicinity of Jacksboro.

The day was warming rapidly and Sioux was swinging along, lightened of her customary load by Hurshel's car. We dropped off a slope and approached a complex of ranch buildings near the roadside. A driveway looped in between lantern-decorated posts and swung around in front of a white-stuccoed two-story ranch house with a tall pillared veranda reaching across the front. New open-faced sheds and a barn skirted the drive to the left, and back in the distance where the mesquite and oak-clad hills rose to encircle the little valley stood old, weathered frame buildings that looked to have been the original ranch headquarters. A slow, measured *putt-putt* beat was faintly audible as we started down the slope and for a moment it was reminiscent of the old one-lung marine engines that used to power the lobster-fishing dories along the Maine coast. As we drew closer, the sound led to a large piece of machinery that was slowly bobbing its head up and down in a rhythmic way that made me think of those trick wooden birds which, when set on the edge of a glass of water, dip down to drink, then rise, pause and dip again. We came to our first oil well and I thought with amusement of the old farmer's comment that a li'l ol' oil well or two shore does he'p run a ranch.

From time to time, the sound of the oil well motors was heard for a considerable distance. When first detected, it was almost like a muffled hoofbeat, more felt than heard. The pumps were ugly-looking devices. I had an ambivalent feeling about them: I would certainly be delighted to own a few of the things, but they reminded me unpleasantly of some sort of mechanical leech, busily sucking the lifeblood out of the earth. I'd like to enjoy the fruits of the gadgets but I'd prefer not to have to look at them. Were I to own a batch of them, I think I'd build some kind of fabricated, fake, weathered old shed to conceal them from view.

Hills with outcroppings of rock, covered in mesquite grass and post oak, climbed upward and by noontime we reached Wizard Wells, a tiny town with an ancient frame hotel building. Mineral springs were the reason for the hotel with its bathhouses but now the only activity centered around a small café, where I stopped for lunch. The atmosphere of a sleepy little town, with its grass threatening to creep out over the pavement, would have tempted me to stop over had it not been for my agreement to catch up to Hurshel in Jacksboro. As I climbed up away from the town and looked back down, I promised myself that should I ever be afflicted with a combination of arthritis and jangled nerves, Wizard Wells would see me again.

The road climbed steeply out of the valley and a vast,

panoramic view of the country opened up. Ragged buttes and mesas, their shadows tinted with reds and purples, swept off to the far horizon. It was so warm and peaceful that I felt a lethargy that goes with summer. The only signs of life were occasional white-faced Herefords seeking noontime shade under the oaks, and the ever-present soaring buzzards. Even these oftentimes seemed to hang almost motionless in the sky. The only sounds intruding on the stillness were the muffled clump of Sioux's hoofs on the sandy roadside and the sloshing of water in my canteen.

We were now in the land of the Comanche and it was easy to visualize the painted ponies and their riders who slid down these rough slopes a scant ninety years before. Movies and television have dulled the hostile Indian into a rather mythical and not too frightening figure. To a lone traveler passing this way a few short years ago, the sight of a band of Comanches or Kiowas must have been bone-chilling indeed.

The sound of a distant automobile cut into the quiet and shortly Hurshel's car appeared. He had spent considerable time scouting Jacksboro and had stopped to talk to occupants of the Chamber of Commerce office. While there he met Mrs. Laura Peacock, a person active in town affairs and particularly interested in its history. Old Fort Richardson still stands about a mile southwest of the courthouse square and Mrs. Peacock suggested that we pull in at the fort for our night's stay. A number of the old buildings, fashioned of cut stone and cottonwood logs, remained intact, but those made only of wood had disappeared over the years with the exception of one of the officers' quarters that was kept in repair.

The fort, built in 1867, was the northernmost of a chain of military posts established in Texas to halt the raiding Comanches and Kiowas, who had become increasingly bold during and after the Civil War. General Sherman, apparently skeptical of reports and complaints that had been flooding his headquarters in southern Texas, decided to take an inspection tour in 1871 and had crossed Salt Creek Prairie, which lies a few miles west of Jacksboro. A few hours after he passed through, the Warren wagon train was massacred almost in his wake. Actually, it was later determined that Sherman had been under surveillance by the Indians but was passed up in favor of the wagon train with its possibilities of greater loot. This incident triggered Sherman into ordering Colonel Ranald Mackenzie to follow through with an arduous campaign which was to eventually bring this phase of the Indian wars to a close.

The large amount of money spent on Fort Richardson attracted a wild element to the tiny frontier community and Jacksboro suffered through some lawless years as saloons blossomed shoulder to shoulder along the banks of Los Creek, which borders the northwest edge of the fort. The stone hospital building, now used as a museum and as a meeting place for community affairs, stands as a centerpiece, with the old post bakery, morgue, ammunition magazine and guardhouse spread out at intervals around it. We'd been invited to use the kitchen facilities of the main building for our stopover, so, with Hurshel directing me, I turned off just south of town and rode through the gates and across the old parade ground.

After eating dinner at a local café we returned to the fort, followed by several visitors from town. Laura Peacock came to offer her assistance and Mrs. Mickey Kendricks, the secretary of the local Jack County Roughriders Club, stopped in to ask if our stay would be long enough for us to attend a dinner to be held the coming Saturday night at the fort. It was to be a joint affair for two organizations, the Jack County Sheriff's Posse and the Roughriders. The

Sheriff's Posse was composed of adult men from the area, while the Roughriders, whose membership in some cases overlapped, consisted of family groups of all age levels. The two units often functioned socially as one and I was tempted to stay over, both for the opportunity of meeting the groups and because Jacksboro looked to be of historical interest.

Hurshel wanted to photograph something of the fort area next day and then would be obliged to return to Dallas for a few days to catch up on his commercial work. The fort kitchen with its gas stove, refrigerator and sink was offered for my use, and there was sufficient grass to last Sioux for weeks. I suspected that if I stalled for only a little while, spring would arrive and new grass would be up in the drier country west of us.

The first night at the fort turned cool and we spread our sleeping bags on the floor in the kitchen with a couple of burners of the gas range turned on to remove the chill. The ceilings were at least fifteen feet high and an open transom over the door provided adequate ventilation for the gas burners. Hurshel shot some additional film next morning, then packed up and headed for Dallas, leaving me to prowl Jacksboro with Sioux.

Riding Sioux over the bridge near town on a grocery shopping trip, I spotted a stone marker indicating the crossing of the old Butterfield stage line, which had been routed this way in 1858. Many of the great longhorn cattle drives were funneled through here enroute to the Doan's Store crossing of the Red River and today Jack County's nearly thirty thousand head of beef cattle are keeping it primarily cattle country. A large herd of polled — naturally hornless — Herefords was north of town and I passed a ranch stocked with the creamy white Charolais cattle while riding in from the southeast. Large bands of sheep and Angora goats occupied much of the country and Mickey

Kendrick's husband Fred ran a herd of prize Black Angus cattle on his ranch south of town. The Angora goats serve multiple purposes, since they're raised as part of a scheme to reclaim the brush-covered land as grassland. Mesquite and post oak trees are knocked down with bulldozers to the level where the goats can complete their demise and the natural mesquite grasses and other types can then grow more prolifically. The goats are sheared in the spring and the silky mohair provides a tough yet soft fiber for numerous products. I'd bought a new mohair cinch for my saddle shortly before leaving Rhode Island, and at this point — and, in fact, at the end of the ride — despite the variety of weather conditions it had been subjected to, it remained soft and silky and virtually as new looking as at the start.

The Saturday-night buffet supper came and went, and here again, as in Virginia, it was refreshing to mingle with a group that ranged in age from two or three to probably eighty. My enjoyment of the food was almost upset when midway in the meal I was approached with a suggestion that I might address the assemblage. This was an entirely new experience for me and I was typically nervous about the prospect, but evidently there's enough of the ham in me so that I found myself enjoying it after the first few faltering attempts to get started. It's difficult to remain nervous long in the midst of a friendly, congenial group such as this was, and the question-and-answer session saved me from the chore of answering the same questions later to the many people with whom I became friendly.

Rain fell steadily throughout the next day and I delayed leaving until it cleared. In so doing I came close to becoming a permanent resident of Jacksboro — the hard way.

Ernest Brock, the young president of the Roughriders, and Hap Jackson, a member of both groups, spent the evening with me in the kitchen of the fort and after they left

I, as usual, unrolled my sleeping bag on the floor of the kitchen and turned in. I left two burners going in the gas range as I had done since the first night. I wasn't really familiar with gas, except that I realized that an unlighted burner, left on, would be capable of doing one in.

Somewhere around two A.M., for what reason I don't know, I awakened and tried to get up. I have a vague memory of falling down and an almost impossible struggle to get up and then, in a fog, I somehow made my way to the coin phone in the large dining room. I succeeded in extracting a dime and dialing the operator and I must have told her that I was in trouble out at the old fort. My first clear memory of the whole event is of standing in the open front door watching a police car drive in, stop at the caretaker's house and then come over to where I was.

Mr. Black, the night policeman, and the hastily awakened caretaker, Reverend E. R. Perritt, came in and we reconstructed the affair. The Perritts had been sound asleep when Black pounded on their door. By the time they answered the door Black was about ready to break it down, assuming, of course, that the emergency call had been from them. Perritt decided that the call must have come from me, so they came over to the door to find me staggering around, blood leaking from several lacerations. My head presently cleared and we looked around to find that in my blind efforts I'd wandered into the museum section, fallen over a section of picket snow fence that roped off a display and engaged in a wrestling match with an ancient wooden washing machine. The huge machine was overturned but undamaged. However, I had stuck a picket through my left eyebrow and acquired a number of other gashes on various parts of my anatomy.

There was no odor of leaking gas, the burners were still going and the transom was open, so for a while we ruled out

203

gas. It wasn't until Mr. Perritt drove me over to Dr. Mask in the morning for some stitches over my eye that we determined what had felled me. I should have had sense enough to realize that an unvented gas stove produces carbon monoxide, and in this case the damp air resulting from the rain held a blanket of the heavier gas down on the floor level where I was sleeping. The transom was too high up to provide ventilation and, as the doctor put it, had I not awakened when I did, I probably wouldn't have awakened at all.

Afraid to go back to my bunk that night, I rode around for the remainder of the dark hours with Mr. Black. I'm sure there were a number of uncharitable souls in Jacksboro who looked at my stitched-up eyebrow, listened to my sad story about the resulting headache and privately snorted, "Gas, hell! The sunuvabitch was drunk!"

Sioux and I wandered around town the following day and stopped at one point for a talk with Fred and Mickey Kendricks. What resulted from this conversation was a three-week pause in Jacksboro for the dual purpose of painting a portrait of Mickey on her quarter horse Ginger and giving Sioux a rest while the grass turned green.

The Kendricks owned a small unoccupied house several blocks out of the center of town which they made available to me. In its rear was a fenced yard ideal for Sioux. I had no materials for an oil portrait and that called for a trip to Fort Worth. The opportunity to go came up when Laura Peacock proposed driving in with Lou Comer, a local artist, and his wife.

I was surprised to be able to get everything I wanted at an art supply store in Fort Worth. Frankly I'm a snob about paint brands and professional-quality materials, but I had less trouble in Texas than I've experienced in Rhode Island. The canvas available was the finest piece of imported linen

I'd ever used, and esoteric potions such as the stand oil that
I'm addicted to were right on the shelves.

We were able to take in several of the art galleries while
there and I saw several examples of what I considered to be
excellent painting. One in particular by a painter whose
name I'm unable to recall depicted a young Mexican boy on a
sorrel horse against an adobe wall background. The lighting
was skillfully handled in a sort of outdoor Rembrandt style
which not only made it a dramatic picture but also por-
trayed accurately the startling contrast of the light and
shadow of this sunny country. One of the plusher galleries in
town gave me the opportunity to see a large panel of Peter
Hurd's and I was completely humbled by the man's ability
at depicting sunlight from a low horizon. In this painting
the sun was hidden behind a handsomely rendered, semi-
silhouetted metal tank. A tiny figure of a lone horseman rode
off into the distance and all around was that damned beautiful grass, its shadows melting forward toward the observer.

The days spent in my little house went quickly. Sioux
rapidly learned to come bang on the back door for attention
and often stood peering in at me through the kitchen window while I painted. Inside, the smell was something my
nose had been numb to for years. The odors of turpentine
and linseed oil equal studio to me. Now, having been away
from it for a number of months, it was once again noticeable
and I relished the pungent fumes. Outside, the smells were
those of earth and spring and horse. It was a good-smelling
place.

Each day I saddled Sioux and rode to the nearby post
office and grocery store. By now Sioux had learned that
grocery stores sell apples and carrots, and she had to be held
down on the way. She was completely officious about the way
I stowed groceries in the saddlebags, turning and twisting
about to see where the apples were put and forcing me to

bribe her with one or two in order to get her to stand reasonably still. Fred Kendricks offered me the use of a pickup truck, but except for a trip to the lumberyard for easel materials I preferred to use Sioux. Many of the back streets were unpaved. I was in no hurry and a certain amount of action each day kept our circulation going.

Evenings we often rode over to the Kendricks home for dinner, which usually involved a fine Black Angus steak, and at times I took a late ride up to the café for pecan pie and coffee. Often the clop of hoofs succeeded in arousing the neighborhood dogs; quite possibly the neighbors didn't enjoy the spring-evening rides as much as I did.

Hurshel arrived one day, walked in and sprawled full length on my bed.

"You are indubitably the biggest fraud I've yet to meet," he said, lying back with his dirty shoes on my clean bedspread and flicking ashes carelessly in the general direction of my ashtray. "Featherbeddin' it again. Supposed to be out roughin' it. Come down to Jacksboro an' what do I find? Sleepin' in a house — roof — windows — screens — runnin' water and a bathtub! Even cookin' on a gas range! Get rid of this bed." He pounded the soft mattress. "Take that bedroll out in the backyard and sleep with your horse the way you're supposed to!"

"I'm glad to see you finally got your dam' dirty car washed," I replied. "I hope you vacuumed the horsehair out of it. It was getting so I hated to ride in the thing."

"Put your hat on so the bald spot doesn't show, get an intelligent expression on your face and get your horse. We got some more Kodakin' to do." He got up and stalked into the kitchen to raid my fig bars and coffee while I saddled up.

We went up to Spy Knob on one of the camera trips. This jagged promontory of mossed-over rocks juts up from the prairie like a lighthouse in the sea. In former years it was used as an observation post by both the Indians and the settlers and its occupation usually depended on who got there first. A story was told about Oliver Loving, who with Charles Goodnight laid out the Goodnight-Loving Cattle Trail. It was related that Loving and one of his cowhand employees were being pursued by hostiles and were attempting to beat the Indians to Spy Knob and its rocky fortress-like cover. The cowhand had often ridden as a jockey in the frontier races and had several times been accused of intentionally losing races. The Indians were gaining; Loving's horse was in a dead run but the cowhand was falling behind.

"Can't you make that horse run any faster?" shouted Loving as the Indians closed the gap.

"Hell, Mr. Loving," called the cowboy with piteous righteousness, "you *know* this is one race I'm not fixing to throw!"

Evidently they won the race to cover at Spy Knob, since Oliver Loving continued for some years as a leading rancher and trailblazer.

The Knob is heavily infested with rattlesnakes and Hurshel and I were extremely careful about where we walked. The weather was warm enough for the snakes to come out at any time and from here on I was always watchful. The sound of their warning rattle was refreshed for me one evening when I was with Hap Jackson.

Hap and his lovely wife Gay invited me to have dinner with them and their two boys. He was scheduled to breed his black quarter horse stud to a local ranch mare, so I accompanied him in the pickup with his stallion riding behind in the trailer. We'd driven out into the country and bred the mare and we were on the return trip to his house for dinner. It was nearing dusk and several times Hap pointed out large numbers of the small Texas white-tailed deer that were grazing near the brushy hills. We passed some land of Hap's that he was planning to build his ranch on, then drove by the neighboring ranch of Carl Ramzey and his wife, an older couple whom I'd met at the buffet supper. As we passed and blew the horn, Carl shouted at us to stop in. A small group stood around in the rear of the ranch house with a large box and a tub.

"I don't know that I really want to see what they've got in that box," Hap commented as he turned in the drive. He was apparently aware that they'd been snake hunting that afternoon.

When we dismounted from the pickup and I heard the old familiar buzzing noise emanating from the box, I knew dam' well I didn't want to look further. Still there's an irresistible fascination to snakes regardless of whether or not a person dislikes them and we approached and looked in at the dirty tan and brown undulating pile of rattlers.

The equipment used to catch these rattlers is an insect-type spray gun which blows gasoline fumes into a den. The snakes crawl out and are caught with a stick and lifted into the collection box. This box contained thirty-five snakes, thirty of them having been taken from one den alone on Carl's ranch. They ranged in size from small to medium with probably a half dozen fat old bruisers. They were all whirring angrily and Carl and his friends were in the process of lifting them from the box to the tub in order to get an accurate count. They used a stick with a clamp on the end, similar to the gadget for reaching the high shelves in old-time grocery stores. To me a rattler, at least this type, has none of the saving grace of beauty that some snakes undeniably have. These were dull in color with broad ugly-looking snouts and I hoped that this would be the only way I'd run into the things for the remainder of my ride.

The batch of rattlers had to do with a public snake hunt that was to be held in Jacksboro about two weeks hence and when I was invited to remain and attend, I turned the invitation down with no reluctance at all.

Shortly after I'd arrived in Jacksboro, the Roughriders and the Sheriff's Posse joined forces and organized a trail ride in my honor. It was a very flattering gesture and a lot of fun. We gathered near the square — an assemblage of some sixty to seventy horses and riders — and, as was customary, paraded through town in formal column of twos with flags flying. When I, a damyankee, was handed the Texas flag to carry at the head of the column, it must have been the all-time ultimate in Southern hospitality. I almost felt as if I'd been voted an honorary Texan. Hap Jackson on his big black stud carrying the American flag and I on Sioux with the Lone Star flag headed the parade until we reached the high school building, where the flags were deposited. At that point, the ride slipped into jovial informality and kids and oldsters rode up and down the line at will. A refreshment wagon, loaded with cold drinks, kept pace and occasionally kids or those with weary derrières swapped seats on the wagon for their saddles. The happy-go-lucky picnic atmosphere of the ride out into the country and the supper held on the ranch grounds where the ride terminated was such that I wished my own kids had been along. When the buffet supper was done and the fires had burned low, a number of men drove up with their trailers. Sioux was loaded with Fred Kendrick's Ginger for the trip back to Jacksboro, and another warm Jacksboro experience was chalked up.

The living was easy. The painting was progressing satisfactorily, I had time to read several books on the history of the region supplied by Laura Peacock, and the thin spot in the hair on Sioux's back was rapidly filling out. I'd been concerned about her near baldness behind the cantle for fear

209

of a saddle sore that would have put us out of action for a long period.

The morning came when it was time to pack up and say goodbye. We rode down to Fred Kendrick's ranch in his trailer to watch the goat shearing and from there headed southwest to Possum Kingdom.

Sandstone and post oak changed to the milky-colored limestone which seems to be generally accompanied by live oak and cedar. A high dam on the Brazos River backs water into a large lake, providing both power and recreation. George White, a distant relative of Hurshel Farrow's, lived near the dam at the fish hatchery and he and his wife invited me to stay over a day so that Pat and Hurshel could join us.

George was very obviously deeply enamored of the wilds and its animal life. After supper, we drove across the bridge and down a little-used ranch road that followed the south shore of the Brazos. The old tracks followed a shelf that stepped up above the willow-lined shore. Sheer limestone canyon walls towered above us; the late sun, catching facets of the cliff, caused long shadows to extend far out ahead of us. A bald eagle, his white head glinting, sailed high overhead as he followed the bends of the river. I felt that George wanted to share something he felt was beautiful with someone who would appreciate it and I was pleased that he'd asked me to see it.

An errand in Palo Pinto with George allowed a tour of an old abandoned jailhouse that sits in a weed-strewn lot on a side street. Double-barred windows are the only remaining indication of its identity; any ghosts of the former inhabitants have easy egress through the doors, which now hang ajar. We prowled up to the second story, watchful that no beams were dislodged by our passing, and carefully skirted the trapdoor that had been part of the indoor gallows. The

210

rusty ringbolt for the noose still hung ominously from the ceiling just above the yawning metal trapdoor, where it must have been a constant and cheerless reminder to the condemned. What appeared to be a solitary-confinement cell had been occupied at some time in its history by a prisoner with considerable talent as an artist. A couple of life-sized obscene murals filled the walls, testifying to the subject matter dearest to the hearts of most prisoners. Considering the materials probably available and the lack of female models, these genuine examples of primitive art were not badly executed. The old stone calaboose could make a great frontier museum building and the controversial murals would certainly pack in the tourists.

Sioux and I crossed the Brazos as we left Possum Kingdom. It was the kind of spring morning that poets write of. Loving Valley swept off behind us and the old Brazos swirled lazily between sandbars as it headed off to divide the limestone canyon walls to the south. Willows and cedars lined the shores. We were hardly more than across when Sioux's ears shot up and she swung her head sharply to the right. Within fifty feet of us, a pair of white-tailed deer peered through the cedars, then started their seemingly slow-motion bounds that carry them with such consummate grace over logs and blowdowns. The canyon wall directed their course so that they paralleled our path for some distance. With a final crackle of brush, they vanished and I was able to breathe again. In some respects that moment idealized what I'd had in mind when the trip began. Here it all was in one package: a soft spring morning with its pale blue sky and white drifting clouds, the indescribable smell of a clean, flowing river mingled with the earth scents, a companionable horse, and wildlife that bounded along not so much in fear as to express the joy of being alive. The only missing ingredient in a situation of that nature is another human, able to share it. But then, perhaps, one's awareness would be less sharp.

Stopping for lunch at a tiny crossroads village one day, I ran into one of the few hostile persons I met in the whole state of Texas. A combination store, gas station and café, with nothing on either side for a number of miles, occupied a corner of the intersection. I rode Sioux up to the building, hitched her in the shade of a live oak tree and walked in as a sour-looking woman emerged from the kitchen and stepped behind the counter. The place was attractively paneled, and the walls were adorned by mounted heads and some interesting photos of old-time cowboys and their horses.

"Are you serving meals?" I asked the woman.

"Well," she scowled, "what did you want?"

Her reluctance wasn't lost on me, so I avoided anything that she might deem too complicated. "I don't care. A hamburger and coffee?"

"Well," she relented, "I guess I can fix you that."

She started for the kitchen and I said casually, "I'm traveling horseback. While you're making the hamburger, I think I'll unsaddle my horse." It was hot and I wanted to avail myself of the respite to let Sioux's back and saddle blanket air out.

The lady turned suddenly and accusingly. "You got a horse out there?" She peered out a window.

"Yes," I admitted, it being difficult to deny the evidence.

"Don't *you* tie your horse to my shade tree," she snapped.

"Oh," I faltered, "I'm sorry. I'll take her across the road and tie her to the fence."

She folded her arms and glared at me. "Come to think on it, I don't guess I will fix you a hamburger!"

Somewhat dumfounded and still a little unbelieving I said, "Can I get something in the line of groceries?" It was at least a three-hour ride to the next town.

"No," she said flatly.

I looked at her incredulously, then fished a dime out of my pocket and walked to the cold drink machine. "I guess you don't mind if I drink a Coke." It was not phrased as a question.

"You takin' the bottle with you?" she asked.

"Certainly not," I said icily, hoping vainly that the Coke would enable me to dredge up a resonant belch.

It was not my day. When I stomped out, letting the screen door fly, it didn't bang as I'd hoped it would, nor had Sioux committed the prayed-for nuisance in the driveway. Her behavior had been impeccable. She hadn't even peeled a leaf from the precious live oak tree. Then, of course, the withering retort failed to come to me until I was a mile down the road. When it did, I was tempted to ride back, dismount, sweep off my hat, bow low and say, "My sympathies to your husband, madam." I didn't, but he has my sympathies anyhow.

Some three hours later, as I neared the next spot on the map, a pickup truck slowed and a kidding remark was shouted at me from a neatly dressed young rancher behind the wheel. I looked up and he suddenly got a crestfallen expression on his face.

"Excuse me," he apologized, "I thought you were a friend of mine. He rides a paint horse like yours." Then followed the question, "Where you headin'?"

"Caddo, I guess," I replied, amused at his discomfiture.

"Hell, there's nothin' in Caddo nowdays but a store," he said; then, without a pause, "but my ranch is about a mile down the road on the left. I'm headed out to a party an' I won't be home till maybe two. I may be a little corned an' fall over my feet an' cuss, but I'll try to be quiet. Why don't you go on down and put your horse in the corral? The feed's in the barn and the back door's open. Go on in. Help yourself to the refrigerator. There's a spare bedroom on the west side of the house. The television set's in my room. The only thing that'll make me mad is if you don't eat anything you want!"

"That's a pretty tough deal to beat," I said. "By the way, my name's Tom Powell."

"Bob Coody," he grinned. "Think of the bug."

We talked awhile by the side of the road and I mentioned the fact that I was hoping to contact a horseshoer as soon as possible.

"My cousin Nancy's ranch is the place just before mine," Bob said. "Gary Smith from Ranger should be there now. His business is horseshoeing."

I rode on down to Nancy Coody's ranch and found a group standing in the dooryard of a well-kept ranch house. Nancy, a very attractive girl, had long, almost waist-length red hair and Gary made me think immediately of the actor James Drury of the television series *The Virginian*. After a brief talk, Sioux and I went on down to Bob's ranch and made ourselves at home. Sioux took over the big corral next to the barn; I made myself comfortable in the brick ranch house.

During the evening, having fed myself as ordered, I was sprawled in an easy chair watching television when Gary Smith stopped by. A tall, lean, dark-haired man, his wide shoulders and powerful arms were accented by the near absence of hips and the easy, limber, slightly swaying walk of the long-time horseman. He was quite shy and so soft-spoken that at times I had to ask him to repeat himself, but for one of those inexplicable reasons we seemed to warm to each other in an unusually short time. My plans were to cut south to Ranger the next day, which tied in conveniently with his.

"My folks own a motel — the Sunray Courts — just about a mile east of Ranger," he said. "If you want to come down

214

there tomorrow, I'll get your mare dressed up in her new shoes Saturday morning."

"Fine," I said. "Is there a place I can tie a horse at the motel?"

"Sure," he smiled. "I've got a couple of pens out back where I sometimes keep a horse that I'm working on."

Bob pulled in shortly after I'd retired for the night and if he fell over his feet, he did it quietly. We arose at an early hour, breakfasted together and he left for some ranch work with his father, who stopped in to pick him up. I got saddled and paused at the little store in Caddo for a few supplies before heading south. The proprietor and his wife were both friendly and interesting and I lingered awhile to accept their offer of coffee. One of the local men stopped by and, seeing my horse tied outside, made the usual inquiries.

"Hell's bells, man." He looked at me earnestly. "You're missin' the best part of a deal like you've got."

"What's that?" I asked.

"Why hot dam'," he roared, "if I was doin' what you are, I wouldn't shave or take a bath for the whole dam' time. When I got through, I'd look like a man an' I'd smell like a man too!"

"More like an old goat, you mean," sniffed the lady behind the counter.

With that I exited laughing and got off with a late start for Ranger.

Twenty miles of broken country sprinkled with cedar separated the two main east-west highways. Except in the immediate vicinity of the through roads, human habitation was becoming less frequent. From here on a town listed on the standard road map often turned out to be nothing more than a weatherbeaten frame building or two at a dirt cross-road. Cars were seldom seen and one of those turned out to be Gary's pickup — another, Nancy's car.

Nadine and Waymon Smith were expecting me at their motel in Ranger and Sioux was staked out in the tall grass behind my room. Like Gary, they were attractive, soft-spoken and completely friendly, and after an evening's conversation we were old friends. The family was born and raised in Texas, but had spent a number of years elsewhere. When Gary was in his late teens, they'd been in the Medicine Bow section of Wyoming and there Gary had been able to run some of the last of the wild horses. Nadine had a number of photographs of the wild ones after they'd been corraled, and additional pictures of Gary bronc riding at rodeos confirmed my suspicions. When we'd met, I'd noticed that his boots were zippered in the manner of the rodeo bronc riders. Now twenty-eight, he'd quit the bone-bruising business of the rodeo and the rough ones he climbed on these days were only those that were to be broken into well-behaved saddle horses.

The Smiths and I got on the subject of dialects and regional accents and I told them about a Texas woman I'd met who confessed that she'd always been a little irritated by the movie and television actor's exaggerations of the Texas drawl.

"Then," she said, "Ah heard mahsef on one of those little bitty ol' tape recorders? Why don't yew know, Ah sounded jes' like one of those ol' heelbeelies?"

Hurshel had educated me as to the pronunciation and, more important, the identity of a tow sack. I knew that a burlap bag, often called a feed bag in rural New England, is called a gunnysack in the Northwest and, for some reason, a sho'ts bag in Maine. When I breezed into a Jacksboro laundromat bearing my soiled clothes in a feed bag and a woman asked me where I'd gotten the tow sack, I'd have been completely bewildered had it not been for Hurshel's coaching a day or so before. The pronunciation of tow sack is something else. The accent is on tow and it's spoken, if not quite in one syllable, at least as one word.

"That's right," Waymon laughed after I brought up the Texas tow sack. "When I worked with a man in Arizona one time, and asked him to hand me a tow sack, I couldn't understand how he could be so dumb as to not understand what I meant."

Following an early breakfast with the Smiths, Gary heated up the portable forge in the back of his fully rigged pickup truck and started replacing Sioux's worn-out shoes. Nancy joined us bearing a formidable array of schoolpapers that were to be corrected. She'd attended college in Middlebury, Vermont, and was now teaching at Ranger Junior College. From time to time both she and Gary's mother interrupted their chores to photograph the shoeing.

"Are you in any particular hurry to head out?" Gary asked as he finished the job and put his tools back in the pickup.

"Not particularly," I replied.

"I've got to shoe five horses at Stamford — northwest of here — this afternoon," he explained. "If you want to go along, I'd be glad of the company."

The run to Stamford would allow me to see a section of Texas that I otherwise would have missed, and I was enjoying Gary's company, so we headed out.

While shoeing, Gary had gone into some of his theories about horseshoes and horses in general. His views about keeping a horse's foot as close to its natural shape as possible made sense to me and now he elucidated on facets of the training of horses.

"I'm pretty much convinced that a horse does a lot of thinking," he said, warming to the subject. "What I try to do when I run up against a problem is to put myself in the horse's position and think like a horse. I always want the

217

horse to think that Gary is his friend. When he's got to be punished, I want him to associate his punishment with the misbehavior. Gary doesn't hurt him, his bad habit does."

He was a strong advocate of what he referred to as "the gimmick." This was a bridle rigged to have the effect of the old war bridle, a rope device that simultaneously puts pressure on the mouth, under the chin and on the nerve centers behind the ears.

"Give me five minutes with the gimmick on the meanest, kickingest man-eater in the barn and I'll guarantee I can shoe him with the lead rope tucked in my hip pocket."

In the two hours spent going to and returning from Stamford I think I learned more about ways of handling tough horses than I would have in two years in other circles. Gary loved horses and his life was devoted to them. He wasn't completely satisfied with shoeing as an occupation but it permitted him to make a reasonably good living while spending the bulk of his time with the animals.

Later I watched him work with a blue roan stallion. At that time the stud was little more than half broken. Before Gary saddled him up and worked him out, he showed me how the horse would come up to him in the corral and put his head over Gary's shoulder as a result of training with "the gimmick."

A light rain started to fall as I left the Smiths'. Nadine had fixed a huge breakfast for me and when I tried to settle up for my room she wouldn't hear of it. Hoping to be able to return the hospitality at some later date, I gave in and left them with nothing more than my thanks.

A four-day ride west and then south brought me down as far south as I planned to go. The cedar hill country was left behind and the mesquite-covered plains opened up. Heat was now suddenly upon us and I carried a full canteen of water for the first time. The gallon container weighed a little over eight pounds when full and for that reason I'd rarely carried it full in the cooler weather. Before leaving Jacksboro I rid myself of most of the heavy winter clothing, so the load for Sioux remained approximately the same.

Habitual whistling is one of my less endearing addictions and the loneliness of this particular stretch of country may have influenced a streak of rather silly behavior that I indulged in along the way. For a good many miles our only associates were cattle and jackrabbits and I noticed that my whistling brought startled stares in return.

Most of the music I'd heard in this part of Texas emanates from Nashville, Tennessee; however, the hot sun was high overhead and, whether as a subconscious result or not, I found myself whistling the jazz ballad "Something Cool." The bewildered reaction of cattle accustomed to the Grand Ol' Opry sound was doubtless all in my imagination; nevertheless, the thought of broadening their cultural horizons amused me. "Something Cool" was followed by Duke Ellington's "Sophisticated Lady," then Billy Strayhorn's "Lush Life." When I gave my bovine audience "Round Midnight," the thought of Thelonious Monk sitting hunched over a piano composing this lovely ballad for the edification of a bunch of half-wild cattle nearly convulsed me. I rounded them out further with J. S. Bach's "Jesu, Joy of Man's Desiring" — badly executed as a result of technical problems involved in whistling contrapuntal effects — and left them at a cross fence with a satisfied feeling. Sioux, of course, has long been subjected to everything from George Shearing to Beethoven due to the presence of a loudspeaker in her barn that's hooked up to a record player in our house. I think she's rather obstinately retained simple tastes, though, because my musical experimentations indicate that she swings along best to the rhythm of the Civil War ditty "Goober Peas."

Somewhere I'd once heard that a jackrabbit will stop

219

short and sit up at the sound of a sharp whistle. I tried it repeatedly and it always worked, although the rabbits seldom stopped until they were a couple of hundred feet away, where perhaps they'd planned to stop anyway. A man sitting on a horse seems to be less frightening to most forms of wildlife than the same man on foot and often I was able to approach within easy camera range of animals.

On one occasion I spotted the brown form of a large jackrabbit huddled under a mesquite and decided to try for a close-up photo. I stopped Sioux and quietly got out the camera, adjusting the focus to about fifteen feet, where I calculated he'd be after the first jump. I wanted to catch him in midair with the long, ludicrous ears sticking straight up as they do in flight. Camera at the ready, reins looped over the horn, I eased Sioux forward and moved in. At a distance of about five feet, my rabbit lost his cool and jumped just as I'd expected him to. I framed him in midair, flicked the shutter release and found to my utter disgust that I'd neglected to advance the film from the last photo. I rectified the situation as quickly as possible with the result that I now have a color slide with a great close-up of mesquite trees and a microscopic rabbit that no one seems able to discern but me.

Late one afternoon, while I was looking for a spot to camp, a pickup truck pulled up and a tall, good-looking rancher stepped out. The rancher, Horace King, introduced himself and after the first opening questions started eyeing Sioux.

"How do you come to be making this trip on a paint?" he asked.

The quarter horse, with little or preferably no white on him, occupies top popularity in Texas and I expected another testimonial to its qualities.

"Well," I laughed, expecting to be reproached, "she was

a paint when we started and she hasn't changed color on me."

"That's a good enough reason," Horace said. "The reason I'm interested is that I'm mighty happy to see you using a paint for the trip. Tell you what. Keep going to the next left turn — bear left — and I'll be back with my trailer in about ten minutes. I want you to stay at my ranch tonight and see some of the paints we've got."

The dust from the pickup had hardly settled before King was back with his trailer. We loaded Sioux, and a few miles down the road arrived at a modern ranch house on a gentle hill that overlooked miles of surrounding countryside.

Hy Diamond Boy, a handsome paint stallion, occupied one of the corrals. His mares and colts were in adjoining pens.

"Those of us in the Paint Horse Association are trying to breed quarter horse conformation into the paint horse," Horace explained as he and his wife and I sat at the dinner table. "The paint is beginning to get more popular as a result and a trip like yours certainly doesn't hurt us any."

"Those old-time paints like your mare are tough ponies," his wife said with obvious warmth. "Head like a mule and a constitution to match."

"Sioux's tough as a boot," I agreed. "She's had to be to stand up the way she has."

I left this friendly household next morning and that night camped on the bank of the Jim Ned Creek at a crossing made famous in the cattle drive days. It was a warm early-summer evening and a mockingbird made my attempts at whistling seem crudely amateurish as he flirted his tail around in the trees lining the creek bottom. The mesquite buds were swelling, new leaves were unfurling and the grass was fresh and new. After the sun was gone and my fire died out, I lay listening to the small noises that become magnified by the dark. The Jim Ned Creek muttered softly between its banks. Sioux, long since finished grazing, shifted sleepily from one hip to the other, finally wandering over to settle down with a grunt, then rolling over to stretch out on her side. As always when she was stretched out full length, the intervals between her breaths seemed incredibly long and I found myself listening for the next breath and wondering if it would actually come. As was her habit, Sioux rose with a great grunting around midnight, chomped a few mouthfuls of grass, then flopped down again on her other side, where she generally stayed until just before dawn.

I found that I had a very persistent alarm clock in the presence of this horse. An early riser, she was content to graze up to a point. Then a soft but insistent nuzzling of whatever part of my face was uncovered made further sleep out of the question. I was supposed to arise and feed her the grain and that was all there was to it. A few sleepy mornings I tried extricating an arm from the zippered sleeping bag so as to take a swing at her big head. She never jumped back in alarm but, with a wise, all-knowing look in her eyes, merely lifted her head just out of reach of my flailing arm and waited patiently for me to get it back under the covers, at which time she renewed her attack.

I'd thought my camp on the Jim Ned was completely out of sight of the road. This morning, however, after Sioux had forced an early start and while the smoke from my breakfast fire was still showing a faint trace, a pleasant-looking white-haired man with a deep tan eased down off the slope that led to the road.

"Mornin'," he called. Then as he approached he said, "My wife and I saw you camped down here last night. We'd have been glad to have you come to the house but you looked like you were all set up. Will you stop in at our place for a cup of coffee? I've got a barn full of oats, if your mare could use some."

I dumped the remainder of my canteen water on the embers of the fire, climbed aboard and followed Henry Davis's pickup across the bridge and through a gate to the house.

Once while talking to a Texan I'd commented on the unusual friendliness of Texans. He remarked that I shouldn't be completely taken in by it. "Some of them figure you're working on a book and they're just putting on an act to build up the Texas image," my cynical Texas friend cautioned me. Perhaps I'm more ingenuous than I realize. I've always flattered myself that I'm a skeptic, even at times an iconoclast. Four years in a combat organization — part of the time in a foreign land — pretty well inures you to the best and the worst in human nature, including your own. Too, I think such an experience helps develop the ability to recognize the phony. If I come across as naïve in my acceptance of these country people at face value, it's because they accepted me the same way.

We sat in the Davis kitchen and talked of many things while I absorbed great quantities of coffee with the warmth of the room. The discussion covered the country, the old days, the Davis's semiretirement, horses and children. When I brought my family into the talk, Mrs. Davis looked up with surprise. I explained that I was making the ride both for the pleasure of the experience and for an illustrated book, also that I planned to return to New England by trailer at the end of the ride.

"Well," she said, "of course you always wonder about people, but a long time ago I decided not to criticize anyone's way of walking till I tried his shoes on."

When I left this couple I was sloshing with good coffee, my grain bags were full of oats and I was sorry that I hadn't spent the previous evening with them. I make no claim to familiarity with the big-city Texan, since I made every effort to give the cities a wide berth. I do assert a certain expertise as to the country men. My means of travel introduced me to a great many people the convertible coupe is totally unaware of. Ingenuous, naïve, call me what you will; anyone who tries to convince me that the Texan is less than a genuine, warm person has one hell of a battle on his hands.

Entering the outskirts of Coleman, I passed a small radio station. A few minutes later a mobile unit caught up to me and a live radio interview was conducted from the roadside. I'd hardly gotten a mile from the encounter when an old blue Ford station wagon pulled up, driven by an old man in a battered black Stetson accompanied by his black border collie.

"Hey, boy," the old man called, "I want to talk to you."

I climbed down and bent over to the car window. Bright blue eyes in a deeply lined craggy face peered out at me from under the stained hat brim. A faded flannel shirt topped the tan khaki trousers that he wore. Traces of tobacco showed at the corners of his wide mouth.

"If you ain't in a hurry, come over to my place and stay a spell. I cowboyed all over that country you're headin' into an' I'd sure admire to talk a spell," he said.

He'd been home with his radio on, had heard the interview and headed out to cut me off. His name was Tom May. He was eighty-two years old and I was in no hurry. I guided Sioux off the first side street and down across the railroad tracks, and pulled up at a small weatherbeaten frame house. Tom, having been in the lead, had the gate open as we arrived and I led Sioux through to unsaddle on the old wooden front porch. The backyard was fenced in for chickens and we turned her loose with the hens.

"Let's set on the front porch and talk a spell," Tom said

224

as he hobbled laboriously back from the chicken yard. For me it's an effort to get my knees closer than a couple of inches apart, but compared to Tom May I'm knock-kneed. He was the living example of the man who was said to be unable to stop a pig in an alley.

"They's a lot I kin tell you about that country west of here," Tom started. "I cowboyed on the ol' T O Ranch from the time I wuz just a li'l ol' button-peckered kid. Thirty years I worked that country — an' it used to be tough in them days." He pulled up his right trouser leg to show me the unmistakable large white dimple of a bullet wound that repeated itself on the inside of his calf. "Got that hole shot in me by one of them Messican snipers. Went plumb through my laig an' kilt my horse."

He pulled open the neck of the flannel shirt and showed me another scar on his left shoulder. "Got that one shot in me down in the Big Bend country back about 1905 — another one of them dam' Messican bushwhackers. Remember oncet when I wuz bringin' in the hawse herd an' the rest of the camp wuz still asleep, 'cept for the cook. A bunch of Pancho Villa's boys surrounded us an' took us 'fore anybody could git to a gun. They run us, our hawses an' all our supplies down acrost the river three days south into Messico. Stuck us in a ol' rock corral an' then they commenced gittin' drunk on that ol' tequila cactus juice. We bided our time an' in the middle of the night one of our boys succeeded in bashin' the guard's head in with a rock an', I guess you know, we stole our hawses back an' theirs too an' hit for the river in a high lope. Left ol' Pancho plumb afoot. That wuz the week afore he got hisself kilt."

We moved into the house, and Tom lighted the kitchen stove and commenced cooking sausage and eggs. While standing at the stove, he now and again fired a jet of tobacco juice at a coffee can on the floor, wiped his mouth on the back of his hand, then his hand on the seat of his old khakis.

"Shore would like to see thet ol' country one more time but I don't reckon I ever will. Too dam' old now." He made a warning gesture with the spatula. "You gonna have to do some figurin' west of the Pecos, boy. Thet country's drier'n a popcorn-fart. An' don't you drink none of thet Pecos River water."

"Salty?" I asked.

"Salty!" he exploded. "That ain't the half of it. You know about the green apple two-step?"

I laughed and said I did.

"Why say, boy, you drink any of thet ol' Pecos an' guaranteed you'll fire plumb acrost the top of an eight-rail fence!"

We sat at the oilcloth-covered kitchen table and ate the sausage and eggs and drank our coffee.

"Finally settled down around here when I married up with a widder woman with four kids," he continued as we ate. "Best dam' woman ever drawed breath — she died some years ago. Dam' me if I didn't marry agin when I wuz eighty. Eighty years I dodged the lightnin', then had to play the ol' fool an' get caught with a witch!"

Tom mopped his plate with a piece of bread and meditated a minute. "Dam' if that warn't the devil's mother-in-law — I run her off a year or so back. Now me 'n ol' Nigger here git along jes' fine." He handed the egg-impregnated bread to the collie, who lay patiently at his feet.

"Worries me some what'll come of ol' Nigger." He fondled the dog's ears with rheumatic fingers. The dog's eyes glowed up at him. "Reckon somebody'll walk in here someday an' find me dead. Then what'll happen to my ol' dawg?"

Tom set our plates down for Nigger to scour, then stacked them in the sink under a running faucet. After he had shaken them off and put them on the drainboard, we moved back to his front bedroom-living room.

"You packin' a gun, boy?" he asked as we sat down in the chairs that, together with a double bed, a trunk and a radio, constituted the furnishings.

I said that I had a pistol in my saddlebags and, in answer to his next question, explained that it was an old-style Colt frontier model with a seven-and-a-half-inch barrel.

"Well, now." He heaved himself out of his chair and walked over to the trunk in the corner. "I got somethin' in this here trunk thet you better have. I used to have a ol' .45 six-shooter just like yours an' I had this made down in Angelo in 1910." He rummaged around and, from near the bottom, pulled out an old sweat-blackened shoulder holster.

"Some sunuvabitch snuck in an' stoled my gun a few years ago. Now I ain't got nuthin' but a shotgun. So you take this – it'll fit. Git your pistol out."

I went into the other bedroom, where I'd piled my belongings, and dug out my pistol. Tom took it, slipped it deftly into the holster and then, holding it under his left armpit, shucked it out to show me how easily it cleared.

"Works as slick as the diamond button on the outhouse door," he said with obvious pleasure. He handed it to me. "Try 'er on under your shirt. She ain't legal, but never you mind."

I put it on under my shirt and Tom adjusted it snugly in place by means of its buckskin thongs. For a large revolver, there was surprisingly little bulge.

"Now I'll tell you how you operate west of here," Tom lectured. "They's some mighty empty stretches of country an' you gotta watch out for them Messican hijackers. You get about three of 'em comin' up on you, here's how you do 'er. Turn your hawse sideways between you an' them an' as

227

you drop off, slip that ol' smoke pole out from under your shirt an' lay 'er acrost your cantle. They'll know you got the hawse for a shield an' you sure gonna get one of 'em, so they'll light out a-runnin'."

He repeated the instructions to make certain that I understood the technique, then went into additional directions.

"You get any a them sneaky li'l boogers slippin' around when you're fixin' to camp, here's what you do. Most of 'em'll figure you're packin' a gun, so's they'll wait till you're asleep. Make up your bedroll agin' some brush an' then when your fire's died down, slip around behind the brush an' set there for an hour or two. They mostly liable to wait till you're asleep, then come sneakin' in to thump you on the head. If you're camped out behind a bush, you got 'em.

"You got a hair rope with you?" he asked next.

I told him I didn't.

"You stop at the saddle shop in Angelo and git you one," he said. "I allus run a hair rope around my bedroll an' many's the mornin' I woke up with a big ol' rattlesnake camped down right outside the rope."

I knew that years ago the myth of the hair rope was exploded by herpetologists and snake experts. On the other hand, every old cowboy I'd met who'd spent years sleeping out in rattlesnake country swore by a hair rope, and whether it worked or not, I determined to get one. I certainly couldn't lose anything by giving it a try, and every now and again some old wives' tale backfires on the experts and proves itself true.

The old holster's stitching was rotted out and reinforced with a couple of copper rivets, and although my real reason for wanting it was for its souvenir value, I spent the afternoon repairing it with the linen thread that I carried. Reminiscing about World War I, Tom remarked that he'd

toted the holster and six-shooter all over France with no one
the wiser. It had once settled a drunken dispute in a Paris
café. He chuckled remembering the puzzlement of the by-
standers at where the big gun had suddenly emerged from.

We went out to a chili parlor for dinner that night,
although it took considerable diplomacy on my part to avoid
giving the impression that I didn't want to deprive him of
his food.

"Shore do like a good hot bowl of chili once in a while,"
Tom said as we sat at the counter, "but by gawd, she's liable
to give me the Messican heartburn tomorrow."

We talked far into the evening and I thanked my good
fortune for the radio interview that had brought us together.
In the morning, over coffee, Tom poked wistfully at a
wooden box on the kitchen floor that held an old iron skillet
and a few odds and ends of rusty camp gear.

"Dam', I shore wisht I could pack my bed in the back of
the old Ford an' go along with you," he said, half to himself.
"Guess I'm too dam' old to straddle a hawse. Guess I'm flat
too old to do anything. Shore would like to see that country
once more before I die though."

I saddled and packed Sioux, feeling miserable about
leaving this lonely old man behind, and as I looked back
from time to time to wave goodbye I could see him, still
standing by his gate, his dog at his side, his old black hat
shading the eyes that followed me out of sight.

From Coleman on, my route curved almost due west. The
Texas sun was now turned on full blast and I was surprised
to find myself getting sunburned. Several times while seated
in cafés with mirrors behind the counters, I noticed that the
left side of my face was two shades darker than the right.

The land began to break into cotton country with spotty
sections devoted to livestock. It was becoming perceptibly

drier and small stunted sagebrush began to make its appearance.

The scissor-tailed flycatcher, a strange-looking bird common to these parts, had been catching my attention for some time. A softly hued bird with a rose-tinted gray body, it has a ridiculously long forked tail. Usually it perched on a fence post or wire until closely approached. In its eventual flight the long tail operated with a scissors motion in time with its wing movements.

A steady dry wind from the west prevailed at this season, and for almost all of the remainder of the state we were to buck a head wind. For some reason west of San Angelo the rainfall decreases and my first real thirst was experienced on the way into San Angelo, although the forks of the Concho River make Angelo itself a verdant oasis.

A pleasant happening now and then was the chance meeting with people I'd become acquainted with a week or so before. Two-hundred-mile errands are not uncommon for people in this big land; I'd recently run into Henry Davis and his wife while picking my way down a hill seemingly far from their territory. Nearing San Angelo and having given Sioux most of the canteen water, I was hot, dry and thirsty. Three or four miles from our destination a car pulled up with a couple of smiling familiar faces. The Carl Faubions, with whom I'd spent an evening back in Talpa, had spotted me on their way into town and now on their return had brought me an enormous container of Coke, still tinkling delightfully with cracked ice.

Old Fort Concho, now a well-maintained museum, sits across the river from the business section of San Angelo. I spent the afternoon perusing the collection of old army and frontier paraphernalia and, like any kid, climbing up into the cab of an old Sante Fe steam locomotive that stands alongside the transportation building. Sioux passed the time

230

profitably by grazing on the lawn beside the administration building and entertaining a group of schoolchildren.

One of the biggest sale barns I'd seen was in San Angelo. As the result of a conversation with an old rancher named C. F. Fant, I was introduced to Howard Morrow, who was due to head west across the oil field country with an empty stock trailer. The flat, dry stretch ahead, bristling with oil derricks, pumps and gas wells, wasn't anything of great interest to me and we wound up hitching a ride through with Howard. No doubt the smell of the oil fields would have soon become unnoticeable to me had I spent a week crossing them. As it was, I was glad to pass through quickly.

A long, dry ride through empty sandy wastes brought me one evening to a gas station-grocery store where the only water for nearly fifty miles was pumped out of a windmill that had been converted to electricity. The place was run by a short, stocky man and his wife and when I rode in and asked if I could stop overnight, the man indicated that I could park out by the windmill.

"Lotsa good grazin' out there for your hawse," he stated.

The only thing I found anywhere around the mill was sand and the tiny burs that stick with vicious persistence to anything up to and including slick leather surfaces. Fortunately for Sioux, a scout of the neighborhood produced a good growth of Johnson grass around a culvert some distance up the road. I tethered Sioux to the fence and returned to the store, where the man and his wife held sway over their domain.

I ordered a Coke, then another and paid the stipulated thirty cents. While I was standing by the counter, a car with California license plates pulled in at the gas pumps and the proprietor walked leisurely out to wait on the driver. He was gone for some time and meanwhile I made the usual small

231

talk with his wife. When he returned, his face was wreathed in the first genuine smile he'd produced since my arrival.

"Hah," he chortled delightedly, "Ah jes' fixed me one of them Californy Jee-ews. The sunuvabitch needed him four quarts a oil. Ah done made him put it in hisself an' charged the bastard fifty cents a quart. You know what that re-cleaned oil costs me?"

I confessed that I didn't.

"Thirteen cents a quart, by gawd," he exulted. "Stuck the little bastard fifty cents a quart an' made him put it in hisself!"

I allowed that he'd done all right by himself.

"Got plenty money," he preened. "Don't give a goddam' if they buy 'er or not. Besides, where'n hell else they gonna go? Nowhere, that's where. Yessirree, I don't keer if it's a Nyew Yawk Jee-ew or a Californy Jee-ew. They stop here, I fix 'em."

I soon gathered that his only test of religious faith was the license plate on the car. New York or California plates automatically proclaimed the occupants Jews — which, if a fact, would swell the ranks of American Jewry. The atmos-phere of this friendly little oasis was rapidly becoming less refreshing but, as I reminded myself, this spot had the only water for over fifty miles and opportunism had reared its ugly head.

A local rancher drove in for a Coke, then left after being charged a dime. My host continued to regale me with a recital of his victories.

" 'Member oncet a carload a niggahs come in, wanted some beer. Stuck them boogers sixty cents a bottle. They didn't like it but they took it. I didn't give a dam' if they did or not. Let 'em go somewhere else." He laughed at his own joke, then made sure I caught it. "Wher'n the hell would they go?"

232

A row of cars with licenses from a variety of states was parked in the rear and putting things together, I began to suspect that serious auto trouble would result in a cash offer for the car for just about enough money to cover the cost of a bus ticket out. I suppose that few persons stopping there were without trouble and that continual exposure to hard-luck stories hardens the best of men. This man gave every indication of reveling in his position of power. He seemed like a huge, ugly vulture, happily standing astraddle a long and lonely highway awaiting the inevitable appearance of his defenseless prey. I made a mental note to myself to make certain that on my return trip I stopped and filled up with gas, oil, water and air before entering this stretch.

The crowning touch came a little later after I'd made up my bed on the lee side of a wall and, prior to climbing in, went to the store for a can of breakfast fruit. Another couple was there and just before I left, the proprietor playfully punched his buddy on the arm.

"One thing's for sure," he said, exuding self-satisfaction from his every pore. "This fella here with the hawse has just met some genuwine plain ol' Texas folks."

Choking on this gross insult to Texas, I bid them adieu and joined Sioux in the shelter of the wall. The wind was blowing sand and dust but the air was cleaner by far. We got an early start in the morning; there were no signs of life at the store and I was relieved that no further conversation was necessary.

The next night was spent in a fairly good-sized town where I picked up a telegraphed money order. The telegraph office was located at a motel, the proprietor was an animal lover who was perfectly happy to have a horse tied on his lawn and I needed no more than that. After collecting the cash, I tied Sioux on the lawn and stood waiting for the motel man to assign me to a room.

233

A rather pretty young blonde girl sat in an old Ford that was parked behind the office and after a minute or so she got out of the car and walked over, leading a small three-year-old child by the hand. The usual introductory remarks were passed and the little boy was held up to pat Sioux. Then the mother informed me that she was a horsewoman.

"I left Florida with this damned old wreck of a car." She gestured at the tired automobile, the back seat of which was piled high with clothes. "I was headed for New Mexico to get a job at the racetrack, but the car broke down just as I got here and now I'm stuck in this burg with no dough."

I listened noncommittally to the problems without making any suggestions.

"If it wasn't for the kid," she continued, "I'd sell the car and all my junk and try your system. At least a horse isn't likely to leave you stuck in the middle of nowhere."

Our talk was cut short by the appearance of the motel man, who showed me to a room. A long hot shower got rid of the dust, and after shaving and changing, I walked up to a nearby restaurant for dinner. The girl and the car had disappeared and I thought no more about the incident until midway through dinner. The pickings had been slim the night before and that day had been a long tough haul, so I'd ordered a large steak with all the refinements. Sitting there, gorging myself, the thought of the girl and her child started nagging me. She'd struck me as a girl who'd been around, perhaps more than her age indicated. I wanted no part of any problems other than my own; still my experience of the night before made me feel a little guilty about callously stuffing myself while they were, perhaps, genuinely going hungry. I finished the last cup of coffee and walked back to the motel office to talk to the owner.

"What's the story on the little blonde with the kid?" I asked. "Is she really stuck with no money?"

234

"I don't know," he said, displaying little concern. "She'll probably make out all right."

"Well, look," I said. "I'm far from loaded and I dam' sure don't want to get involved, but if you think she's really in a jam, why don't I give you five bucks? You can give it to her without telling her where it came from and at least she and the kid can eat tonight."

He squinted at me for a moment, then said, "I wouldn't worry about her. I think she's already made connections and I'd forget about it."

"O.K." I said. "I just figured five bucks would ease my conscience about stuffing myself if they were really broke."

"It's a nice thought," he said, "but if you worried about all the birds that come through here with troubles, you'd drive yourself crazy."

He was basically a kind, gentle person and no doubt he was right. He'd probably been the victim of confidence jobs times without number until he'd developed an automatic guard reflex.

"You know best," I said. "If she shows up again and you think she needs it, let me know."

I went off to tend to Sioux and followed my chores by an early retirement. A thirty-five-mile waterless ride faced me in the morning and I wanted to get an early start before the heat set in.

We got away reasonably early and I covered well over half the distance by noon. Stopping around one o'clock on the shadeless flats that shimmered in the noon heat, I un-saddled Sioux while I lunched from my saddlebags. The hot sun dried both the saddle blanket and Sioux's back while I ate and after brushing the dried sweat out of her hair, I resaddled. I'd almost finished when a moving speck in the distance became a car that, as it approached, had a familiar look. It was the battered Ford from the motel and as it pulled up, the little blonde rolled down her window.

"Hi," she greeted me. "You must have started a lot earlier than I did. I didn't get out of bed until about an hour ago."

"I had to," I said. "I didn't want to crowd my mare too much in this heat."

"It is hotter than the hinges," she agreed. "Say, do you need any money?"

I think that I successfully masked the startled expression on my face, but I'm not sure. "Well — no, I don't," I replied.

"Well, look," she persisted, "if you need any, I can let you have twenty bucks. I got some dough after I talked to you." With that she held out a twenty-dollar bill.

"I sure thank you," I laughed, "and I appreciate the offer. But really, I'm all set."

"O.K., if you're sure," she said smiling. "Just thought you might be broke."

I thanked her again and her car was soon a distant speck on the horizon.

Fort Stockton, a sunbaked, historic old town that combines the Anglo influence with the Spanish, was suffering from acute drought when we arrived. The greenest lawn in town was at the De Luxe Motel due to the sprinklers that were in action there. The owners very kindly, and somewhat to my surprise, made their lawn available to Sioux and in fact treated her somewhat as a celebrity. It was to be her last green grass for some miles. I always made it a practice in these cases, as I did here, to follow her around with a makeshift shovel. It seemed good public relations, if nothing else.

Bob Mayo, reporter for the *Fort Stockton Pioneer,* called on us the first morning for what resulted in one of the most accurate interviews of the whole trip. He followed up with directions to points of interest in the town, some of its history and a guided tour. Several comments that Bob made while we were together sparked further inquiry and alerted me to a number of dangers that I'd been only dimly aware of before. I knew locoweed was something to be avoided but wasn't sure of the areas in which to be on the lookout. Bob produced a book on poisonous weeds put out by the state. Looking back, if I'd known how many plant types are toxic to horses, I might have been afraid to take on the trip. In my case ignorance had been bliss. From here on out, I steered Sioux away from anything that remotely resembled a weed.

Rabies was causing trouble in the country at this time and Bob Mayo mentioned that in some spots it was nearing epidemic proportions. Coyotes, skunks and other nocturnal prowlers carry the disease and I began to worry about the possibility of Sioux being bitten while I was asleep. Before leaving town I called Bob and he got in touch with Glen Mooney, the local veterinarian. Although it was Easter Sunday morning, he agreed to meet us at his office in town.

Riding out, I passed a little sunbaked, walled-in cemetery where the wind-and-sand-blasted names were almost obliterated from the stones. Some of them retained enough of the original lettering to indicate that the names belonged to members of the old fort's garrison. Soon, I suppose, they — like the few remains of the fort itself — will be little but a memory.

Dr. Mooney was at his office with Bob and he proceeded to give Sioux a rabies shot that looked the size of a transfusion. He first carefully determined how she carried her head and where the reins normally lay on her neck so that the resultant swelling, which he warned would be considerable, could be out of contact. In spite of his Easter Sunday morning trip to the office, he accepted only the cost of the serum.

237

We headed out past the fringes of town, where modern suburban homes mingle with the Mexican adobes and where the long stalks of ocotillo cactus are still used for corral fencing. We passed the modern high school northwest of town, its green lawn serving as a nightly gathering place for the drought-driven jackrabbits.

My map indicated fifty-seven miles of unbroken desert ahead but I was told that a windmill water tank was located about twenty miles out of town. This would serve as a halfway stop. From there we'd make a long one-day haul to Balmorhea.

We took our time in leaving and late in the day still saw no evidence of the water tank ahead. The blazing sun dropped behind barren distant ridges and just as dark began to fall and I was beginning to get concerned, a station wagon with a bale of alfalfa tied on its top caught up to us and pulled over.

Bob Mayo and his two sons were the occupants. Bob had checked with the sheriff's office and found that there was no grazing for a number of miles in the vicinity of the water tank. Howard Morrow had produced the bale of alfalfa and Bob had gathered the hay, his two boys and a healthy serving of their Easter ham dinner. They now preceded me to the camp area next to the water tank that lay ahead.

By the time we arrived, a fire lighted the night and dinner awaited us. To say that I was happy to accept the kindness of these people is to put it mildly. Sioux, particularly, was to have her toughest day coming up; to be able to put in an easy night with all the alfalfa she wanted was like cutting the next day's ride by half. We spent the remainder of the evening in what was now a comfortable and cheery atmosphere. The night was dark and clear, and Bob, a man of wide and varied interests and information, began to point out and identify the stars, which were almost within reach.

238

For one reason or another my stellar education had been neglected. The lesson he gave his sons wasn't lost on me. Up until that time, I didn't know how to find something as basic as the North Star.

The moment arrived, as it always rather sadly did on the trip, for these good friends to leave and I spread my sleeping bag on a bench near the fireplace. Such benches not only provide a flat surface, they also are up out of the way of any wandering snakes, which, regardless of my efforts to "unthink" them, were always somewhere in the back of my mind. Had I ever been awakened to find a rattler in or on my sleeping bag, any bite would probably have been superfluous. I'd have expired on the spot with a heart attack.

The next thirty-seven miles were without doubt the toughest experience of the whole ride. When we were scarcely a mile out of camp, what had started as a clear day began to take on an ominous brownish-tan look. The wind started and almost immediately we were enveloped in swirling sand and dust. The wind was head-on and steady, and the terrain was flat with nothing to slow it down or provide shelter. There was nothing possible except to plow on into it.

I knew this was the season for dust storms and I'd made a couple of unsuccessful attempts to buy goggles for Sioux. Whether they'd have been much help or not, I'm uncertain. My sunglasses did little for me. We were both soon coughing and I got out my bandana handkerchief and tied it over my mouth and nose. This strained out the sand but failed to prevent a sore throat.

Visibility at times was limited to a sepia-tinted thirty to fifty feet and the wind, which must have been of forty- or fifty-mile-an-hour velocity, beat at us unrelentingly. My only way of guessing its speed was to judge by the way the tumbleweeds whipped by us. One of them bore straight down on us; I saw it too late and in endeavoring to turn aside

239

succeeded only in having it scoot right under Sioux's belly. She kicked at it more in irritation than in fear and we plodded on, heads down.

The noise of the wind on my lowered hat brim was a steady roaring drone broken only by our coughing. From time to time I'd dismount and we'd turn tail for a few minutes rest. There was little to be gained by this, since the dust whirled around from all sides and seemed to permeate our every pore.

Mile after mile, the wind slammed into us. On rare occasions the visibility cleared long enough for us to see the dust devils that spun about like small tornadoes. As they moved along in their erratic way, they picked up tumbleweeds and lifted and juggled them high into the air. Some of them passed close by; their only effect was momentarily to change the wind direction.

Near noon, we came to a four- by eight-foot plywood signboard, the only cover we found all day. I climbed off and led the willing Sioux behind it, and although it didn't stop the swirling dust, it did provide a windbreak of sorts. We drank most of the warm water in the canteen and I tried to smoke a cigarette. My throat was so sore that it was small comfort, and I'm certain I smoked less that day than at any time since I started the habit.

Eventually some high mesas to our left seemed to divert the wind and perhaps they were rocky enough to eliminate some of the loose sand. Toward the end of what was seemingly an endless day, the air began to clear and the wind changed from its steady blast to gusty puffs. The dust devils continued to stagger about on the greasewood flats and there were always five or six of them to be seen on all sides. What looked to be a distant farm on the fringes of a town turned out to be just that. The loveliest irrigation ditch I ever saw bordered the road and the farm, and Sioux broke into a trot

240

at the smell of water. She was unable to reach it from up on the banks, so I sprawled on my belly and bailed it up to us with her canvas bucket.

Vastly improved in our attitude, if not our appearance, we stopped at the first store in town. A Mexican grocery store, it stocked two items that I leaped at. The white corn used by the Mexicans in the making of tortillas picked up Sioux's spirits while I soothed my parched throat with quantities of their ice cream.

By now the storm had completely stopped and the village lay in tree-shaded quiet, save for the pleasant gurgle of the irrigation ditches that ran through town on both sides of the main street. An attractive little motel with a shaded lawn made its appearance and we rode across the bridged irrigation ditch to the office building. I was red-eyed, bewhiskered and dusty, but confident that a good prolonged shower would solve my remaining problems. I'd been welcomed at every motel to which we'd applied thus far and the thought never occurred that this establishment might have a different attitude. After all it was in the heart of ranch country, we'd been nickered at by half a dozen horses that grazed in backyards in the village, and in fact a horse was tethered almost next door to the motel. I was not prepared for the jaundiced-eyed reception that was forthcoming.

The proprietor looked at me with ill-concealed distaste. I think he was strongly suspicious that I'd crawled up from under a rock and I'm sure that he wanted me to go away quickly, preferably in a downwind direction.

"They's an ordinance against keepin' horses inside the town limits," he said with finality, starting to turn away. "Why don't you go down to the lake a coupla miles west of here."

Fortunately for the tender ears of this hostile little bureaucrat, I was rendered speechless long enough for him

241

to escape to his interrupted lawn-mowing duties. Fuming with impotent rage, I collected Sioux, who of course to my deep regret had comported herself like the lady that she is, and rode diagonally across the road to the sheriff's office.

The deputy on duty listened sympathetically and shook his head at my encounter with the sandstorm.

"I heard on the radio," he said, "that it was so bad west of El Paso that they've had to close off the highways until they can clear the drifted sand off. Why don't you keep headed the way you are about four miles to Toyahvale? There's a state park, café and motel out there where I'm sure they'll take care of you."

An additional four miles was a soul-withering thought but it seemed the best plan.

"Thanks," I said, and Sioux and I again headed west.

The long four miles out to Toyahvale brought us, just as dark fell, to the state park. Jack Roberts and his wife made us immediately welcome — Sioux to a broad expanse of watered lawn and me to a comfortable room with the hot shower that I craved.

It had been a long time since breakfast, I'd skipped lunch due to the storm, and now I was afraid any delay under the shower would allow the café to close before I made it for dinner, so I slapped and washed the excess dust off and walked over to eat.

As the sole customer at this late hour, I got into a fairly lengthy conversation with Charley Hoefs and his wife, who ran the café. They insisted that before leaving the area, I ride up to the mountain home of Ed and Sophia Bartholomew. Ed, a Western historian and writer, and his wife had their house high on a plateau in the Davis Mountains where the Hoefs assured me I'd be welcome. A cutoff across the Kingston Ranch would be necessary to reach the Bartholomews and detailed instructions were provided by the Hoefs.

Rested and refreshed, Sioux and I headed out in the morning. The Davis Mountains run roughly in a north-south direction paralleling the highway, and after a few miles of roadwork we came to the cattle guard and gate leading into the Kingston Ranch. For those who may be unfamiliar with the term cattle guard, it refers to a ditch that crosses a road at the point where the road goes through a stock fence. The ditch is cut wide enough and deep enough so that a cow won't jump it; across the top and level with the roadway it's bridged by a series of rails or pipes six to eight inches apart. These rails allow a car to be driven through the ditched fence opening without the nuisance of stopping to open a gate. A cow or horse is unable to navigate it, however, since its hoofs would go down between the openings of the rails. Usually a conventional gate is located next to or near the cattle guard so that driven or ridden livestock can go through. I understand the gate is also necessary to permit heavy equipment such as bulldozers to go around, since the rails of a cattle guard are usually inadequate to support so much weight. When I came to a cattle guard with Sioux, I, of course, had to dismount and open the gate.

The gate at the Kingston Ranch had evidently been unused for some time, because a large Spanish dagger cactus plant had grown so close to the opening that I stuck myself while unlatching. After appropriate comments, I led Sioux through, closed the gate more carefully and headed down the ranch road toward the ridge of purple mountains ahead.

It was a cloudless day; the reddish-brown land rolled out in a series of low, sometimes broken undulations. The olive green of the greasewood shrubs, highlighted by the lighter gray green of the mesquites, complemented the flinty reds of the soil. White-faced Herefords lay at this time of day in the shade of the mesquites and although our passage didn't go

243

unnoticed, few of them stopped their cud chewing and only those closest to the road bothered to get to their feet.

At the foot of a rise off to our right, a water tank glinted into view and we cut off toward it. I wasn't particularly thirsty and my canteen was nearly full, but I thought that Sioux might be interested. She was and plunged her nose in to drink deeply. Her enthusiasm caused me to wonder if the water was of a better quality than much of what I'd found, so I cupped some in my palm and discovered that her reaction was justified; the water was unusually cold and sweet. I hoisted myself up on the edge of the tank and hung over to join her.

The road climbed up a sharp little ridge and as we topped it my eyes caught a small band of antelope just below on the flat. The sentinel, off to one side, stood motionless, poised for instant flight, and watched our approach. He allowed us to come surprisingly close before springing into action; when he gave the signal, the little band heliographed their way to a safer distance, then quite casually slowed down to continue about their business.

The purple blues of the mountains were by now not so remote and as we got closer they took on individual shapes. A shiny spot that sparkled in the sun three quarters of the way up the slope later proved to be the aluminum roof of my destination. Perhaps the most striking quality of this country was the quiet, which can only really be appreciated by the horseman or one on foot.

Here, some ten miles from the closest highway, the only intrusion on the monologue of the wind was the liquid sloshings of my canteen. Sioux's feet were nearly muffled by the sand and my soft latigo leather saddle had long since stopped squeaking. I guess that old devil progress is inextricably intertwined with speed, and the ability to cover great distances in a limited amount of time is more important than dawdling along in order to be able to feast the eye on the sun-washed coat of a poised antelope. But not to me, and I suspect not to others. The antelope in a zoo with the element of wild, electric freedom removed by a background of bars is a poor substitute. The diorama with its stuffed figures and painted backdrop comes closer to the truth.

I saw the white plume of dust from Ed Bartholomew's car for some distance before the sound of the motor became audible.

Ed, a tall, heavily moustached man with the sun-squinted look of the Southwest stamped on his face, was behind the wheel of a Dodge station wagon. Sophie, his wife, sat next to him. A soft-voiced woman, her kindly eyes instantly gave you the feeling that her sympathy for any living creature was such that you'd lie your head off to prevent her from finding out about any sort of cruelty. We introduced ourselves and they said they hoped I was headed up to visit them.

"I wish there was some way that we could load you and your horse," said Sophie, "so you wouldn't have to make that long ride up the mountain." She stroked Sioux's nose from the car window.

"We're enjoying the ride and I wouldn't miss it," I replied truthfully, although I'm not sure that I spoke for Sioux.

"There's our house." Ed pointed to the shining speck on the mountainside. "We'll be expecting you."

He repeated the directions concerning the fork in the road near the entrance to Dark Canyon and checked off the number of gates to go through. In the crystal-clear air, I was able to follow their trail of white dust almost all the way as it wound up the steep caliche road to the high plateau.

About an hour later, the road started to climb steeply to the left and began the switchbacks that soon allowed us to look back down on the wide valley below. Small groves of trees clustered in the washes and a flight of doves made soft noises in the brush. We were hardly inside the last gate when an official greeting party of burros picked their knock-kneed, mincing way down the bank to approach us. The boldest of them, a light gray jack, honked noisily and led the procession up to us. As his bravery increased, he followed so closely behind that Sioux laid her ears back and with her unmistakable dirty look let him know that he was to keep a respectful distance. The pecking order established, we continued up the steep caliche road, Sioux in the lead followed by the gray jack and the six jennys.

A welcoming shout from above directed my attention to Ed, who stood atop the last hill, and as we rounded the last curve I saw that the hill had concealed the plateau and house until the last moment. The mile-high, level, grassy shelf spread out before us, ringed with the remains of small individual cabins. The road curved up to the right, culminating at a large stone structure with a railed patio entrance and wings that stretched out on either side. Beyond the smaller cabins the land dropped off into a rocky canyon, then rose sharply by a series of shelving cliffs that were topped off by a fringe of distant ponderosa pines.

Ed and Sophie waited at the entrance to the patio with a bucket of water for Sioux and a cold drink for me. In short order my saddle and gear cluttered their spacious living room and Sioux was staked out in the mountain grasses with the curious burros for company. Sliding glass panels at either end of the living room provided a sweeping view of the valley below. At night, the lights from the city of Pecos were clearly visible, some fifty miles away. From the branches of a tree next to the house came the plaintive call of a canyon wren. The sound was similar to that of a person

246

whistling to a dog except that each note made a sliding half-tone descent.

This particular wren was a regular occupant of the Bartholomews' home. She entered through a small opening that they left unblocked and frequently zipped out from under the piano to various points in the room. Several times when the nesting season was on she'd gotten into Ed's manuscripts and research notes to shred a suitable amount for her nest lining. Except for that minor transgression, she was a neat and unobtrusive resident and Ed and Sophie felt that her lovely clear song was worth many times the value of a few pieces of paper.

Almost everywhere I'd been, the handprints of the raccoon had been visible proof of their presence, provided there'd been enough moist sand or mud for them to put down their "sign of Kilroy." Here was no exception. Sophie left nightly snacks for these Halloween masked bandits and often watched them through the glass doors as they appeared for their midnight suppers. Three shy old horses, one partially blind, were living out their retirement in the hills. They came only at night, and several times we looked out after dusk to see them standing about hobnobbing with Sioux. A movement at the door and they disappeared like wraiths.

The clowns of the place were the burros. Twice daily they tripped up out of the canyon for their supplementary meals. Sophie had early discovered that they approved enthusiastically of her leftover hotcakes. Indeed their reaction had been so gratifying that Sophie had been known on a number of occasions to cook up a batch of hotcakes specially for the burros, regardless of whether she and Ed wanted them or not. The story had magnified to the point where mere mention of Sophie's name in the area was likely to bring forth the remark that she was that wonderful lady up

247

on the mountain who cooks hotcakes for burros. Before I got away from the country where the Bartholomews were personally known, several people mentioned the hotcakes to me; what was especially surprising was that here in stock-raising country where the burro was a tough little animal used to pack such things as fencing materials and salt into the otherwise inaccessible mountains, Sophie's softness about her animals was never spoken of with ridicule. A lesser person doing something similar might have found himself snorted at as being mawkishly sentimental.

It took a minimum of effort on the part of the Bartholomews to get me to stay over in this setting. In the quiet of the morning, we stood on the front steps and listened to the distant rattle of a falling rock. It was followed by a faint "Ho!" We searched the slopes of the far ridges and at last there came in sight the reddish glint of a sorrel horse ridden by a Mexican vaquero. Another faint shout echoed out of nowhere and in a moment a second mounted figure could be spotted slowly working his way through the treacherous rock slides. With the aid of Ed's field glasses, we watched these incredible riders moving their sheep down off the mountains. The terrain they covered so casually made the Appalachian Trail look like the bridle path in Central Park. Many of the saddle animals used here were mules, and as I watched I found it hard to see how the sheep themselves could navigate.

Most of the ranch hands in this country were Mexicans. One who stopped by on another day had worked for the same ranch for seventeen years. A slim, wiry man, Tomás spoke very little English and we did little better in his tongue. He'd ridden up out of the canyon driving the burros before him on what looked to be a half-broken horse, and at Sophie's invitation had tied the spooky animal to a tree to come in and join us for a "cerveza" and lunch. While

248

waiting for lunch and sipping at his can of beer, he sat his easy chair with the lithe grace of a born horseman. Watching him, I felt that he didn't entirely trust the chair and that if it suddenly spooked he was not going to be caught and unseated. Ed attempted to explain what I was up to.

"Señor Powell" — he pointed to me and I nodded — "el caballero y caballo" — he pointed outside to where Sioux was tied in the shade of the breezeway.

"Si." Tomás smiled agreeably.

"Señor Powell," Ed continued with a great all-encompassing sweep of his arm, "rides the caballo from Bos-tone, Mah-sah-chusetts" — he then pointed to the west — "to el Grande Canyon, Ahree-zona!"

This, of course, was not strict truth, but Boston was close enough to Rhode Island to make the point, and evidently Tomás understood. His eyes widened and he shook his head in polite amazement.

"Mucho trabajo," I said, not too modestly. I didn't know how to say "helluva long ride" in Spanish. It was all right, however, as Tomás laughed and agreed that it was a lot of work.

The original cadre of the Bartholomews' gang of burros had come from the Kingston Ranch. They'd been obtained by the Kingstons for use as pack animals and also as breeding stock. The crossing of a female burro and a male horse would have produced a hinny, its only technical difference from the hybrid mule being that the mule results from the breeding of a mare to a male burro or jackass.

Their ludicrous long ears and sad eyes had appealed to the Bartholomews and they'd succumbed to the extent that five burros had moved up to reside on the mountain pasture. Two additional members had since been added to the little band, whose friendly presence was their only duty. On rare occasions they were asked to supply a little reluctant transportation to visiting grandchildren, but for the most part they were free to wander about the canyons as their whims directed them.

"Maybe you ought to have a burro as a pack animal for the remainder of this ride," Ed suggested.

It didn't seem a bad thought and we hashed it over at some length. There were some long dry stretches ahead with questionable grazing and a burro with pack saddle would be capable of carrying a good supply of concentrated horse feed plus a five-gallon can of water.

"We'll give you one of these," Sophie interjected, "if you think you'd want one."

"Actually, we're up to our neck in burros," Ed added.

In addition to my needs, it occurred to me that my children in Rhode Island would doubtless be delighted if I brought one of these charming little west Texas donkeys home, and so a dark-colored, sad-looking female burro was selected to accompany Sioux and me. The Spanish word for rabbit is conejo. One look at this long-eared little donkey suggested Conejo as her name and it stuck.

Location of a pack saddle presented a problem until the following evening. It was Saturday and we were asked to visit the Kingston Ranch, where a number of the younger set were planning to get together with guitars. Ed, Sophie and I got into the station wagon and drove down the steep mountain road to the fork where the road turned back toward Dark Canyon. On the way down, Ed pointed out the unlikely route taken by Johnny Kingston on a hair-raising ride with a half-broken horse.

Johnny, Duncan Kingston's son, had called on the Bartholomews one afternoon. On leaving, Ed noted that he was having difficulty in mounting his spooky bay. By dint of a quick move he found his stirrups, but before he could turn the horse to the roadway, the horse "came apart" with him and bucked straight off the steep, rocky hillside. According to Ed, at one point Johnny kicked his feet free and raised up on the saddle looking for a reasonably soft place to jump. Rocks, cactus and a series of almost vertical drop-offs made bailing out a very unpromising solution, so Johnny decided to ride it out and settled down in his saddle.

"I've seen a lot of rodeo rides in my time." Ed shook his head. "Johnny topped them all with that one. Sophie and I jumped in the car and drove around by the road expecting to find the worst. There they were down by the gate — the horse standing spraddle-legged and both of them soaked with sweat."

Horses raised in this country are surefooted out of necessity, but coming down off that hill would have made a goat pay close attention. Merely thinking about such a ride gave me a cold chill.

The ranch house sat in the wide entrance to the canyon, a stout stone building dating back to the 1880s. It was built by the first of the Kingston family in what was then Apache-inhabited country and is still the focal point of a twenty-thousand-acre spread. A fenced green lawn surrounded the house and separated it from the barns and corrals. Once through the gate, wide, railed steps led up to a veranda that stretched across the entire front.

A Walker hound heralded our approach and we were welcomed into the house, where the family and friends were gathering. A long, wide central room divided off the bedrooms that were on either side, ending at the dining and kitchen area. Rugged oak furniture lined the sides of the room; the center was reserved for the guitarists. A rifle rack with its nested Winchesters sat against one wall, where I suspect it had been placed when the house was new. A large gilt-framed, hand-colored photograph of the house — taken years back — showed it looking only slightly different from its present appearance, and other photos were of successful bear hunts by earlier generations of Kingstons when the men wore beards and the ladies rode sidesaddle. Duncan had been the champion bear hunter of these hills before the bear population was thinned and Ed mentioned that he probably knew the mountains better than anyone else in the country.

Branding season was in full swing, and added to the older family members and Johnny and his young wife were several part-time cowboys. John Stevens, a clean-cut young man, was there with his guitar when we arrived and he was shortly joined by another part-time cowboy who played lead guitar.

Country music has seldom appealed to me, but after the first few minutes of the players' shyness wore off, what I heard was pure, unaffected and great. From the sad, minor sounds of "Streets of Laredo" to a toe-tapping, spur-jingling recital of the problems encountered in the city by a ranch-bred cowboy, it was an evening of home-brewed fun. It differed from its commercial counterpart in the same way that the dusty-toed, stirrup-worn boots of the musicians were a pants-wrinkling six months' ride away from the glittering costumes of the record makers. Attracted by the sounds, the grinning Mexican "segundo" came in from the rear of the house and with great coaxing was prevailed upon to do "El Rancho Grande."

Later, during a respite, the subject of Conejo the burro came up. When I asked for information concerning the purchase of a pack saddle, Johnny said that there would be no problem.

"Come on out to the barn a minute and I'll get you one you can borrow. No need to buy one. You can drop it off to us on your way home."

Again the Texas attitude toward a total stranger came to

252

my mind. There was no question and no complicated deal involved.

The next day's packing involved a certain amount of consideration because the dead-weight load that goes on any pack animal must be carefully balanced in order to ride evenly. Conejo caused no trouble while being loaded; I'd led her once or twice before and she seemed to be reasonably willing. I knew little or nothing about mules or burros but I'd been told that after a few days of following a mare, the burro would be all but impossible to leave behind.

Sunday morning we left Ed and Sophie at their mountaintop home with a promise to return on the way back. Ed gave me a number of his books that I was very anxious to read but unable to take with me and, too, I was using his canvas panniers on the pack saddle which itself belonged to the Kingstons.

Instead of taking the long road back out to the highway, I took a shorter route that went by way of the Kingston Ranch. Partway down the mountain, a trail cut to the left which led through a gate in a barbed-wire fence. At that point I was to find an old wagon road which led directly to the ranch house in the valley below. Another ranch road would take me to the highway some ten miles above the point where I'd left it.

All went well on the downhill stretch to the Bartholomews' gate. Conejo stepped along quite briskly and the pack seemed to be riding as it should. Once through the gate, with the other burros left behind, I began to detect what seemed to be a drag on the lead rope. Thinking that perhaps Sioux was walking too fast for her shorter-legged companion, I attempted to take her in a little. About then Conejo, without warning, braced all fours firmly into the ground and set the brakes. The lead rope zipped warmly through the palm of my hand, so I took a turn on the saddle horn and started

253

Sioux up again. Conejo dragged back a few steps, then lunged forward and came along quietly. Obviously, a little patient firmness on my part would teach her to follow without pulling. I didn't know that Conejo was even then formulating her plan to fill the gaps in my neglected education regarding burros. Perhaps a hundred yards were ticked off when — *slam* — friend Conejo sat back on the rope again. Sioux laid back her ears in irritation and jerked her forward with but slight urging on my part. This time Conejo lunged sideways, and I noticed in looking back that the pack saddle appeared to be slipping. I stopped, dismounted, dropped the reins on the ground and went back to straighten the pack saddle and tighten the cinch, which had become slack.

We started up, cut off the road in the direction of the gate and after a quarter mile of picking our way through the rocks and cactus, interrupted by several more grinding stops, came to the fence. I stood up in my stirrups and craned my neck but was unable to find any evidence of a gate. Catclaw cactus was abundant at this spot and its name makes further description unnecessary. While hitching my animals near the fence in order to scout for the gate on foot, Conejo jerked back and caused me to snag my hand in the catclaws.

Stumbling along the fence line to the top of a ridge, I finally located the gate and then returned to where I'd left the animals. I was met by a sad-eyed, reproachful-looking burro who stood innocently hipshot next to Sioux with her capsized pack saddle hanging upside down beneath her, its contents spilling out. With what I considered to be admirable patience, I removed the mess and started from scratch.

Neatly repacked and remounted, we proceeded through the gate and found the clearly defined, wagon-rutted trail. We had gone some distance, gradually dropping down toward the valley, when we came to the top of a ridge that

fell away quite steeply. Conejo was still applying the brakes at intervals and I began to notice that her backward pulls coincided with the times when Sioux was precariously balanced in the rocky path. We continued to pick our way forward.

Eventually we made our sliding, slipping, stumbling, cursing way down off the mountain and got to where the valley leveled out. Coming to the road with great relief, we headed in the direction of the fork to the ranch house. At various times during the descent I'd been able to see the distant house, which had, if nothing else, at least supplied a ray of cheer.

A dust cloud coming our way from the direction of town developed into a car and, as we met at the fork of the road, it proved to be Mrs. Kingston returning from church services. Our descent had taken so much time that it was by now almost noon and Mrs. Kingston insisted that I make certain to stop off with them for lunch.

Pulling up to the hitch rack that fronted the house, I was welcomed by Duncan and Johnny. I tied the horse and burro and followed them into the dining room, which contained what must have been one of the largest tables in the world. The "lunch" to which I'd been invited was composed of enough food to feed a small army, and the variety was such that a small helping of each course would have left me staggering. Duncan occupied his place at the head of the table, Mrs. Kingston was opposite, and family members and their wives, household help and ranch hands filled in the spaces on either side.

"We were watching you coming down off the hill," Duncan said in the deep resonant voice that always boomed out of the depths of his barrel chest. "Thought for a while you were about to get in a wreck."

"Us greenhorns should learn not to take shortcuts in

257

strange country," I admitted, demonstrating the catclaw-wound chevrons that decorated my knuckles.

"You won't have any trouble from here on out," Duncan consoled me. "There's a road all the way. Unless you want to cut across another way. It might be shorter for you."

"Thanks, but no thanks," I laughed. "The last shortcut added two hours to my time."

Leaving by way of the road this time, we worked our way across the comparatively level valley. A series of tanks and windmills were laid out so that the sweet water with which this ranch was blessed was spotted out at convenient intervals. By now I'd gotten tired of holding Conego's lead rope in my hand, so I fashioned a large loop that I dropped over the saddle horn. It was loose enough to be readily thrown off in case of trouble, but in taking the strain off my arm, it transferred the jerks to Sioux. Conejo was by now giving us more trouble rather than less, even though she was rope-burning the hair off her jaw in several places.

I'd planned to make twenty miles the first day to Davis Mountain Station, where there were a restaurant, a motel and water, but by the end of the day we were barely more than out to the highway. We still had ten miles to go when dark fell, so I was forced to make a dry camp in a grassy wash alongside the road. The animals had drunk at the last windmill and my canteen contained plenty for me.

In the morning I saddled Sioux as usual and packed Conejo. When I led Sioux over to where the burro was hitched and started to get the lead rope and mount up, Conejo sighed sadly and lay down, pack and all. Coaxing and pulling on the rope got me nowhere. With no other course available to me and glad that Sophie wasn't looking, I prodded her in the ribs with my spurred heel and that did the trick. Conejo got up, but she didn't look happy about it. The first time we tried to cross over the pavement on the highway the little burro made her stand clear on the subject of concrete. Setting her legs firmly in position, she forced Sioux to drag her the entire distance and when we came to our first bridge, the performance was repeated.

Sioux was becoming downright waspish by now and almost sighed in exasperation each time she had to haul our unwilling companion. The lead rope was beginning to cut into my hip from the point where it was attached to the saddle horn and, apart from the discomfort and annoyance, our progress was being cut in half.

The only enjoyable part of the next ten miles was afforded us by the antics of a young mule deer that we came up to. He was either unable or unwilling to jump the fence that paralleled the road, so he moved along ahead of us for a mile or so, stopping every hundred yards to peer at us from behind a mesquite tree. He'd brazen it out until we got within fifty feet, then slip quietly ahead to stop and watch us approach again. Somewhere, at a spot unseen by me, he either got through the fence or hid successfully and we saw him no more.

By midafternoon we reached the Davis Mountain Station, by which time I was completely disgusted with the grand plan to haul a burro to Arizona. I hoped to find a phone so I could try to arrange to get Conejo back to her mountain home, but the nearest one was another twenty-odd miles ahead. Fortunately in the café when we arrived was a young salesman who was headed for Balmorhea. He offered to take me back to the Bartholomews', some distance out of his way. It was rather embarrassing to back out of the situation, or would have been with people less understanding than Ed and Sophie. Neighbor Kingston came to the rescue with his pickup and trailer, and before long Conejo was loaded in the trailer and headed back to her old friends. I probably insulted Duncan by attempting to at least pay for his gas.

"Hell," he snorted, "I don't often get a chance to help neighbors like Ed and Sophie. When I do, don't try to spoil my fun. Come back and see us on the way home."

As we watched the trailer disappear on its way to the distant mountains, Sioux, despite her annoyance of the past two days, threw up her head and nickered her farewells.

A dreary continuation of sand, greasewood and Spanish dagger cactus rolled out in front of us for nearly fifty miles. Gomez Peak in the Davis Mountains finally dropped out of sight over our left shoulder and the Apache Mountains came up on our distant right. A heat-blurred ridge on the third day shaped itself into the Van Horn Mountains and I was getting close to country that I'd known long before, yet, somehow, only yesterday.

We pulled in at one point to where a sizable growth of grass lined a wash. I was about to step off Sioux to allow her to graze when she spooked sideways for no apparent reason. Looking to see what had attracted her attention, I caught a glimpse of the moving tail of a rattler, the first and, as it turned out, the only one we were to meet. I reached for the revolver that I'd been carrying loaded ever since it had been seasonal for snakes to emerge. Normally Sioux isn't gun-shy but now she was fidgety about the snake. She was not alone in her reaction and, as a result, it took three shots before I connected.

The scoring bullet was unquestionably fatal but not instantly so, and the rattler thrashed into some rocks edging a culvert. I entertained brief thoughts about getting the rattles for my oldest boy, since they doubtless would have been a status symbol in Rhode Island; however, the snake wasn't aware of his decease as yet and I wasn't about to tell him by attempting to "count coup" on his tail. We left him for the buzzards and headed on toward the approaching Van Horn Mountains.

Van Horn sits at the foot of these mountains and I knew that as soon as I crossed them I'd once again see the familiar whitish peak of Sierra Blanca, a landmark visible for a great distance in all directions. Our old 7th Cavalry border patrol camp had been located near the town of Sierra Blanca and I began to feel a sort of excitement at the prospect of once again seeing the town and perhaps an old friend or two.

McVay's Courts in Van Horn was a Western Union office as well as a motel and located conveniently next door was a store selling baled alfalfa. My finances replenished and Sioux with a whole bale of alfalfa at her disposal, we stoked up the fires in preparation for a blistering thirty-three-mile one-day haul across Eagle Flats to Sierra Blanca. Ol' McVay, as he was called, although his age was no greater than mine, and an El Paso salesman whose name I should recall but don't and I were standing about bemoaning and solving the ills of the world when the salesman observed Sioux with a whole bale of alfalfa. Knowing I planned to move on to Sierra Blanca next day, he wondered what I expected to do with the remains of the hay. I told him I'd be obliged to leave it behind, since I had no way of carrying it along.

"That's no problem," he said. "I've got the back of my station wagon empty. Put it aboard, along with your other stuff, and I'll drop it off wherever you plan to stop tomorrow night."

"Back in 1942, the Owl Courts was our beer-drinking hangout. I'd like to pull in there just for old times' sake," I said. "I've heard they're still at the same old stand."

"Be glad to leave it there for you," he said, "and I'll tell them to be sure to save you a room."

Bright and early Sioux and I, lightened of everything except canteen and saddlebags, started the ascent that would take us through the notch in the Van Horn Mountains to where Sierra Blanca lay ahead. We passed the old familiar turn to our left that would have taken us south to Valentine and Marfa, where we'd once ridden the Sierra Vieja mountains bordering the Rio Grande. I'd been told in Fort Davis that the Miller Ranch was still intact, although old Espe Miller was now dead.

In 1942 a group of us had camped on Espe Miller's land with our cavalry horses and pack horses at an old tumbledown army post that perched high on a lonely shelf of land halfway up Vieja Pass. One of our pack horses, a handsomely built brown, had a penchant for blowing up for no apparent reason whatever. With equal lack of reason, his name was Frank, and the preceding day on the way up the pass Frank had gone into a bucking spasm that had nearly been the end of him. I'd been leading him when he suddenly went into action, pitched over the edge of the rocky canyon and cartwheeled into a nest of boulders with his load of baled hay. I'd had no saddle horn on my McClellan saddle with which to snub him and I had no intention of going with him, so I let him go and turned my head away. Mentally calculating how long it would take on my army pay to reimburse the government for a horse valued at one hundred sixty-five dollars, I galloped back down the trail with Billy Pratt, a Montana cowboy, to survey the bloody wreckage that by all rights we were sure to find amidst the rocks.

We picked our way around a bend in the canyon floor and there lay old Frank wedged upside down on two bales of hay in a nest of boulders. We cut the cinches and Frank scrambled to his feet with nothing but a dime-sized spot scraped off one leg.

Next day, at the old deserted army camp, we were engaged in packing Frank while conversing with Espe Miller, the rancher, who sat watching us on his buckskin cow pony. All went well until we dropped the breeching of the pack saddle under Frank's tail. Whether he considered this to be an indignity, I'm not sure. At any rate he lunged away, fully loaded, with a sack of pancake flour riding the top of the pack. The container withstood the strain of riding a bucking horse for less than the ten seconds customary in rodeos, then split open to punctuate each ensuing buck jump with a billowing cloud of flour dust. I thought for a while that Miller would fall off his horse laughing and it must have presented a pretty ludicrous sight. Once in control of himself, he loped his horse after Frank and roped him, to return the now placid and meek horse to his army custodians.

Espe Miller has been dead for some time, but his land remains unchanged. The sight of the familiar mountains made what had seemed at times to be figments of my youthful imagination once again clearly remembered events of only a day or so ago. It would have been fun to head south toward Valentine once again to invade the Miller Ranch, and someday maybe I can round up a few old balding ex-saddle bumpers like "Booger Red" Kitchens and "Will Bill" Keas to join me on a pack trip through the unchanged hills.

Booger Red, a California cowboy, was saddled back in '42 with the nickname that has followed him to his present position of respectability as brand inspector for the state of California. A big, jovial, redheaded, hell-raising Irishman, he'd gone out of his way to be assigned a cavalry horse called Big Booger for the reason that the horse was the most likely to buck of any in the saddle string. Booger Red Kitchens he

263

was from that day on and it is a distinct possibility that there are merchants in Van Horn who might still recall some of his exploits with less than amusement.

Frank, Big Booger and my little cavalry horse Curly are doubtless long dead, as are many of the young men and boys who left from this border country for the more serious business in the Pacific.

Sioux and I were halfway up the notch in the Van Horn Mountains when a familiar station wagon pulled over as it came abreast of us. Ed and Sophie Bartholomew, on their way to El Paso, had figured with considerable accuracy where they'd "cut our sign." As always, Sophie was equipped with cookies and cake – some for me but mostly for Sioux. We established a plan to pick Conejo up with the trailer on my homeward route and they headed on to El Paso.

A new multilaned highway cut over the mountain and down onto the flats and the old Route 80, still visible off to one side, seemed incredibly narrow. It had once been the main highway across most of Texas and now it looked the width of a New England country road. Over the top, the whole familiar panorama opened up before us. To our right the harshly barren Sierra Diablos stretched along the way, on our left the ragged, impassable Eagle Mountains broke up from the flats, and thirty miles ahead lay Devil Ridge, where our old base camp had been. At the edge of Devil Ridge was the town of Sierra Blanca and off beyond to the right loomed Sierra Blanca mountain, for which the town had been named. The sun's glare in this country has an almost whitish quality, at times enhanced by a breakthrough of white caliche clay. Cactus and greasewood cover the rocky, sandy soil and a stranger would think it impossible to raise livestock or, indeed, rabbits. The traveler generally sees little animal life except for the horned toads that live among the rocks and the swift little lizards that appear as tiny flickers of cerulean blue. It is, nevertheless, livestock country. The cattle are there but the sparse feed causes them to be widely scattered and hard to spot.

I couldn't begin to explain what there is about this land that attracts me. I think it was General Sheridan who, when asked about his views on west Texas, said something to the effect that were he to own west Texas and hell, he'd rent out Texas and live in hell. There were times when the sand was blowing and the fine grit had penetrated to my teeth that I swore to myself and my dust-caked mare I wouldn't take the country as a gift, if residence was a requirement in the deed. But maybe the very brutal hardness appeals to the masochist in me. For a good many years I had nostalgic thoughts about it and even now I'd be glad to go there again. Certainly it's a tough country and it produces a tough breed and always has, from its Apache residents and those that were here before them on. One of the men in our small horse cavalry troop, Bill Hines, was a circus trick rider and roper from California. His hatred for Sierra Blanca was so voluble that it earned for him the nickname Tex, which stuck throughout his army career. In a group of men outstanding with their proficiency for profanity, his descriptions of Texas still stand out in my memory.

Now I was in a hurry to get there. Our load was light and I frequently broke into a slow lope that made the miles pass by faster than usual. Tiny buildings ahead broke through the shimmer of the heat waves and gave me tantalizing glimpses of the town. A toy-sized freight train crawled across the wide country to the south – I'd forgotten that the track went through that way. When we came to a railroad siding sitting out in the middle of nowhere, the lone boxcar was a misplaced Yankee like myself, its painted sides announcing that it was of the New Haven Railroad.

The sun was making a flashy red descent behind Devil Ridge as we rode into Sierra Blanca, and there was the old town as I remembered it — but something was wrong. The new highway stood high on its white concrete base and sliced loftily across the south side of the town and on to El Paso, completely ignoring the village below. The dirt road that should have turned left and led to our old camp now dead-ended against the concrete base of the new highway and the structure itself blocked my view of the area. Moving on down the main street, we passed the fire-gutted remains of an old beer joint that sat on the right of a kink in the street, all that was left of the scene of numberless escapades. Vacant stores spotted both sides of the road, the inevitable result of progress and a shiny new highway that no longer needed the facilities of a town.

The Owl Courts came up on the left; the units appeared as I'd remembered them but a face-lifting job had modernized the front of the café building. Hitching Sioux to the sign post, I went in and found that I was expected; my bedroll, grain bags and the partial bale of alfalfa were stored in the office. The Spanish-style units enclosed three sides of a rectangle, with the café in the center fronting on the road. A narrow alley cut in alongside and around in the rear. My room was ideally situated for a horse traveler, since the window facing out on the alley was equipped with a tree to which I could fasten Sioux. The layout enabled me to lie on the bed and talk to Sioux through the open window not more than a foot or so away. This feature proved to be fortunate on our second night in Sierra Blanca.

Showered and shaved, with Sioux hitched under her tree contentedly munching alfalfa next to my window, I walked over to the café for dinner. The friendly proprietress began to fill me in on the people in town that I might have known. I was aware that Mrs. Rodway Keen still lived in town. She had been active at the small frame U.S.O. building during the war and had cheerfully and patiently put up with a great deal from the group of young horse soldiers. The unfailing kindness of this lady and others like her had been responsible for unusually good relations. My first move after eating was to call her on the phone and make plans to see her next day.

"Did you know that Will Nardine has lived here ever since the war?" she asked after we'd talked on the phone for a while.

I didn't and hadn't seen nor heard from Will since we'd parted company at Fort Devens, Massachusetts, in 1945.

"He lives at Allamoore. I'll let him know you're here," she said.

Another of the old cavalry friends had been a native cowboy from the region and I asked the café owner if she knew of a man named Bud Meixner.

"I guess I do," she replied. "His wife works here — she'll be behind the counter at breakfast time. Bud cowboys out at the Slaughter Ranch north of town."

The interior of the Owl was not greatly changed. The front windows and doors had been modernized and the stove that had occupied a space near the left wall was gone, but the counter and stools remained the same. I thought about an evening when Booger Red Kitchens had sat at a table with a friend and his friend's wife from the Midwest. It was spring and a sign behind the counter advertised "mountain oysters" as being on the menu.

The girl read the sign and turned to her husband.

"What are mountain oysters?" she asked in all innocence.

267

Her fairly new husband looked a trifle embarrassed. Then, grinning, he turned to Red. "Tell her, Red."

Red looked a little sheepish for a moment while choosing his words.

"Well," he said, "you know what a bull is?"

"Sure," she replied.

"You know what a steer is?" he continued.

"Yes," came the answer.

"Well," Red explained, "mountain oysters is the difference between a bull and a steer."

After a session with the nearby coin laundry I turned in early, looking forward to spending the next day checking out some of my old haunts.

When Will drove in early next morning I recognized him instantly, although the twenty-odd years of Texas sun had etched his face deeply and grayed his hair.

"I'll be damned," Will said, looking over at Sioux where she stood hitched by my window. "I passed a nut riding in this way yesterday. I wondered who the crazy s.o.b. was on the paint horse, but I sure never figured that it was you."

It was Saturday and Will spent the day with me. We went out to the old camp area and without Will as a guide I'd have been hard put to know exactly where it had been. The old road was cut off by the new highway and now it was an unused dirt track almost erased in spots by the drifting sand. Where once had stood corrals, a barn, a saddle shop and blacksmith shop, there was nothing but greasewood — spotted desert. Two weathered fence posts, the rusted-out barbed wire trailing off into the sand, marked where the gate and sentry box had been; nothing remained to mark where the faded tents and kitchen building once stood. Only the changeless ridge that backed the site and old Blanca Mountain remained as unquestionable proof to me that this

268

had once been home base for one hundred sixty-five men and some two hundred horses.

We drove south on uncharted ranch roads through Quitman Canyon and on to the Rio Grande, this part of the famous river bone dry as it has been for over ten years. The Rio, now a dry gully grown up with salt cedars, is proof of the contention that the country has been steadily drying up. We turned "downstream" on a brutal road that follows the course of the river and wound through heat-blistered rocks and cactus to Indian Hot Springs, where we headed back north through a rugged canyon which not too many years ago was the route taken by large herds of cattle smuggled in from Mexico. The cattle, said to have been stolen south of the border, were driven in at night, followed by a band of goats to obliterate the trail, then trucked out to far markets where they could be quickly auctioned off.

Back in Sierra Blanca, Will suggested that we drive out to the Slaughter Ranch to see if we could run down Bud Meixner. The only sign of life at the ranch was a pair of saddle horses that stood dozing in the corral. It was nearly noon, so we decided to wait, and shortly three riders came in off the flats for the dinner hour. They told us that Bud was out setting wolf traps and should be back for dinner, and in a few minutes a rider came down off the hills on a saddle mule.

As tall, thin and wiry as he'd been in his twenties, Bud greeted Will, looked at me curiously for a moment, then broke into a slow grin of recognition.

"What the hell are you doin' out here, T.B.?" Bud drawled, using my old army nickname. Another of our cavalry buddies was a Boston Irish jumping-horse trainer named Walter B. Sullivan. Bud had convulsed us numerous times when he tried to imitate Sully's Boston accent. I reminded him of these attempts as we sat down and joined the

269

riders for their noon meal, and the old wry grin twisted the corner of his mouth.

"Is auld Sillivan shtill roidin' thim joompin' harses, you reckon?" Bud tried to say.

"Last I heard he was an electrician in Ohio," I said, "and you still can't do a Boston Irish dialect worth a dam'."

I told him that I hoped to locate Walt Drye in Winslow, Arizona, when I got there and Bud said he'd tried some years back with no luck.

"If y'all find ol' Walter, yew tell him Ah still owe him two bucks," Bud drawled. "If he'll send me his right address, I'll shore mail it to him."

We left Bud as he was heading back to the hills on his mule. That evening I walked over beyond the old adobe courthouse to visit Mrs. Keen. As spry and alert as ever, she still put in her days at the county courthouse. She filled me in on a number of friends I'd lost track of over the years and I was genuinely saddened to hear of the death of Gus Chiles, our first sergeant. A thirty-year man in the army, he'd been killed in an accident in east Texas shortly after his retirement.

In 1942, arriving at the old border camp by horse truck as fresh new recruits, we'd been greeted by Gus after the trucks rolled through the gate. Trained on spit and polish at Fort Riley, Kansas, we were warned of the strict military formality we were to expect when we joined our permanent regiment, Custer's old 7th Cavalry. We leaped out of the trucks with precision and lined up snappily for inspection and assignment by the first sergeant.

The camp was on a sandy flat at the foot of Devil Ridge, surrounded by a barbed-wire fence. At one end was a heavy-timbered horse corral and a water tank; at the other a series of pale, faded, yellowish tents on wooden platforms ending at the rough-sawn wood building that housed the kitchen.

Blackened stovepipes stuck out of the tops of the pyramidal tents and brighter-colored canvas patches indicated that sparks from the Sibley stoves had burned more than a few holes.

The flap of the orderly tent pushed open and Gus Chiles made his appearance. The left sleeve of his faded shirt was dominated by the large, yellow, horsehead 1st Cavalry Division patch, his first soldier's chevrons, and some twenty-seven years worth of enlistment hash marks. The shapeless blob of a sweat-stained, faded campaign hat would have been the envy of a Hollywood prop department. Its brim was bent up rather jauntily in front and back, and a chin strap was nowhere in evidence. His bowed legs spindled down into high, laced cavalry boots that were almost completely innocent of any association with shoe polish, and blunt cavalry spurs drooped listlessly from his heels. The outstanding feature of his squinty-eyed, saddle-leather face was a formidable black handlebar moustache, and as he eyed us standing in our neat and shining alignment it almost visibly curled with disgust. He stumped stiffly to a central vantage point, pushed the old felt hat back on his forehead and stopped to stand for a long moment, hands on hips, with an attitude that bespoke pure contempt.

"Ah'll be gawddammed," he said at last.

We'd learned rapidly and were scarcely ever caught again in the proper uniform. We soon wore Levi's, usually topped by the army shirt and field jacket, and for the most part we looked more like a horde of bandits than soldiers. High-heeled cowboy boots were frequently substituted for army footgear. Toward the end of the days of horse soldiering, when we were being trained to march on foot, we were scheduled to do a twenty-five-mile march through the desert. Bud Meixner, who'd never learned to walk in the first place,

271

approached the old first sergeant to ask if he could make the march in cowboy boots instead of army boots.

"Ah cain't walk in them dam' flat-heeled Li'l Abner shoes," he'd protested.

"Son," old Gus said paternally, "Ah don't give a rat's ass if you do 'er barefoot, jes' so you do 'er."

Gus was one of several old-timers in the troop, some of whom dated back to Black Jack Pershing's pursuit of Pancho Villa into Mexico. "Foghorn" Clark, the choleric stable sergeant, "Pop" Lane, the wizened old-timer with a voice like an enraged Donald Duck, and "Sandbag" Smith were all career soldiers — hard as nails and, once you got to know them, soft as butter. Foghorn, named for his voice, although it was closer to the sound of an outraged bull, was to be blown up by a mortar shell on Luzon Island in his twenty-ninth year of service. Gus, who'd survived his thirty years and the Pacific war, followed a short time after in an automobile accident.

Thoroughly unloved by the dewy-eyed recruits at first, these tough old birds had taught us the realities of army life and eventually commanded, if not affection, certainly respect — and speaking for myself, it was a lot closer to affection. They were, almost to a man, hard living, whiskey drinking, profane and complete realists, and in the army of that day, they were what made it go. Years of boozing and hard living should have made them the first to drop out when the going got hard, but they were the last. Youngsters with football star physiques fell by the wayside with regularity; these old-timers didn't know the word quit.

Back in my room for the night, I thought about old Gus Chiles and about a scene that took place when we went into the Philippines with MacArthur. It was one of the rare times when the kitchen trucks had caught up to us with hot chow and we lolled around near a grass-thatched village that

272

we'd just come through. A handful of hungry, naked Filipino children approached to watch us eat and two of them stood staring at Gus, who squatted nearby, a fire-blackened steel helmet replacing the old felt campaign hat. Gus rose after a couple of bites, scraped the contents of his mess kit into a couple of empty cans, handed them to the kids and stomped past where I was sitting with a young Mexican soldier.

"Gawddam' li'l bare-ass sunuvabitches," he growled, "standin' around with their dam' li'l peckers pointin' at you like a row of artillery."

"El Grande Viejo," my Mexican friend grinned, using their Spanish name for Gus, "ees sure wan tough guy, no?"

"No," I agreed.

While walking back to my room that night I'd heard a far-away rumble of thunder but had thought little about it, since the land was so dry that rain was a dream. Some hours after dropping off to sleep I awoke to a loud rapping noise that momentarily baffled me. Just outside my window Sioux was snorting and nickering with a distressed tone, and a quick glance showed what was taking place. Hailstones the size of golf balls were bombarding the outside world. I jumped into my clothes as rapidly as possible, grabbed a tarp and ran out to throw it over her back. It was a pointless move, since the hailstones were falling with painful force. I quickly unhitched my jumping, snorting friend and without further delay ran around to the front of the motel and led her into the empty garage unit adjacent to my room. Getting under cover made her as happy as I've ever seen her. By the time I walked back to my room, the hailstones were drifted six to eight inches deep on the ground.

In the morning my clothes were still soaked from the brief encounter with the storm, and though I'd just laundered everything I owned at the nearby coin laundry, I took time to return and run the soaked articles through the washer and dryer again. We finally got on our way headed out on the old road to El Paso. In 1943 I'd ridden out this same road as part of a long column of horses headed for Fort Bliss. At that time we covered the eighty-seven miles in just over two days. Now I planned to take a little longer, because I wanted to stop in Fabens and attempt to contact Hugh O'Donnell, another ex-member of our cavalry troop.

Sierra Blanca had left me with a strange feeling akin to loneliness. A reasonable degree of common sense tells anyone that a familiar scene revisited can never be as it was, yet there's a lingering childlike hope that perhaps it will be. I'd expected to find no one I knew besides Mrs. Keen but I had a bonus in Will Nardine and Bud Meixner. I'd also met a friendly and helpful young couple, Leon and Darlene Snyder, who brought me horse feed and were to prove particularly kindly during a car breakdown on the way home some months later.

The road into El Paso closely follows the course of the Rio Grande and dating from the time I'd gotten to within seventy-five miles of the border, I'd been under occasional scrutiny by the United States border patrol. Small planes had buzzed me the first time and in my ignorance, I'd thought them to be merely friendly ranchers flying low to wave. Some border patrolmen drove radio-equipped Scouts and I'd stopped to talk with several at intervals.

They'd always been friendly to me after they got close enough to determine that I was not a Mexican wetback; however, after hearing numerous discussions of treatment accorded to the illegal Mexican laborers, I was happy that I happened to be a gringo. As a mere passerby I don't pretend to know the intricacies of foreign or domestic policy or the

274

reasons behind such things; I did form a strong opinion about our actions toward these people.

As I saw the situation in passing and from what I heard of discussions between local people and ranchers, these illegal Mexican entrants are helpless and needy neighbors of ours. They are not looking for free handouts of any sort but merely for the chance to work at hard and disagreeable labor for the few dollars that it takes to enable them in some cases to live and feed their children. Many of them cross over the harsh mountain ranges barefooted, thirsty and near starvation, desperate in their need for work. They continue to take the chance even though they're aware that they'll be arrested by the authorities and shipped back again with the same empty stomachs they arrived with. The ranchers and farmers of this section need them, want them and usually feed and clothe them even though they may not at the moment have work for them. One person I met stocks up on old clothing from rummage sales just to have something on hand to help the Mexicans on their way. It seems unlikely that these people are depriving any of our native citizens of work, since I personally had four job offers from area ranchers who thought I was just an itinerant ranch hand. All the way to Arizona I heard little talk that did not include at one time or another the shortage of ranch help.

We seem to be able to spend vast sums of money in attempts to persuade people of all parts of the world to love us with the result that they stone the windows of our embassies and disport themselves by feeding their celebrant bonfires with the American flag. Here, right at home, when hungry neighbors express a willingness to perform labors that we appear reluctant to do ourselves, we chase them with airplanes and clap them into the backs of suffocatingly hot vehicles for deportation back into Mexico.

The wetbacks not only contribute their needed labors,

they also spend a considerable amount of the money they earn at small local stores. One store where a sale was in progress tempted me to stop and buy a new length of rope at half price. The store was selling out for the reason that the absence of Mexican farm labor had cut their volume of sales to the point where they could no longer make a go of it.

Ranch gates are often found locked today that have never been locked before in the history of the Southwest. It was explained to me that this was done to prevent the border patrol from entering the premises to arrest the wetbacks who might be busily working in the branding corrals or sheep pens.

I was told of one case of a patrol plane diving so close to a Mexican on horseback that the man was beheaded by the propeller. Another story told to me was about a federal forest ranger who climbed off his horse to open a gate. A border patrol plane buzzed him and stampeded his horse, and the ranger had to walk some five miles back to the ranger station.

Others told me of intentional baiting of the patrolmen. Upon observation of a plane showing signs of going into a glide, the ranchers would pretend to hide behind mesquite trees. The evasive behavior seldom failed to get the patrol stirred up and the inevitable radio-summoned jeeps found nothing but a legitimate rancher minding his own business.

I have no desire to castigate individual members of the border patrol, who are only performing their duties as they are prescribed (although a few would appear to have been overzealous at times). It does seem to me, however, that our policies toward our Mexican neighbors could stand a realistic revision.

From the little town of Tornillo, I made a phone call to Hugh O'Donnell and Hugh met me on the highway just out of Fabens. I'd last seen Hugh at a machine-gun emplacement in the Philippines. Artillery fire had driven us into a tunnel mouth on the face of a dam at a reservoir site near Manila. I'd bent forward to untangle the ammunition belt just as a shell burst at the mouth of the tunnel. The shrapnel had somehow missed me in my stooped position and badly smashed Hugh's upper right arm. I'd gotten a pretty good look at the damaged arm at that time and the fact that he can still use it pays tribute to some army surgeon.

Hugh's mother was hospitalized and he made arrangements ahead at a motel with facilities for Sioux in the rear at a horse-owner friend's corral. On the way through town to the motel, I cut off the main street to take a side lane that went in the same direction and ran up against a situation that was to repeat itself several times.

The houses off the main street were largely occupied by Mexican families and hordes of Mexican kids came running from all directions at the sound of Sioux's hoofs.

"Mira, un caballo!" they screamed. Lookit the horse!

Grinning joyously, the little five- and six-year-olds scooped up stones and, yelling, flung them with disconcerting accuracy. My only defense was to pick up as much speed as possible and get the hell out. At first I took this to be a sort of El Paso area version of "Yankee Go Home" but several people more familiar with the kids said no.

"As long as they're smiling, they're not mad at you," one man explained. "It's only a friendly gesture. Did you get hit?"

"No," I admitted.

"You see," he said, "those little bastards grow up killing jackrabbits with rocks — can't afford .22 rifles. They coulda hit you right between the eyes if they'd wanted to."

Following a visit to his mother, Hugh came over to the motel, where we had dinner and spent the evening together hashing over old times. As I planned to make the thirty

277

miles to El Paso next day, I tried to reach Tom Lea by phone — with no success.

Trying again after breakfast, I still got no answer, but I headed out for Ysleta, the old Spanish mission town that is now included in the El Paso city limits. From there I had no better luck with the phone, so, in search of advice, I called Bill McGaw, editor and publisher of the *Southwesterner*, a monthly publication devoted largely to the history of the area. Bill's name had been given me by Ed Bartholomew back in the Davis Mountains and this was a stroke of luck, because Bill gave me directions to the Red Mill Motel on Alameda Avenue, where I could tie Sioux on the lawn almost in the heart of the city.

Taking his advice, I cut over to the levee at Ysleta and rode the broad top the remainder of the way into the city. Here the Rio Grande contained water, although it looked shallow and sluggish. Looking off from the top of the levee, I saw El Paso spread out in all directions. It had been a fair-sized city when we'd been stationed at Fort Bliss in the last days of the horse cavalry. Now it was expanded beyond belief. When I came to a grassy park containing a lake, I mistakenly assumed that it was Washington Park, where I was to leave the levee. Too late, I found that it was Ascarate Park and that I had several miles of Delta Road to take in order to make the motel. The late-afternoon outward-bound traffic was murderous and again I was pursued by screaming, stone-throwing small fry. I thought of a remark attributed to W. C. Fields. When asked how he liked little children he replied, "Fried."

After a nerve-wracking, apparently endless bout with city traffic, I rounded the corner where Bill McGaw has his newly opened New Orleans-style restaurant.

A number of plans I'd had involving El Paso didn't work out. Bill McGaw suggested several names of people to call and through them I found that Tom Lea was out of town and was not expected to return until the middle of the following week. One of my plans was to revisit Fort Bliss. The present size of El Paso made that scheme out of the question by horse, since I'd had more than my fill of traffic getting in to the motel and was due to take on an equal portion on the way out.

Bill drove me downtown to pick up a telegraphed money order and I spent the next day getting my boots repaired at Tony Lama's shop, where they'd originally been made. I also made some changes in gear in El Paso. Rain pants and a parka in the dry part of the Southwest seemed excess baggage, so I got rid of them and one of the two tarps. A poncho would serve if it ever decided to rain and it also would double as a substitute for the abandoned tarp.

Bill's publishing offices were a part of the motel that was adjacent to the restaurant and Jim Coates, an employee, gave me a helping hand.

"Before you leave," Jim said, "why don't I drive you over a couple of alternate courses so that you can see which is the easiest way out of town?"

I accepted his kindness with gratitude and it was of inestimable assistance. Had I plowed my way out by way of the levee as I'd originally thought to do, I'd have gotten enmeshed in downtown traffic. With Jim's suggestions and the presence of the Franklin Mountains, which jut up on the north side of El Paso, I was able to keep my bearings in a city that was no longer more than vaguely familiar to me.

Bill McGaw, his wife and daughter and Jim Coates saw me off and I headed north across the heavily trafficked Alameda Avenue, nervously fearing the worst. As it turned out, El Paso is laid out in a way that made the exit relatively simple. The main residential streets run roughly east-west and between each paved street runs an unpaved alley. By

279

heading north toward the mountain for a block or so and then shifting west for a while, I was able to edge my way northwest and over to where old Route 80 heads out to the New Mexico line. The bulk of these maneuvers were accomplished on unpaved alleys with no traffic at all except at the crossovers, and shortly past noon we were well beyond the heavily settled area and nearly out of Texas.

The new and at that time incomplete superhighway Route 10 cut overhead in several places, and we unintentionally left our mark on El Paso where 10 crosses old 80 on the way out of town. A sidewalk goes under the bridge on 80 and I swung over to the left side onto the sidewalk to avoid the cars. I noticed several dark spots on the cement walk, but as they were unguarded, mistakenly assumed that the cement was hard. It wasn't and I looked back to see that Sioux had left her tracks permanently scored in the concrete.

Both banks of the Rio Grande have wide levees for some distance into New Mexico and they made good traveling for a horse. I bore left toward the Rio and just before leaving Texas came to a small motel with good grass surrounding the parking area. It was early for a stop, but the nervous tension of getting out of the city once relieved left me somewhat let down and I pulled over for the night.

Jim Coates spotted the familiar paint mare tethered at the motel and joined me on a stool at the café across the street. I was glad to see him again and let him know that his suggestions had worked out far better than we'd expected.

Jim typified the kindly Texan that I'd met so often in this vast state and it seemed somehow appropriate to end my stay in Texas with still another warm, compatible friend.

8.

Texas came to an end with the crossing of a small bridge that took us to the west side of the Rio Grande. The river separates a small strip of Texas from New Mexico and here it's a pleasantly flowing stream bordered on either side with the grassy banks that edge the levees. Most of the surrounding country is devoted to cotton farming with its flat cultivated look, but the riverbanks are grassy and shaded by cottonwood trees. Riding quietly along, I noticed weasels busily scouting out the contents of gopher holes in the bank. They paid little attention to me as I rode by.

The Franklin Mountains faded to our rear and soon the Organ Mountains came up as we approached Las Cruces. A mile or so from the valley of the Rio the country is barren and dry, and the mountains are devoid of growth. The stark rocky spires have their own special brand of beauty, but I'd certainly have been reluctant to leave the Rio Grande Valley. I'd often thought about the old-timers during the last few hundred miles of desert country and wondered what kind of courage they'd had, or perhaps what desperation drove them into taking on this unforgiving land back in the days when the trails were uncharted. My conveyance was no plusher than theirs, except possibly for the foam rubber pad on my saddle seat, but I, at least, always knew from accurate maps where there would be a settlement with food and water. To think of taking on this enormous country with nothing more definite than a rumor of a waterhole that well might be dry on arrival must have taken a special brand of man. It is an accepted fact that grazing was much better in those days and wild game was there for the taking; still a minor accident today could have been fatal at a time when no help was around for hundreds of miles.

There were times when I'd probably have been overjoyed to trade automobile traffic for Indians, although truthfully most drivers that I met were reasonably careful. I'd read a number of colorful accounts of motorcycle clubs and so once on a lonely stretch of highway when I saw a large gang headed my way in a column of twos I expected the worst. I eased way over on the shoulder with a close rein and my thoughts strayed to the loaded Colt in my saddlebag. To my great and pleasant relief, they throttled way down as far over on their side as possible, waved as they rode quietly by and left without so much as one backfire. I've entertained much more kindly thoughts about motorcycles ever since.

There are always the idiot drivers who mean no harm and these can be more dangerous than the smart punks. Walt Drye told me about an affair that took place on Route 66 in Arizona when a cowman friend of his was driving a small herd of yearling steers across the highway to another pasture. A tourist car came roaring down the highway, saw the steers crossing but still continued his pace, blowing his horn. To many cattle, fed from a pickup truck, the blowing of a horn is an invitation to eat and not an invitation to panic. At the last moment the car screeched to a halt, knocking down one of the steers. The groggy steer got to his

282

feet and ran off and the tourist, ashen-faced, got out of his car.

"I thought he'd get out of the way when I blew the horn," the tourist said shakily.

"I sorta thought," said the cowman dryly as he sat his horse, "that you might have slowed down just a little."

"Well," the tourist said brightly, "I guess I didn't hurt him any."

"If you want to leave me your name and address," the cowman drawled, "I'll sure be happy to let you know if I find out you done him any good."

The route I was following now is one of the oldest trails in the United States, having first been traveled by the early Spaniards who made their way up the valley to Santa Fe. By continuing to stay with the river to Caballo I could then cut sharply west and be in the timbered mountains from then on. It was a little longer but I'd had enough desert by now and the thought of the pine and juniper country ahead was a welcome one.

Near the little Mexican village of Berino, a movement along a levee caught my eye. It was a quiet Sunday morning with little activity and the flash of red approaching from the rear soon proved to be a young Mexican boy on a white horse. The horse was in a dead run on top of the levee and the flying white mane against the boy's red shirt made a handsome sight. After catching up to me he slowed down and then angled over to the edge of the road where I was riding. He spoke almost no English but rode along with me for two hours or more. Evidently he'd seen me pass his home, because I'd noticed the white horse standing in a pen. He must have run out, thrown on a bridle, jumped on bareback and caught me just for the ride. We came to a little store where I hoped to be able to get him a bar of candy or a

Coke, but the store was closed, and after I got him to pose for a photograph he waved and headed back toward home.

As we were approaching Las Cruces in the latter part of the day, the sky above the mountains that lay ahead began to darken. Purplish black clouds roiled up and brilliant slashes of lightning split their way through. I unlashed my new poncho so as to have it handy, but the storm as it approached looked to be the type that would hardly be put off by a mere raincoat. Ahead on the left stood a handsome white-stuccoed, two-story, adobe ranch house. To its rear was a large brown adobe-brick barn with a wide-open door. It looked to be the only cover in sight, so I moved Sioux into a fast trot in an effort to beat the rain. We made the driveway with plenty of time to spare and I hitched Sioux and went up to the house to ask permission to pull under the barn roof until the storm passed over. One of the children answering the door informed me that his parents would be right home and that he thought it would be all right.

While I stood talking to the kids with a wary eye keeping tabs on the sky, the clouds began to dissipate. In a matter of minutes the sky was completely clear, so I decided to move on. I'd just climbed on Sioux and started out the drive when Jay and Barbara Borrett returned in their station wagon. Thinking to explain to them that their children had not been approached by some sort of depraved character, I climbed down and introduced myself, explaining why I'd stopped in.

"Those clouds always do that," Barbara laughed. "When we first moved here, I thought sure that it was about to pour. They seem to break up over the mountains."

"Are you headed any place in particular tonight?" Jay asked.

I wasn't and said so.

"Why not stay over with us?" he suggested.

This time, quite literally, a dark cloud turned out to have

a silver lining. Jay, a former British naval officer, had come to this country some years back, had taken up citizenship and is now a nuclear physicist at the White Sands Missile Range west of nearby Las Cruces. Barbara, his Chicago-born wife, and their children ranging from the toddler age to the teens lived in this lovely old thick-walled adobe ranch house that was formerly the headquarters of the Corralitos Ranch, a huge operation that had at one time extended over most of southwest New Mexico and part of Arizona. The high-ceilinged house with its broad veranda, handsome staircase and paneled walls made me think of the plantation manors of the deep South, although the Spanish flavor of its architecture was unmistakable.

The fields in the rear of the house were being farmed and ranched by a neighboring rancher, and the corrals were occupied by cattle and a couple of fine saddle mules. Virgil, the rancher, was an avid hunter and used the mules for his saddle trips into the remote mountain areas. Sioux moved in with them while I carried my "luggage" houseward.

I'd had a Las Cruces horseshoer recommended to me, and Jay and Barbara suggested I stay long enough to have the work done at their place. However, an early-morning phone call brought the news that the man I sought was to be out of town for several days. The rear shoes were paper-thin by now and I was leery of taking on the mountains that lay ahead without Sioux's starting out newly shod.

Barbara drove me into downtown Las Cruces, where the Cliff Yarborough saddle shop solved the problem. Cliff was busy on a handmade saddle as I walked into his leathery-smelling shop. After I explained my problems, he agreed to come out to the Borretts' early in the morning to shoe my mare himself.

Cliff Yarborough arrived bright and early in the morning and in short order equipped Sioux's feet for the moun-

tains ahead. While being shod, Sioux did considerable fussing about her ears and I suspected that the type of tick
common in this region might be the cause.

Barbara suggested that Dr. Johnson's office would be
convenient to my route through Las Cruces, so with thanks
to the Borrett family, I saddled up and headed out.

Following the railroad right of way through town made
Las Cruces an easy maneuver; once through town, the
veterinarian's office was only a block away. While Dr. Johnson was treating Sioux's ear condition, it occurred to me
that the mosquito season would soon be upon us, at least as
long as we were in the Rio Grande Valley, and that the
mosquito-borne sleeping sickness virus was a danger in this
country as it was at home. Sioux's annual booster shot was
almost due, so Dr. Johnson took care of all our needs and,
like others charged me a token fee.

Before leaving town I made one more stop to pick up a
supply of grain and found that an El Paso television news-
cast had preceded us. I bought as much grain as I could
carry with convenience but in leaving mentioned casually
that Sioux liked the white tortilla corn, considerably more
expensive than standard horse feed. While I was packing up
the grain, the young Mexican store clerk came out with a
bag of the white corn as a bonus. My protests were in vain,
so I piled it on top of the rest of the usual gear and we
headed out. Our errands had taken so much of the day that I
didn't expect to get far, and I knew that Sioux would lighten
her burden of extra feed that night and the following
morning.

A few miles out of town we came to George McKinney's
motel and grocery store. The store and motel fronted a pecan
grove with irrigation grass between the rows and I was
tempted to pull in for the night. We hadn't gotten far but
Sioux was newly shod and when possible I preferred to give

her a chance to get used to the change as gradually as possible. In addition, it was a hot day and I felt it wise not to overtax her after she had just had an innoculation.

George and his wife, an instantly congenial gray-haired couple, were behind the counter and they were willing to install Sioux on their grass with no reservations. A short conversation informed me that George had grown up in the Davis Mountain country of west Texas and was an old schoolmate of Duncan Kingston's. He seemed determined to prove to me that my Rhode Island money was no good in Las Cruces and not only refused to charge for the room but insisted that I join his wife, his grandson and him as their dinner guest at the famous Mexican restaurant La Posta in nearby Old Mesilla.

Old Mesilla is a quaint little Mexican village near Las Cruces steeped in early New Mexico history. Almost all of its buildings are constructed of natural adobe brick and the streets are unpaved. The old courthouse still stands where Billy the Kid was tried and sentenced to be hung. Nearby is the old Wells Fargo building and La Posta itself is the building that originally housed the Butterfield stage station. Its visitors have ranged from Billy the Kid and Pancho Villa to Douglas MacArthur.

After closing hours at the store, we got in George's car, picked up his teenage grandson and drove down to La Posta, where the wildly effervescent hostess Katy all but embraced me, following George's introduction. Potted trees and vines with live parrots and birds gave the restaurant an outdoor garden look, set off by warm Mexican color. My aging digestive system rebels at times against highly spiced foods; however, this doesn't prevent me from enjoying them. In this instance, my liver cooperated and I had no trouble.

My hosts went so far out of their way to show me points of interest and entertain me that I felt much more like some

287

sort of honored guest than a "tourist" who'd stopped by looking for a night's lodging. At times I wondered if I'd developed an underfed, woebegone appearance that made me an object of pity.

Heading north out of Las Cruces, we followed the banks of the Rio Grande for a while, with the Organ Mountains on our right. Toward the end of the day a commercial campsite came up and we turned in. The camp was situated on a loop of the Rio Grande in a salt cedar grove with some fairly good grass. A couple of groups were picnicking and fishing, but it was fairly unoccupied this early in the year.

I'd just finished up a dinner of tortillas and dried beef when a young couple returned from fishing with their children. The kids came over to visit with Sioux and then went over to where their parents were preparing a picnic supper on one of the tables. Shortly one of the children returned bearing his parents' invitation to join the family for watermelon. I walked over and found when we had introduced ourselves that the man, Don Horner, was a mathemetician from the University of New Mexico.

Personally, I'm unable to make change for more than ten dollars without considerable brow-furrowing; however, there are a number of mathemeticians in my family, one of whom, a cousin, is of considerable prominence.

I name-dropped the cousin, Saunders MacLane, and my status rose immediately. Don had attended his lectures, met him and was enthusiastic in his admiration. Being aware of my personal arithmetical shortcomings, I couldn't take on a too greatly inflated sense of importance from the connection.

Dusk brought mosquitos out in some force, and the Horners piled in their car and left Sioux and me as sole occupants of the park. I bedded down on top of a picnic bench with Sioux hitched to the end and hoped that the whine of the mosquitos would cease with the cooler night

288

air. Some granddaddy bullfrogs chimed in to add to the racket but I finally dropped off.

At about one-thirty in the morning, Sioux stamped and awakened me and I peered out of the sleeping bag to see what she was fussing about. The parking lights of an automobile were coasting quietly and slowly toward us from the point where the entrance curved through the trees from the highway. Earlier in the evening there had been a few unsavory-looking types fishing nearby. They'd left before the Horners, but now, as the car came closer, I began to entertain faint suspicions. When the car eased to a halt directly opposite the opening of the campsite where I was parked, my sense of uneasiness was tripled and I reared up on one elbow. So many people had cautioned me that now I always slept with gun and flashlight inside the sleeping bag and, whether the occupants of the car knew it or not, they were thoroughly covered. It was too dark to see more than the outline of the car, but as they were no more than twenty feet away I'd have heard a door opening. For a long thirty seconds the car sat idling; then it backed up, turned around and drove out. I had probably interrupted nothing more serious than romance by my presence, but I decided to stay awake for a while longer and burn up a few cigarettes.

We passed the ruins of Fort Selden next day. An adobe brick fort, it had been first built in 1865, later abandoned and then reoccupied in 1881 during an Apache uprising. Douglas MacArthur had spent some of his childhood years here when his father was in command of the post. Now nothing remains but crumbling roofless walls. Rumors of buried treasure hastened its end, because treasure hunters dug holes in the walls, which weakened the structures and allowed the weather to get at the adobe.

The road to Hatch was hot and arid. From there an additional forty miles of desert country would take us to

Caballo Lake and at that point a westward turn would head into the mountains. By noon I was heartily sick of the heat, sand and greasewood flats; and worst of all I was beset with mosquitos from the Rio Grande.

I stopped at a small motel in Hatch to freshen up for a two-day ride to the mountains and was on the verge of packing up to start out when there was a knock at the door. To my surprise, the Borretts were outside in their car. Jay, Barbara and the kids were on their way for a weekend ride and picnic in the mountains when they'd noticed Sioux grazing outside my room.

"Why don't you leave Sioux here for a day's rest and go with us for a preview of the mountains?" Jay suggested. "We're going over the Black Range to Silver City and we'll have you back here before dark."

It sounded like a pleasant day's change and I'd noticed a large grassy area near the feed store, so I took them up on their offer. A quick trip with Jay to the feed store secured permission to tether Sioux in the grass for the day and we were off. At Caballo Lake, a left turn started a steady and gradual climb. The dark-shouldered mountains ahead were now clearly visible and soon we rose to juniper country. The road followed a cleft in the hills and crossed back and forth over a clear mountain stream.

Almost suddenly the clear pungent smell of pine was all about and Jay drove off on a dirt side road that led us into a grove of towering ponderosa pines with the cold mountain brook cutting through the center. It was a wonderful spot for a picnic and my only regret was that Sioux was still down in the heat of the flatlands. This fact apparently also bothered Barbara, who began to conjure up a scheme to remedy the situation.

"After we get back to Hatch and drop you off," she

290

suggested, "why don't we drive home, pick up a trailer and haul Sioux and you to Hillsboro?"

"Thanks for the thought," I demurred, "but that would make a long drive for you and be a hell of an imposition. Anyway, we'll make Hillsboro in two days."

Frankly I was not enthusiastic about the forty miles of dry country separating us from the mountains. We'd had about all of that sort of going that I needed. However, the Borretts lived at Mesilla Park back on the other side of Las Cruces and after a day of driving over the Black Range it seemed to me that Jay would be ready to quit. He wasn't, it seemed.

"I enjoy driving," he insisted. "We can take the kids home, pick up the trailer and have you in the mountains in no time."

My refusals weakened and the outcome was that we drove over the Black Range, which enabled me to spot out likely campsites, dropped down the mountain road from Emory Pass to Silver City, headed south to Deming, and across to Hatch. The Borretts then drove all the way home to Mesilla Park, picked up a trailer and returned to my motel.

By the time they got the trailer attached darkness had fallen and they had difficulty hooking up the lights on the trailer. Consequently it was well into midevening by the time they got back to Hatch. Sioux should certainly have been everlastingly grateful to these people, as was I. It was late evening by the time we got loaded and hauled to Hillsboro, where there was a small motel, and by the time we got settled, which involved waking up the lady who ran the place, the Borretts had to return back down the long road to Mesilla Park. I had enjoyed the interlude at the Borretts' home, had been hauled across the last forty miles of desolate country and had wound up with a preview of the mountains ahead.

Hillsboro, where we awakened in the morning, is a partially inhabited ghost town where some six million dollars worth of gold and silver was extracted over the years. It's now a sleepy little village with a tree-lined main street and lovely mountain-foothill surroundings. I stopped briefly at the museum in the building that once housed a hotel and restaurant run by Sadie Orchard, a well-known madam. A quick onceover of the collection gave me the impression that the Hillsboro of the late eighties and early nineties was indeed a lively place. Today it looks much like a movie set with its high sidewalks and false-front buildings quietly awaiting the appearance of the actors.

It was a warm spring day; with each foot of elevation the country became more beautiful and I lingered longer than I should have. The clear mountain stream that I'd seen the day before with the Borretts is called Percha Creek. It comes out of the high mountains over a clean gravel bed and flows the length of this valley that we were ascending. Sioux and I had drunk so much alkali water over the past months that the change was a real treat. I bellied down alongside her and we drank our fill. I got up conscious of the incredible fact that there was no mud on me.

The road wound upward through the notch worn by Percha Creek and some nine miles above Hillsboro we came to Kingston, another reminder of the mining boom that took place in these mountains. The little town, virtually empty at this time of year, was once active enough to support Lillian Russell and her troupe. I stopped once to let Sioux graze and climbed over the fence to look at the old cemetery just out of town. With the civilian markers, some of them illegible, were a number of army headstones that must have related to the days when the Apaches raided these mining communities.

Out of Kingston, the road climbed swiftly and switch-backed its way through pine-clad ridges. By midafternoon we looked back and down on the little toy villages of Kingston and Hillsboro and, far beyond, the Rio Grande Valley. The elevation became a thing to contend with; prior to this our highest climb had been at the Bartholomews in the Davis Mountains in Texas. Sioux's breathing was becoming labored, and when we came to a steep climb where I dismounted and led her, I quickly found out why: a mere hundred yards of walking had me gasping for air. From then on to Emory Pass, we made the trip in short laps with time out for breathing.

From time to time small tumbledown cabins and the dark openings of long-abandoned mine shafts spotted the slopes below. The timber at this level was almost exclusively ponderosa pine with the wonderful smell of Christmas; it was hard to believe that the sandy desert was still within visible range. The day before I'd been excited by the sights and smells as we passed through by car. Today, by horse without the restrictions of roof and windshield, the feelings aroused were more than redoubled. The tassel-eared squirrels, looking like a cross between large gray squirrels and rabbits, paused in their business of stripping pine cones to watch us pass, and the quiet of the mountains was broken by the plaintive cascading call of the canyon wrens. Several times deer browsing along the steep-sided edge of the road moved back to give us the right of way, but they didn't seem particularly frightened – only careful.

The road follows the only possible route by clinging to the sides of the ridges and much of it is a series of deep U's. You come to one of the outside curves and look a short distance across a deep cut to see the continuation of the same road just ahead. To get to it, however, it's necessary to swing in along the convolutions of the ridge and then out again to finally attain the section of road that was so close a long way back. A bird could have flown to our final destina-

293

tion while we were thinking about it, and as it was, dusk was nearly upon us before we finally leveled off at the nearly nine-thousand-foot elevation of Emory Pass. A level area at the pass allows the passerby to look back over the country behind and we turned in for a look and a breathing spell.

The mountain ridges we'd just climbed were now diffused by the pre-evening mists; far beyond where the late sun's rays were still reflected the tiny speck of Hillsboro was as yet visible. Extending far below was the Rio Grande Valley with Caballo Lake making a bluish smear in the desert. Even beyond that, probably some sixty miles away, stretched the pale sandy wastes of the Jornada del Muerto, the old Spanish trail named the Journey of Death.

Our climb had been leisurely and now the mountain air was cooling. We still had several miles to go to reach the camp area I'd decided on the day before. Mountain grasses were sparse and scattered at this height and I'd observed plenty of grass and water at the officially designated camp area at Iron Creek. Now headed down the western slopes, the light lingered awhile longer. When the last rays dropped behind the mountain it was as though someone had turned out the lights.

Iron Creek splashed noisily below on the left side of the road and I'm sure that Sioux was as thirsty as I. The road shelved off sharply to the creekbed below, its shoulders crumbled away in places, so we stayed on the solid roadbed. Making camp in the dark is seldom much fun and I began muttering at myself for having dawdled earlier in the day. Still I knew where I was headed, which eased my mind considerably. Had I also known of the complications of the camp area I might have been less complacent, and I wasn't long in finding out.

The Black Range is part of the Gila National Forest and as such is leased in part to cattlemen. The ranges are open

294

on the road and sectioned off by cattle guards that cross the highway. Each cattle guard I'd come to on the road had been equipped with a gate, most of which worked fairly well. In order to keep the cattle out of the public campground the area was fenced in, and as I came to the entrance I found the usual cattle guard. I got out the flashlight and started looking for the gate. There was none. I stumbled down the fence line in one direction, then in the other, and found no way of getting in with anything other than an automobile.

Sioux was hungry and tired, as was I, and the grazing was all on the other side of the fence. Up to now I'd been entirely virtuous about cutting fences but here, to me, was an unforgivable outrage committed by the United States government. With righteous anger and a touch of unholy glee, I got out my lightweight hatchet, selected a likely location for a gate and went to work on the wires. The fence was stout and I was obliged to hold a flashlight in one hand and chop with the other. But with justice on my side, I whacked my way through the strands, all the while mentally composing a blistering note to Stewart Udall. For a while I even contemplated sending the Department of the Interior a bill for gate construction.

Once inside with Sioux contentedly cropping grass, I found my mood considerably ameliorated by fire and dinner, but I still rather hoped that one of the park rangers would stop in and inquire how I got in with a horse. I'd have been happy to explain in some detail. I'm no longer mad at Mr. Udall but I would like to suggest that the federal government place gates next to their cattle guards — at least until a law is passed prohibiting anyone from going camping other than by automobile. My only regret about my actions was over the series of nicks put in the edge of my hatchet by the wire.

In spite of the difficulties, the camp was a particularly

enjoyable one. There were great quantities of ponderosa pine branches lying about and although this wood soon piles up a thick patina of char on cooking utensils, it has a delightful aroma. Thanks to the very thickness of the coating, I was able to enjoy the smell long after leaving the ponderosa country by merely heating up one of the buckets or pans. The sounds of Iron Creek were as pleasant as the smells. The creek itself chattered throughout the night, several coyotes started a high-pitched falsetto duet, and with each passing of the night breeze the pine branches high overhead set up a soft whispering.

With the coming of day, I let Sioux graze to her satisfaction while I cooked a leisurely breakfast. I'd had a cyst between my shoulder blades for a number of years that had never caused me any trouble — one of those things that could be taken care of someday when it was convenient. With the coming of hot weather and dust in west Texas it had started to get troublesome; however, I'd continued to ignore it in the hopes that if I did it would go away. It hadn't and by now the point had been reached where medical attention could no longer be stalled off. Much as I would have enjoyed a leisurely trip down through the mountains on the west slope of the Black Range, I decided I'd better get to Silver City without delay. It was a much longer day's ride than I usually attempted but at least the path lay downhill.

We came to the main road entering Silver City from Deming and I continued pretty well into town, finally selecting an attractive motel, which as usual I judged by the quality of grass on its lawn.

Once again low on funds, I hurried down to Joe Hurley's Drugstore, where preliminary reconnaissance with the Borretts had indicated there was a Western Union office. I had to speed up the last few miles in order to catch the

298

pharmacy before closing time and once again luck was working for me.

Joe Hurley evinced immediate interest in my project, and when I explained my aches and pains and need of medical attention, I found that the telegraph office's location in his store couldn't have been more adroit. Directly behind the store was a new and modern clinic building, almost a small hospital, staffed with several excellent physicians and surgeons who also happened to be fellow horsemen. Clark's Motel was a short two or three block walk from the clinic and across from the motel was an excellent restaurant.

Bob Cecil and his wife, owners of Clark's Motel, were perfectly willing to have Sioux tied outside my room, although their establishment was close to the center of town. This turned out to be a wonderful convenience when I found out that I'd be forced to lay over for a full week.

When I phoned Dr. Richard Walsh, one of the surgeons who ran the clinic, he gave me an appointment for the next day. On hearing of the complications involved he offered to put Sioux up at his home in the event that my difficulty took longer than a day, which, as it turned out, it did.

Dick Walsh laid me out on the table next morning and got out his tools. I thought I detected swearing noises and asked how it looked.

"Like hell is how it looks," he snorted. "What were you waiting for, your birthday?"

With that he went to work on me. He was one of the leading surgeons in this part of New Mexico and enjoyed the respect and admiration of ranchers and hunting guides throughout the entire wilderness area surrounding Silver City. A young man not much over forty, if that, he'd come to this country from New York some ten years ago and had become a New Mexican with a vengeance. He was an avid horseman whose hobbies were cowboy polo and lion hunting, and a call for assistance from deep in the mountains immediately had him and his medical kit winding the steep trails on horseback. I later heard of occasions when he had whisked into the clinic for a fast leg-setting job with his white tunic covering Levi's, boots and spurs. This was probably a slight exaggeration; however, the rancher who mentioned it to me claimed with obvious delight that he was pretty sure Dick Walsh would operate with his spurs if he could fit them into the sterilizer. Out of the office, dressed in faded Levi's, blue shirt, scuffed boots and a thoroughly disreputable old black hat, he was a far remove from the Park Avenue surgeon he might have become. It was also evident that he was enjoying life to the hilt.

Now he wanted me to stay in town for a week of treatment, following which I'd be able to go on my way, stopping for further checkups along the road

I wasn't certain I would be able to keep Sioux at the motel for a week, and if not Dick offered to let her stay with his horses. But a check with Bob Cecil indicated that he didn't object to her presence and, as always, I preferred to keep her nearby.

If I had to get laid up anywhere, Silver City was an ideal location. I'd been in the town some twenty-odd years before and at that time it resembled a Hollywood version of a cowtown. The high sidewalks still bordered the downtown streets, but it was now a lively, bustling city that had become quite modern in appearance. Despite its new look and burgeoning size, it had retained the friendly, casual attitude of the small town. Located in a dip in the rolling foothills of the mountains, it was at the point where the desert country to the south merged with the timber country to the north. The climate is favorable almost year-round and the elevation and sparklingly clear air combine to make the sunlight the most brilliant I've seen. My first day in town made the purchase of sunglasses an essential move and I wore them almost constantly.

Clark's grocery store was across the street from the motel and although my purchases were limited to little more than a few apples and carrots for Sioux, I was assigned my personal coffee cup on my first visit. With the cup came an invitation to tap the ever-brewing coffeepot at any time of the day.

Sioux occupied a small railed-in section of lawn next to my end room. A tree provided shade, and from her vantage point above the sidewalk she was free to observe the town's activities or doze as she desired. A local feed store cheerfully delivered a bale of alfalfa and such feed as I could use; my problems were nonexistent.

The week passed restfully with little more for me to do than make the daily trip to the clinic, eat, read and nap. Joe Hurley stopped by almost every noon to take me to lunch and I'm sure I kept him from his work at the pharmacy much more than I should have through the long and interesting conversations in which we got involved.

The only trouble of any sort came during our fourth or fifth night, when Sioux broke loose. The day before, I'd saddled her up and taken an exercise ride across the hills in back of the motel. At two A.M. my room phone rang and Bob Cecil told me that some kids had stopped by to report that Sioux had been seen running up the road. A glance outside my room proved her missing and I hurriedly dressed and got my flashlight. The woven nylon stake rope was neatly snapped at a point a foot or so from her halter — a situation difficult to explain. I got her bridle and started out.

I tried tracking her by flashlight with little luck. I found the tracks we'd made on our ride across the hills but was unable to detect any others. Normally, if frightened, she wouldn't go far and I squatted and tried to see her silhouette

301

against the night horizon. My efforts earned me nothing but cactus scratches and sore feet, so after a couple of hours I walked back to my room to wait until daybreak, at which time I'd stand a chance of seeing her. I wasn't sure which course she might have taken and my chief fear was of the main highway, where a certain amount of all-night truck traffic would be a menace. I'd observed a few batches of locoweed when riding into Silver City, but I doubted that she'd bother with it, since ordinarily a well-fed horse won't touch it unless he's become addicted.

At the first trace of dawn, I headed out toward the hills along the main highway, a section I hadn't checked before. I saw several horses far off to the east, but the rising sun made it impossible to ascertain their color. A long walk allowed me to determine that she was not among them and I headed back toward the motel to try the other direction again. By now I was sick with worry, for I was certain that normally she'd have returned to my room after recovering from whatever fright had caused her to break away.

Stumbling down the last hill before reaching the motel, I looked up and there on the crest of the hill in back of the motel was Bob Cecil's station wagon driving slowly over the ridge. Bob's arm was stuck out the window on the driver's side; in his hand was a rope to which was attached a demure and innocent paint mare walking daintily alongside the car. Where a moment before I'd have welcomed her with open arms, I now was tempted to lead-pipe her on top of her thick head. When I reached the motel Bob was sitting behind the wheel still holding Sioux and grinning broadly.

"Bet this is the first motel where you've had horse-wrangling services," he said.

I agreed that it was and asked him where he'd found her.

"The phone rang about an hour ago," he explained, still

302

chuckling. "A retired army man with horses a mile or so up the back road said she was out next to his fence visiting his horses. He'd seen her out here at the motel so he knew where she belonged."

I led her back to her place under the tree and fed her before I spent the next two hours pulling cactus stickers out of her sides and legs. A greenhorn in the land of cactus, she, I hoped, in the future would rely on me to do the path finding. The day before, we'd ridden quite close to the horses she'd gone to visit. She probably smelled them and once loose had decided to make their acquaintance.

On Sunday, which was to be my last day in town, Dick Walsh invited me to have dinner with him and his family and then accompany him to the polo field where the team was to have a practice game.

If I recall the number correctly, the Walshes had thirteen children. The atmosphere of their home was a testimonial to large families; every family member presently at home seemed busy, cheerful and interested in what he was doing with the same sort of enthusiastic energy displayed by the parents. Somehow there was far less confusion than is found in many much smaller families and I was amused by a sort of military precision Dick employed in the loading of the car after we had dinner. He stood at the rear door of a large station wagon. The children lined up and, with a gesture similar to that of a ticket collector at a theater entrance, he directed them to their seats in the car. Their weimaraner dog, who waited at the end of the procession, jumped in after the last of the children. We got in the front seat and were off. No one whined about which seat he'd gotten; there was no fuss whatsoever.

Monday morning Dick Walsh checked me out and gave me the name of a practical nurse in one of the small mountain towns that I'd be passing through. Bob Cecil, a rock hound, woodsman and motorcycle buff, drove me to the post office on the back seat of his motorcycle so that I could mail some materials home, and I was ready to take off in a northwesterly slant for the Arizona line.

I'd planned the route from this point on to stay in the high-altitude forest country as much as possible. It was to be an uphill climb from here to Arizona. The entire area is steeped in comparatively recent history. Ghost towns, a few still lightly inhabited, are the sites of mines that produced millions of dollars' worth of gold and silver. Old fort locations are almost as numerous, since the army was hard put to protect the gold seekers from Mangus Colorado and Apaches that followed after him.

On the first day's ride out of Silver City, shortly after we'd crossed the continental divide, a young couple, Gerry and Darlene Billings, stopped me on their way into town. Their ranch, which I would come to by the end of an average day's ride, lay about a mile off the road. They directed me where to turn in and said they planned to be back by the time I got there. A large ranch, it was built by her grandfather in the early days of New Mexico; the only change was that new dwelling houses had replaced the old originals. The young Billingses were Mormons and, although they invited me to a sumptuous dinner and breakfast, they apologized several times for the fact that they had no tea or coffee, both beverages banned by their religion.

The Mormon religion is strong throughout much of this part of New Mexico and Arizona. I don't know whether to attribute it to the religion itself or to the fact that the religion is not an easy one to belong to, but I do feel obliged to comment that I have yet to meet a Mormon I haven't admired. It would be difficult for me to agree with all their views, particularly when it comes to the efficacy of abandoning coffee, but in my contacts with members, from the young

306

missionaries in the East to the ranchers in the West, I've found them a close-knit and self-sufficient breed.

For the first time on the entire trip I became plagued with a rather severe headache, and when I came to the crossing of the Gila River a general store was a welcome sight. I popped a healthy dosage of pills and sat about for a while washing them down with cold drinks when a man named Bill Heron came in. He asked where I was stopping for the night, I admitted to no firm plan, whereupon he suggested I turn in along the bank of the Gila to where he had a couple of trailers parked. The larger of the two trailers was occupied by Bill and his wife; the other was used for their overflow but was also available for guests. I surmised that mosquitos would be out along the river as soon as dark fell. Also, I'd never stayed in a trailer, and Bill, a former native of the Gila country who'd returned to his original home territory, would be a source of interesting information. A large pasture was fenced in all around the trailer where I'd be able to turn Sioux loose; this would give her freedom to move around and to roll if the mosquitos got too voracious.

Like most newcomers to trailers, I was impressed with the economy of space and convenience possible in small quarters. The screens would assure a restful night. After an excellent dinner, Bill spoke of some old Indian dwellings recently uncovered on the high bluffs overlooking the river valley. We walked up the steep slope a hundred yards away from the tree-lined river and coming out on top found the uncovered walls and floors of the six-hundred-year-old houses of this ancient tribe.

A new highway was being surveyed, with a modern bridge destined to cross the Gila from one bluff to the other, and in the process of surveying and testing for the footings, the village had been unearthed. Bill mentioned that in his

307

childhood years he and his friends had known of the grassy mounds on both sides of the river but hadn't attached any significance to them. Now carefully uncovered by archeological teams, a fascinating complex of square, connected apartments has come to light. They were built of adobe bricks, and had doors and fireplaces. In the center of the floor of several of the units, the teams had unearthed tiny skeletons of infants buried below the floor level.

Just above on a slightly higher bluff, the rocks had good-sized round holes in their surfaces where the Indians would grind their corn with a sort of mortar and pestle technique.

When I'd driven up this highway in the early forties, it had been a dirt road all the way from Silver City to Springerville, Arizona. Now it was paved, a disappointment to me; nevertheless, traffic was almost nonexistent. Approaching Buckhorn, a one-store town in which the store was closed, I was a little disconcerted to find myself sharing the road with a light plane that made one pass, then landed behind me and came taxiing along the road. The lone occupant, an Arizonan, was checking on a well-drilling crew nearby and casually landed his plane in the road at the point closest to where the crew was working. A passing automobile was a rare sight, and human contacts were scarce from here on.

Winding down into the canyon where Dry Creek flows, we seemed miles from anyone or anywhere. I'd planned to take Bill Heron's recommendation and go on to Frisco Hot Springs, but on coming back up out of the valley we approached a particularly attractive ranch off to the left of the road. As usual a hound announced our passing and Ray Foster stepped out to see what the dog was commenting on. A ruggedly built ranch house, barn and corrals occupied the level area. In moments Ray was serving dinner to me in the kitchen, although he'd already finished his, and Sioux was ears deep in the feed rack of the corral.

The ranch, dating back into the last century, was known as the SI ($\frac{\omega}{I}$) and belonged to Jim Henry, who with his wife was off vacationing. Ray Foster, Henry's nephew, was keeping an eye on the place during their absence and he seemed happy to have company. Far from public power lines, the hum of a diesel generator provided electricity and all the conveniences of city living.

Moving into the comfortable living room for the evening, I almost felt that I knew the Henrys. A framed photo of the rugged-looking rancher, a mountain lion slung across his saddle, gave me a verification of my picture of him; the warmth, comfort and solidity of the place told more than the photo. An anachronistic touch came just before we turned in for the night when Ray turned on the television set and we wound up watching the *Tonight Show* with Johnny Carson. Five miles up Dry Creek, the maps list the country as primitive area; a short run with hounds would be more than likely to produce a mountain lion. I wouldn't see another house for a good many miles, yet here, with the aid of a generator and electronics, the show which to me more than any other typified the show business flavor of the big city was as close as the dial.

I'd been told that there was a nurse named Gladys Clanton in Glenwood who would be able to change the dressing on the incision between my shoulderblades. This troublesome cyst was in the most unreachable spot it could have chosen.

Glenwood was probably one of the most attractive little towns along this stretch. High red bluffs surround the village, which sits astride White Water Creek where it flows into the San Francisco River. The bluffs are sprinkled with juniper; the big craggy pine-covered mountains supply the

309

background. The river, at least at this time of year, boils swiftly over a gravelly bottom, its ice-cold water indicating its origins in the mountain snowbanks. A motel situated on the bank of the stream made us comfortable for the night. An excellent and congenial café next door with a broad expanse of grass in its rear took care of both our dining requirements.

I took a short walk up the shady street to stock up on horse feed and contact Gladys Clanton. By the time I returned to my room, I felt acquainted with half the residents and wished I knew the remainder. There's an undefinable something that some places have which makes a stranger feel completely at home. Whatever it is, Glenwood has it, and I left in the morning with a strong desire to someday return.

A steep climb and turn and Glenwood was out of sight. Miles of pine-covered mountains lay ahead to the Arizona line and beyond. Although we were well along into spring, gleaming white patches showed on the flanks of the mountains where shade had delayed the sun's rays in their job of melting the drifted snow. "Breathtaking beauty" is a hackneyed phrase that anyone should cringe from using. I don't know how else to describe the scene. Deep rocky canyons, the dark greens of tall pines, the lighter fresh tints of willows along the streambeds, cerulean blue skies, and maybe most of all the hugeness of it all. At times I felt that Sioux and I were like some sort of tiny brown and white ant and its even tinier rider struggling with unbelievable slowness and even more incredible presumptuousness to cross over a great upheaval of earth, rocks and trees that was simply too vast to be undertaken. Automobile and plane travel have reduced the land for us to the point where we no longer can grasp its full impressiveness without returning once in a while to a simpler way. Perhaps a comparison with modern ways of getting about actually enhances the greatness of the country and perhaps our forbears were less impressed for the reason that they expected it to be big. The pungency of pine and the more delicate scent of the grasses are aspects of personal contact with the land that the color camera for all its skill misses entirely. Even olfactory senses like mine, numbed by tobacco, can't fail to make the smells an integral part of the whole. And the whole is a stirring experience. It's breathtakingly beautiful — that's what it is.

Our last visit to a New Mexico ranch was the result of an invitation left for me at the café in Glenwood. Billy Ray Littlefield and his wife had mentioned to the proprietor of the café that a twenty-seven-mile ride would take me to the ranch where they were located and that I'd be welcome to stop over with them.

The ranch was known as the Maxwell Ranch, although it was in the process of changing hands. It was located high in the heart of the pine country, and all the buildings and corrals were of log construction. As we rode in through the gate, I felt as though I was entering a calendar picture.

I hadn't met the Littlefields but I guess I was easily recognized by Sioux, because they came out and made us welcome before we'd covered more than half of the distance in from the gate. They were a young couple. Billy, having majored in range management, was following up the college courses with practical ranch experience.

After dinner we walked over to the main house to meet the foreman, Dee, a tall, slim man with pale blue eyes. We sat down with our coffee and Dee appraised me with a sly grin hovering around the corners of his eyes.

"Bet you got a fair set of callouses on your butt," he suggested.

I admitted that the nurses in Silver City had complained about my dulling the points of the penicillin needles.

311

"I once rode a hundred miles in one day," Dee observed, "but not on one horse. We'd finished working cattle up in the mountains a hundred miles from the home ranch. We piled all our gear in a truck and I drove the horse herd into the ranch. I'd strike out in a lope driving the herd and when my horse got tired, I'd drop a loop on a fresh one and change horses. I swapped horses seven times that day but we made it in. Guess I was some ready to get off when I got there."

"I'll bet you were," I agreed. At this time, I doubt that any amount of riding would have made me sore; however, cramping in the hips was something that did bother me toward the end of the longer days. That may have been due to the fact that I was no longer nineteen years old. As it had worked out, I never had to make more than forty miles at any time. For the sake of Sioux with her heavy load, I tried to keep the rides to twenty miles. Scarcity of water had forced a number of longer days but for the most part we'd been able to keep the daily mileage reasonably low. When you're in condition for it, twenty miles a day is a pleasant ride, twenty-five to thirty isn't too bad, but from that point on it's no longer fun but a race and I'd started out to have a pleasant and leisurely tour by horse. Sioux was in the peak of physical condition that would be enjoyed by any athlete in daily training. She could do forty miles when called on with little perceptible tiring, but I'm sure that loaded as she was, a steady diet of that sort of treatment would have taken the edge off.

The little town of Luna was the last stop in New Mexico and the first encounter with a lumbering operation of the type found in much of the country ahead. A column of smoke rose up from the little clearing in the valley and I soon saw that it was emanating from a large conical stack near a sawmill. Evidently the bark and other waste runs out of the mill on a conveyor to be burned in the huge inciner-

312

ator device that disposes of the material safely. A strikingly handsome building on the edge of town proved to be the Mormon church and I found that Luna was largely a Mormon settlement.

I hadn't really planned to stop at Luna but as always I found it tempting to pull up at an attractive-looking village, as this one was. A heavily constructed general store was centrally located; its walls were of squared-off logs that dated back to the days of hostile Apaches, as indicated by a few remaining rifle ports. Adjoining the buildings to the rear was a pleasant motel unit and café run by Rilla McNeil and her son. She turned out to be not only an excellent cook but a trained nurse and kindly offered to change the dressing for me. Springerville, Arizona, would be the first town of any size and that was several days ahead. I was glad of the opportunity to start out with a new bandage.

For six months people had asked where I was headed. My stock answer, Arizona, usually drew a wide-eyed reaction. After Luna I was to remind myself that I finally had made Arizona . . . but the Grand Canyon still lay ahead.

.

 **9.**

Along climb through pine country brought us at last to a cattle guard and gate that straddled the state line. A sign bade us adios from New Mexico, another welcomed us into Arizona. Sioux, who always availed herself of the opportunity to graze while I opened gates, tried the grass on both sides of the line but was not visibly impressed with the difference. The country leveled off at this point and after a few miles began to slope down. We'd climbed so much from Las Cruces on that Sioux's horseshoes were nearly worn through at the toes, although the main body of the shoes was not badly worn.

Gradually, the timber began to open up into a mixture of grass and pine. The impression was of being in a great park with rolling, smooth, grassy swells spotted by clumps of ponderosas. It could have been the carefully nurtured greens of a country club golf course except for the absence of man-made devices. Small lakes and ponds were scattered about reflecting the blue sky above. The wonder to me was that there were no hordes of people picnicking or fishing.

We camped that night in an area designated as a public

314

campground; however, I had the whole thing to myself until after I'd finished cooking and eating dinner. Just before dusk, as Sioux was finishing grazing in the heavy grass alongside a mountain stream that cut through the camp, a pickup truck with a large camper rig turned in and stopped nearby. The license plates indicated that the occupants were from California and they were the first of the summer campers that I'd seen. It was now the latter part of May and from here on out the official campsites that I'd had all to myself would doubtless echo to many voices from all points of the map.

Don Gedney came over to chat while his wife Gerry got their dinner going on an outside charcoal brazier, and I offered a cup of my boiled cowboy-style coffee which came complete with floating grounds but no cup. He got a cup and returned to join me. The Gedneys were a young couple who spent their weekends and vacation taking in as many national parks as possible. They were now on an early vacation that would take them over much of the Southwest, and some of the country I had covered.

Don invited me to join them in the camper and we walked over for my first look inside one of these arrangements. To look at it was to covet it — not for me at the time but certainly for later travels. This particular camper had everything from stove to bathroom and the space inside was hard to believe. Four people could have been comfortable at the table. For camping trips with a family, particularly one with small children, it was an ideal arrangement. Then and there I decided that an outfit like this with a two-horse trailer hooked on the rear was a must for my future.

Gerry mentioned that they were planning to stop at the Balmorhea State Park near the Davis Mountains in Texas the following night, so with the smugness of an old China hand, I asked them to convey my greetings to Jack Roberts

315

and his wife and the Hoefs at the café there. If there ever again is a need for a wagon train guide across this part of the country, I'm ready. I'm confident that there are few people currently around with such gems of information as the fact that a water faucet is located in the left rear lawn at McVay's Auto Courts in Van Horn, Texas, or that fossil remains may be found twelve miles west of Denton, Texas, merely by looking in the bar ditch next to the road.

The gobble of unseen wild turkeys awakened me early in the morning. I heard them a number of times from then on but it was useless to look for them. I never actually saw one of the handsome birds in the wild state, although I'm reasonably sure that a little time and effort could have made it possible.

The Gedneys and I left at about the same time but in opposite directions. They would cover in one day's time what had taken me nearly six weeks to travel. Again, as a self-appointed expert, I recommended a slight detour to them so that they wouldn't miss the spectacular scenery of the Black Range east of Silver City.

Elevation all along this section averaged in the nine- to ten-thousand-foot range and the tall pines continued until the country started to drop off toward Springerville. Then pines were replaced by piñons and junipers until we started climbing again.

Horseshoers were slightly more difficult to find in this country, for the reason that most of the local horsemen did their own shoeing. I met a group of forest rangers at Springerville and, due to a delay in waiting for a telegraphed money order, followed their directions to one of the ranger stations four or five miles south of town. Camping there for the night, I met a young ranger and his wife who had recently moved in. Buck Buckner, having graduated from a university where he'd studied forestry and range management, had just joined the Forest Service. He'd earned most of his money while in college by a combination of rodeo bronc riding and horseshoeing, and when I mentioned my problem he offered to do the job for me.

I'd hardly finished my crack-of-dawn coffee when Buck appeared, ready to replace the worn-toed shoes. Equipped with what was to be the last set of shoes we needed, we rode back to Springerville to replenish funds and once more headed west toward the pine country.

The White Mountains of Arizona are as lovely as any I've seen. I think many people visualize Arizona as an arid desert country with little more than rocks and cactus. While this is true of much of the state, a great swath of high pine country starts at the eastern central border of New Mexico and swings northwest two thirds of the way across the state. I had intentionally avoided the drier country in order to stay near water and grazing land. The temperature was also much cooler in the mountains. It was warm by day but the nights were always crisp, and frequently mornings found a skim of ice on the banks of the mountain streams. We'd been bothered by insects at times and these were driven under cover in the cool of night.

A particularly annoying type of fly had made its presence known from the middle of New Mexico. It was grayish in color, and similar in looks and persistence to the yellow and black deer fly familiar to New England woods. Like the deer fly, it refused to be shooed away; only a well-aimed swat was effective. These flies went after Sioux's neck, ears and shoulders, probably because her long tail kept them away from her rear quarters; I was kept busy leaning forward and swatting whenever the breeze died down and allowed them easy access. My spoiled little mare soon got to expect my services, so that when a fly landed low on her shoulder unseen by me, she'd stop and turn her head to look

317

back at me with clear reproach for not tending to my end of the job. She became quite officious about it and always, as soon as I acceded to her demands, she started right up again with no signal on my part. Except in traffic I always rode with a loose rein, and she was pretty much a free agent. She was one of the few horses I'd seen with a completely natural mane and tail. Because I'd never cared for the fads that come and go with the years, I had left her mane and tail completely functional so that she could defend herself from insects when they attacked from the rear.

Another theory I'd developed, possibly foolish, applied to an untrimmed mane and foretop. I'd found that during periods of extreme heat the slight lifting of my hat allowed the dry wind to blow through my hair. The hair, usually wet from perspiration, immediately became cold — in fact almost icy. Probably it worked rather like an air-conditioning unit; anyhow it worked. Using the same idea, I often poured a dollop of water from my canteen on Sioux's foretop. The dry wind made it evaporate quickly and I'm reasonably sure it made her more comfortable, as it did me. A roached or clipped mane and foretop would have been more stylish, but styles be damned when it comes to nature's protective design.

Most of our route now lay through national forests, and at this time of year we saw few people except the rangers and not many of them. Cattle grazed on leased sections but there were no ranch houses, since the actual ranches were located on deeded land some distance away. Camping posed no problem, for the numerous mountain streams were bordered by stands of grass adequate for grazing. The piney mountain surroundings satisfied any aesthetic desires. Of the big game, we saw mule deer most often. They were not usually overly frightened by my presence on Sioux, although on occasion one would remain frozen behind a clump of

318

junipers to spring out and bound away when we inadvertently got too close.

My path led me from the Apache National Forest across the line and into the Fort Apache Indian Reservation. From there, near a little town called Pinetop, we'd go into the Sitgreaves National Forest, where I planned to follow the Mogollon Rim country, locale of the sheepmen-cattlemen wars made famous by Zane Grey. As luck would have it, my back troubles flared up again and the nearest medical help was located in McNary, a sawmill town on the reservation.

Since I was aware of the abuses we've committed on the person of the American Indian, I expected the twenty-odd miles of reservation land on the way to McNary to be a cast-off wasteland unwanted by anyone. Quite to the contrary, some of the most awe-inspiringly lovely land I'd ever seen stretched out as far as the eye could see. Open mountain pastures with fine herds of white-faced cattle reached out on either side for miles. Pine covered the flanks of the mountains with the pale, light green aspens accenting the stream banks; on the shaded side of the peaks, and in fact on several cutbanks near the road, snow still defied the sun.

In spite of my physical miseries, I was so swept up by the grandeur of the place that late in the morning when I came to a small cabin and saw a man come out the door, I decided to speak to him. I was so exhilarated by the clear mountain air and the beauty of the surroundings that I felt a need to speak to someone about it and this man, a Basque sheepherder, was the only person I was to see in the entire day's ride of some thirty miles. He glanced briefly at me as he crossed the road and started to open the gate to the sheep pen. I rode up, stopped Sioux and greeted him.

"I think," I said, gesturing at the mountains, "that you live in one of the most beautiful places on earth."

He looked at me with a certain amount of suspicion, as though he thought perhaps I was being sarcastic.

"She too dam' cold," he said wrapping his arms around his torso and making a shivering motion, and then turned again to open his gate.

The growth of timber got somewhat more dense as we approached McNary, and huge log-hauling trucks began to emerge from woods roads heading for town. We soon saw the smoke of a sawmill operation, and then the town came in sight.

Norm Anderson, a forest ranger I'd met at headquarters in Springerville, had photographed Sioux and me next to the Madonna of the Trail statue near the post office. I'd noticed that he used a four-by-five press camera but I hadn't realized he was taking the picture for a newspaper. A Phoenix paper, the *Arizona Republic,* had carried the picture that day and I found that I was recognized in McNary.

The small hospital in McNary prescribed a week of antibiotic treatment for my back trouble, so I made arrangements at the motel in the center of town. A young horseman, Ruben Douros, suggested that I park Sioux in his pasture which was only a hundred yards from my room.

Sioux's feet were hard and dry, the result of so much desert travel; Ruben's pasture was lush, green and almost marshy in places. It was shaded with the ever-present ponderosa pines and I was delighted to give Sioux a much needed foot treatment on the wet, soft ground. I had no idea that I was to take her into broken lava country a short twenty miles from McNary, where her hard feet would have been to her advantage.

The week in town was uneventful. The surrounding mountain peaks were a handsome setting for the small town but the continual smell of woodsmoke from the mill was at times unpleasant. All business on the reservation is operated

320

through a lease from the Apaches, who appear to be dis-interested in running such operations; most of the sawmill labor is done by Negroes, who have been the main labor force here for a good many years.

I don't know whether the usual Apache has a built-in poker face or whether he still bears a grudge against the whites. I tried nodding in a friendly manner at those I met on the street; I smiled at the small children, but the only reaction I ever got was a flat, blank stare.

When we left McNary at the end of the week, Sioux was fresh and full of pep. Ruben Douros, the young man who had pastured her for me, rode with me as far as Indian Pine on his sorrel quarter horse. At one point we pulled aside to watch a large herd of cattle pass. They were being driven by five or six Apaches, evidently from the winter pasture to higher summer grazing ground.

Prior to leaving home, I'd written to my old friend Walt Drye in Winslow, but my wife had told me by phone that the letter had been returned stamped "unknown." I decided now to cut north to Winslow to make some inquiries as to his possible whereabouts. This meant I'd have to leave the pine country sooner than I'd hoped.

Shortly after I left Show Low, a town named for a legendary card game, I noticed a change in the landscape. The vegetation was still coniferous, but beneath the light pine-needle covering a sort of broken lava replaced the turf. With the exception of about four miles of paved road on either side of the small town of Heber, we were to travel dirt roads for the remainder of the distance to Winslow — roughly a hundred miles. Ordinarily we both would have been delighted to get away from pavement of any sort, but now Sioux's feet were soft and flexible and I began to notice her flinching slightly when she hit the ground with her left front foot. I stopped to check her a number of times and

321

finally decided that she'd bruised the sole of her hoof, or the frog. On level going she was all right, since the contact with the ground was confined to the outside wall of her hoof, but in coarse gravel or the broken lava a limp was detectable. I hoped it would work itself out and to some extent it did become less noticeable as the day wore on. Certainly we added considerably to our mileage as we zigzagged about in our attempt to avoid rough surfaces. This took much of the pleasure out of some wonderful country, since I was continually uneasy about riding a sore-footed horse. At times rough gravel stretches were unavoidable, and then I dismounted and led her; when this happened we were both sore-footed.

We stopped one night at a small Mormon settlement where the fine old patriarch who ran the little general store suggested pouring a little turpentine into the touchy hoof. I was unable to get any turpentine until later and it didn't seem to help when I did.

By now my own physical ailments seemed to have run their course and I would have liked to take my original route along the Mogollon Rim. But Sioux's troubles made it out of the question, so I decided we'd call a halt at Winslow. From there it would have been another hundred and thirty miles to the Grand Canyon and to have put the little mare through a week of discomfort merely to humor myself was out of the question. I'd gladly have stopped where we were except that we were in the middle of nowhere.

At Heber our dirt road crossed a highway and I got a small bottle of turpentine at the general store. I also found a telephone and came to the definite decision to call my home and set the wheels in motion for us to be picked up in Winslow. I would be two days reaching Winslow, so while I waited there for the car and trailer to drive out from Rhode Island I could devote myself to looking for Walt Drye.

322

In this high-altitude Arizona pine country, the clarity of
the air is probably the most striking feature. Ordinarily,
when painting an outdoor landscape, intense blues would
never be used near the horizon for the reason that atmos-
pheric haze softens and lightens the color of the sky. In this
part of Arizona there is so little haze that the blues are
almost as bright at the skyline as they are straight overhead. I had long ago put away that old line about "where the
skies are bluer" as poetic nonsense; now a reappraisal was
in order. These skies are so blue that I wouldn't have the
nerve to paint them the way they look.

Wildlife abounds in the mountains. Elk have been successfully restocked, deer are plentiful and the first badger
I'd ever seen in the wild came bustling up the middle of the
track one day.

Nearing the Chevelon Canyon country, I noticed a large
elk, dead on the side of the road. I assumed Sioux had also
seen it, and that she was unimpressed. I was mistaken. The
wind was with us and she must have been looking elsewhere.
Fifteen feet from the body of the elk she got a whiff, and
regardless of any sore foot, she almost unloaded me on the
spot. She must have cleared ten feet in one jump and landed
facing the elk, snorting. Once downwind, the aroma was
gamey enough that I didn't linger to investigate the cause of
death; we moved on.

A steep road turns and clings to the wall of Chevelon
Canyon. The wall drops swiftly to the creek below, a clear,
cold mountain stream that flows northerly to empty at
length into the Little Colorado. It was to be our last camp,
and the rock pinnacles, pines and lush grass made it one of
the most beautiful. Since leaving Heber, we hadn't seen a
sign of a human, nor would we the following day. We
crossed the tiny bridge (although we could as easily have

323

used the old ford) ; I turned Sioux upstream to a heavily grassed, level area where she could eat and drink her fill.

In 1882, units of the 6th Cavalry had almost walked into an Apache ambush that was set for them in the rocky walls of Chevelon Canyon; the Apaches, secreted in the rocky walls, had hoped the cavalry would ride on down to the creek bottom and be at the mercy of their fire from above. Sharp-eyed government scouts had spotted the ambush in the nick of time and the cavalry troopers, dismounted and firing down on the Indians from the rim of the canyon, had reversed the situation to the extent that the battle marked one of the death throes of the Apache tribe.

Now, almost a century later, the canyon was shrouded in silence. I sat for a long while watching the lengthening shadows drive the sunlight up the canyon wall while Sioux grazed along the bank of the stream. With the dark it became quite cold and I built up a larger fire than usual, then brought Sioux up near my bedroll for the night. I crawled halfway into my sleeping bag and watched the dying fire for a long time, attempting, I guess, to squeeze all I could out of the final night. Sioux's head drooped sleepily, her eyes no longer reflecting the firelight, and the last thing I recall after she lay down was trying to stay awake to listen to a coyote chorus high on the top of the canyon.

When the first rays of the sun poked down at us, I found that a light skim of ice made the grass at the edge of the creek crackle under our feet. The chill was short-lived; by the time Sioux and I had breakfasted, the temperature was rising rapidly.

A steep, twisting climb took us up out of the canyon and canceled any hopes I'd entertained of returning by this route with the car and trailer. The hairpin turns and loose gravel surface didn't look promising for an automobile hauling a

324

horse trailer, much as I would have enjoyed returning through these same mountains.

After we passed the top level, the descent was rapid. As always with the lowering elevation, pines changed to cedar and juniper and gradually these began to thin out. At one of the smaller canyons we came to one of many old crossings which mark the route taken by the Mormon people on their trek to Utah.

Once out of the hills, the land leveled off and became extremely arid. Up ahead to our left Chevelon Butte loomed, and as the day progressed it moved alongside and then slowly dropped off to our rear. A hot dry wind was blowing, and the heat (which became oppressive) was only partially relieved by the wind. The road had been graded quite recently and was hard packed and smooth, a help to Sioux's tender foot. About noon we were becoming rather thirsty; between us we finished off the water in my canteen.

The road shimmered on, seemingly endless, and I found myself straining to see some indication of a city ahead. The land became ever drier and more barren; nothing showed ahead, although visibility extended for miles. A herd of cattle came up to our left and some of them stood near what looked to be an earth water tank. I cut over toward them and, happily, found that there was water at the bottom. It was scummy and green around the edge, and the cattle had not been particularly careful as to hygiene, but Sioux was thirsty enough to drink after wading far in from the muddy edge. I decided to pass it up but had it not been for a passing Navajo Indian I would have been sorry.

We'd gone on probably an hour from the water tank, and I was beginning to feel the thirst, when the first sign of human life we had had all day appeared in the form of a pickup truck. The driver, a Navajo whom I'd met a couple of days before in Heber, had in the back of his truck a number of his children and several gallon jugs of water. He stopped and asked if I didn't need water, and I agreed that I certainly did, whereupon he filled my canteen and then offered me one of the jugs for a drink. He was rather shy and seemed embarrassed by my voluble thanks, but under the circumstances my effusiveness was justifiable.

Without the passing of this kind Indian, a bad day would have been infinitely worse. Even with his water, I was extremely thirsty by late afternoon, probably due to the hot wind, and I could guess that Sioux felt the same way. There had been no grazing at all after we left the mountains — I had no idea what the cattle we'd seen found to exist on — and Sioux began to tire in the last ten miles. After she stumbled badly once, I got off and led her for perhaps five of the remaining miles.

We came to some strange stone formations, reddish slabs, some of them sitting on legs like low tables. At another time I'd have ridden over for a closer look and probably photographed them, but now I was only interested in getting to Winslow and water.

At last, late in the day, we came to a bridge that crossed a tributary of the Little Colorado River. The road swung in a westerly curve and there, seven miles ahead, lay Winslow. It was an endless seven miles and dusk was falling as we got to the outskirts of town.

10.

Winslow is a good-sized place stretching for some distance along either side of Route 66. Parallel to the highway is a large railroad yard, and I found on approaching it that I had to enter a heavily trafficked underpass to get to the main part of town. The highway surface was slick concrete, the underpass was narrow, and it was nearly dark. All I could do was cross my fingers and go. We made it safely and emerged to find the town well along on a lively Saturday night. I had no idea which way to head, except out of where I was.

Leading Sioux across the busy thoroughfare, I crossed a block or so to a less traveled street and turned west, staying on the sidewalk. Two men standing on the watered green lawn of some kind of clubhouse accosted me and expressed their curiosity. They were well lubricated and I really didn't want to talk, but standing there gave Sioux a chance to graze on their lawn. I asked their advice about escaping the crowds and they decided then and there to take me in tow and drive me around until they found a motel. Leaving Sioux hungrily chomping on the lawn, I got in their pickup and we made the rounds.

We stopped at a row of motel units several blocks from where I'd left Sioux, and my helpful friends parked while I approached the office. I gave the proprietor my standard introduction and he looked at me coldly.

"We don't want any horses here." He looked haughtily down his nose at me.

"In that case," I snapped testily, "I won't waste any more of your time or mine."

Halfway down the block, a skinny, bespectacled little man greeted my request with even less enthusiasm than the first.

By my third rejection, I was ready to fight. Sorely tempted to collect Sioux and tell this crummy little railroad town to go to hell on a handcar, I tried one last time. My two jovial buddies in the pickup were the only people I'd met so far who were not downright hostile, and finding a place to pull in for the night was becoming a sizable problem.

The Red Hills Motel was the last one I intended to try. I walked into the office with shoulders hunched and jaw stuck out, ready to treat Winslow, Arizona, to some spectacular and scathing billingsgate.

"Why, of course," said the friendly owner as soon as I'd made a truculent request for a room and a place to tie my horse. "You just bring her right down here and hitch her next to your room. We're happy to have her."

Smiling with relief, I hustled back to the pickup, and in a matter of moments I had picked up Sioux and left my escorts with my blessing to continue their Saturday night festivities.

It took only a few minutes to lead Sioux the few blocks to the motel but by the time I got there a large bucket of water was waiting for her. Norma Blumlein was standing by the door with a bag of carrots.

A call to Rhode Island gave me the information that the

328

trailer would be unable to leave until Monday morning; this meant that I had the largest part of the week to wait in Winslow. I made an additional stop at the sheriff's office to ask where I could best quarter myself and a horse for what would be a week's stay. By now I seemed to have hit a string of pleasant people; the deputy on duty made several calls on my behalf and came up with a man named Johnson who had a string of horses a mile or two out of town and would be glad to put Sioux up for me. Fortunately, since I would be obliged to walk to and from the stable, there was a motel on the same end of town. I'd rather have stayed at the Red Hills Motel where I'd been so well received, but there was no grass there at all and I could see that the prolonged visit of a horse would have been an imposition.

Inquiries at the sheriff's office turned up nothing on Walt Drye; however, Norma Blumlein knew of the family. She thought the Drye ranch was some distance from Winslow but wasn't certain about the direction.

Early the next morning I tried to find some sort of grazing for Sioux, with little luck. A small patch of grass next to a railroad track on examination proved to be full of splintered glass where the local winos had bounced their empty bottles off a brick wall. Taking advantage of the quiet of Sunday morning, I headed east through town to its outskirts. I stopped at the motel to unload my personal gear before riding out to the Johnsons' and went into the office to register.

"What are you going to do with the horse?" came a somewhat cautious question before the key was surrendered.

"I've already arranged to take her out to the Johnsons' place as soon as I unload," I replied, by now resigned to a certain lack of enthusiasm where horses were concerned.

As soon as I explained that I had other plans for the horse, my host became his commercially affable self and I

329

transferred my belongings to the room. Actually I had been incredibly lucky where motels were concerned. From various conversations I learned that rodeo people often are unable to park at motor hotels with their animals in trailers. A fairly new development, on the other hand, is a chain of motels with stables attached, specifically designed for people traveling the horse-show and rodeo circuit. The only explanation for my experience that comes to mind is that I stayed away from heavily traveled routes as much as possible and people were generally a lot friendlier in small towns and along lightly traveled roads than on a main thoroughfare.

However, the Johnsons' place was on Route 66 and it hadn't seared *their* dispositions. They put Sioux in a spacious pen, cleared off a saddle rack for my saddle and invited me in for coffee. I asked them about Walt Drye, but while they'd heard of him, they didn't know where he was located.

"One thing you'll have to get done before you haul your mare out of the state by trailer is a brand inspection," Bud Johnson commented. "Sid Griffin is the brand inspector. I'll see him tomorrow and ask him to stop by and give you an inspection slip so you won't have any trouble."

"I'm glad you mentioned it," I said. "It's something I wouldn't have known anything about."

"Come to think of it," Bud said, "Sid Griffin knows every stockman in this part of the country. Maybe he'd know Walt Drye."

It seemed the best suggestion yet and I decided to give it a try. Sid was located some twenty-odd miles west of Winslow toward Flagstaff, so a phone call seemed the easiest way to settle it. I succeeded in reaching his wife and explained my problem to her.

"Why sure," came her answer. "Walt Drye's place is out at Canyon Padre – just a few miles west of Two Guns. I don't think he has a phone out at the ranch but I think you could contact his wife at the Twin Arrows Trading Post."

Having exhausted the police, the post office and everyone else that I'd talked to, I'd almost given up hope of making the contact. Now if this was the right Walt Drye, he was forty miles west of where I'd been looking. I called the Twin Arrows and asked if a Ruth Drye was there. She was, and came to the phone.

"Do you know a Walter B. Drye, formerly in the 7th Cavalry?" I asked.

"I think so," Ruth answered calmly. "I'm married to him."

"In that case," I laughed, "would you tell him that T. B. Powell is in Winslow on horseback? I'll be here for about five days and I'd sure be happy if you two could drive up and have dinner with me."

"Well," Ruth said, "I'll tell him. He's out working cattle today and I think it'll be late before he finishes, but maybe tomorrow. Give me the phone number where you are and I'll have him call you."

I gave Ruth the number and sat back to await results. I had until Friday to wait for the trailer, with nothing to do but eat, sleep and make a daily visit to Sioux's quarters with some hoof dressing that I thought might help work out the soreness in her foot.

Early the next day the room phone rang and I picked it up with the customary hello.

"T.B.?" came a familiar voice from the past.

"It sure as hell is, Walter B.," I said, using an old army nickname that had distinguished him from Walter Sullivan, our Boston Irishman. "What I want to know is whether you can still whistle the 'Garry Owen.'" George Custer's 7th Cavalry Regimental marching air, an old Irish drinking

331

song, was a lively tune not at all easy to whistle, but Walt had rendered it often in the four years we'd spent together.

His soft laugh rolled back the years and without reminiscing further he announced that he'd be around with his pickup to haul Sioux and me out to his ranch. I could leave a note for Tom Atkinson, a young man from Boston who had already left with my car and trailer, telling him where to find me; nothing remained but to await Walt's arrival.

This Arizona cowboy had been one of the most unfailingly cheerful and good-natured men I'd ever known. From our days on the border in the horse cavalry to the more serious life in the Pacific Islands, I'd never seen him lose his complacent, calm exterior — and as we were in the same rifle platoon throughout, I'd certainly had ample opportunity. Most of us had been kids in those days, still wet behind the ears; Walt was a few years older with a touch of gray over the temples. Judging by my own reaction to juvenile behavior today, he must at times have been irritated by our foolishness. If he was he never showed it, but how he escaped without ulcers I don't know.

Seated in the restaurant across from my room, I'd just finished a cup of coffee when a green Ford pickup swung in and parked. Under the wide sweep of his summer straw sombrero, the hair was nearly white, but I recognized the warm, genuine twinkle of the smile. Walter B. stepped out of the Ford as I came out of the restaurant — and it was yesterday. He'd shaved off the big black moustache that many of us had cultivated in the islands, he was dressed in high-heeled boots and a big hat, but otherwise he was unchanged. The outdoor, active life of a cattle rancher had treated Walt kindly, and he looked scarcely older than he did in 1945.

It was twenty-one years since we'd parted in Manila; my slovenly correspondence habits had allowed a complete loss of contact, but somehow we picked up as though we'd seen each other a day before. For some reason I don't completely understand, civilian friendships which have been broken off by separation usually require a rather formal reintroduction and a series of witless questions about wives, children and employment. Friendships born of foxhole relations don't seem to suffer from time lapses. It must have something to do with the sharing of danger that wipes away anything approaching protocol.

After I had left a note for Tom Atkinson with the motel man, we drove out to the Johnsons' place and loaded Sioux in the back of the pickup. A forty-mile drive toward Flagstaff brought us to the Twin Arrows Trading Post, a large tourist gift shop on Route 66. There, a ranch road led south, then west for a couple of miles to Walt's ranch.

A recently built, modern, one-story ranch house occupied the space south of the drive; a rugged frame barn stood opposite, along with the heavy-timbered corrals found in this part of the country. Two bays, a paint and a palomino horse were near the corrals; Sioux nickered her greetings as we backed the pickup over to a loading chute where she could disembark.

Walt and Ruth had a daughter, newly married, living in Greer, Arizona; I shortly cluttered her cheerful, sunny bedroom with my stained gear. Finding that I'd camped within three miles of her home in Greer, I realized I'd probably come within a whisker of passing Ruth and Walt on one of their recent visits. Ruth arrived soon after we did and I found it hard to believe her old enough to have a married daughter. She was completely unpretentious and as easygoing as Walt, and she had the ability to return from the Twin Arrows in street dress, turn into a housewife while cooking dinner, then, in boots and denims, climb on a horse and work cattle with the best of men. I promised her we wouldn't drive her out of the house with stories of World War II — but I lied. In four days we covered everything from Fort Riley, Kansas, to Manila.

"I hope you won't let me keep you from anything you need to do," I told Walt early in the visit. "I'm not a good cowhand, but I'm cheap."

"O.K.," Walt laughed. "We've got to drive the herd up to the summer pasture Thursday. We'll put you to work."

Most of the harder work had been completed just before I landed; calves had been branded and inoculated. All that remained was moving a few portable metal water tanks and the cattle themselves.

Walt's mother and father lived at the old home ranch on the other side of the highway. They'd driven from Texas to this country with everything they owned in a wagon, and had started the hard way with a homestead. Hard work, sweat and tears had produced the two fine ranches on either side of the road; once in the early years, fire had wiped out their home and all their possessions. Probably Walt's cheerful reaction to anything that came along was the direct result of being bred of this fine old couple, to whom fire, drought and struggle were nothing more than expected obstacles.

One day we took Walt's pickup and his father's to move a couple of the water tanks. Walt drove the lead pickup while I followed with his father in the other. I mentioned the high regard Walt had been held in by his army friends and the old man laughed.

"Wal, I tried to raise the boys right," he admitted. "If I ever did anything myself in the old hard days that I wasn't rightly proud of, I never let them catch me doin' it."

Sid Griffin, the brand inspector, came over to the ranch one evening and, after making out the slip for Sioux, sat down in the kitchen where we congregated over coffee. When

334

the current shortage of ranch help was brought up, Sid became serious.

"I honestly don't know what all the ranchers are going to do," he said. "The kids today don't want to go far enough out of town to cowboy. Where are the ranch hands going to come from?"

"I guess they're going to have to do what I did." Walt's eyes twinkled. "Marry one."

The next day I found that his remark was absolutely true. As we saddled up the horses and started gathering the cows and calves from the home ranch pastures, Ruth was the equal of any man — certainly superior to me. She could spin her horse and cut a bunch-quitting calf back into the herd while I was gathering my reins; she and Walt did the bulk of the cutting and working while I dawdled along in the rear keeping the drags moving.

One large bull was reluctant to leave the home grounds and Walt went after him. I sat my horse watching him tearing over rough ground in a hard run, twisting and wheeling his horse to counteract the moves of the bull. He rode with the easy grace of many years of practice; having won a contest of wills with the bull, he followed him up to the end of the herd at an easy swinging trot, his hips and shoulders flexing to the horse's gait with effortless ease.

"How come you never learned to ride the army seat?" I hollered across the drags at him. (Toward the end, the horse cavalry had adapted the Italian forward seat, which had involved sitting well forward in the saddle and posting to the trot. It had not been popular with the old-time cavalry-men or the cowboys who sat farther back and stayed with a trotting horse instead of rising up and down.)

"I don't know," Walt yelled back. "Seems a shame, the army spending all that money trying to teach me."

Ruth was riding swing at the moment and we sneaked in

335

a little more reminiscing. When we took cavalry training at Fort Riley everyone started at the beginning and was placed on a horse to be led around the corral by a soldier on foot. Turk Greenough was one of the recruits; if I'm not mistaken, he was at the same time the world's champion bronc rider. I suspect that even the horse was amused at the sight of Turk being led around like a kid in a pony ring.

"What do you bet Turk Greenough never learned to do it the right way either," Walt said.

The day was perfect, neither hot nor cold, and as the herd became loosely bunched, we headed them south to where the land began its rise to the mountains. The open flat country was left behind and we worked on into juniper and cedar country, with occasional side forays to pick up a few head that had been at the south end of the pasture when we started. When we came to a fence Walt rode up beyond the point and opened the gate, then sat his horse to one side making the count as Ruth and I funneled them through. The red and white color of Hereford cattle against the green background of the cedar country would make me partial to Herefords purely for aesthetic reasons. Fortunately I'd brought my camera with color transparencies and I got a number of shots of Walt and Ruth in action. Beef cattle are driven fast only in Hollywood, since beef is valued by the pound. To prevent unnecessary loss of weight cattle are moved slowly, nipping at the grass as they walk; with careful handling they should arrive at their destination in as good condition as when they left, if not better.

"We'll take a trail that cuts west pretty quick," Walt said, riding over to where his voice would carry over the bawl of the cattle. "The trail drops into Canyon Padre and we can push them right up the floor of the canyon almost to where we're headed."

336

"After you, Alphonse," I agreed, and shortly we turned into a rocky defile that led over a steep slope into the canyon.

The rocks were loose and rolling, the grade became more acute, and the only comforting feature of the terrain was the trees, which would have broken the fall if a horse slipped.

"Aren't you using the word trail a little freely?" I asked Walt when we'd finally reached the bottom and congregated at the rear of the herd. "If this is what you call a trail, I'd hate like hell to follow you cross-crountry."

"It saves a lot of trouble this way, " Walt said, grinning at my discomfiture. "Now all we have to do is follow the cows up the canyon. They can't go anyplace but straight ahead."

Canyon Padre, dry at the moment, had evidently seen a great deal of water at times. Frequently we were forced to dismount and pull our horses under tangled trees and through brush piles that had been jammed up by walls of water during cloudbursts. Gradually the canyon floor broadened and rose, and we came out into open, grassy, wooded country.

Toward the end of the day, the little calves began to tire and hang back. Their bawls caused the mother cows to want to turn back and nurse them, and frequently a calf would try to nurse as he walked alongside his mother. More pushing was required to keep them moving by now and my ineffectual whistles and yells were falling on deaf ears. Elizabeth Pratt, a friend of ours in Rhode Island, runs a telephone answering service and a secretarial office. Using only her tongue and teeth, she's capable of producing the shrillest, sharpest whistle I've ever heard. It would be the pride of any cowboy and I thought with envy and even a little resentment about the waste of such a talent as I attempted to move cattle with my weak little tweet.

When at last we reached a water tank with the by-now

weary and stubborn cattle, Walt signaled that this was the place and we turned the happy horses toward home. Before we left, we'd driven a pickup about ten miles up the ranch road and left it. Now by cutting across, we could ride out to where we'd parked, unsaddle the horses and drive home. The horses would come in cross-country by themselves, making everything easier for all of us. On the way up with the cattle Walt had pointed out the spot where a mountain lion had killed a mule deer and dragged the carcass under a juniper sometime during the winter. Unconcerned with wall trophies, the lion had left a handsome rack of antlers that now lay at the base of the tree, still attached to the skull. When we passed them on the way back, I was unable to resist picking them up, but the struggle I had carrying them horseback through the junipers made me wonder how the deer had been able to maneuver himself. I finally evolved a sideways technique and I decided the deer must have done the same thing to get through the dense foliage with his branching headgear.

When we reached the truck and turned the horses loose, they lined out in a stiff trot. We were hardly more than seated at the dinner table when they arrived home and swung around to the back gate of the corral to be fed. Sioux no longer seemed to be having trouble with her foot but to be on the safe side I'd used Ol' Paint, a roping horse that had formerly belonged to Ruth's brother. He was no longer young but he made up for his age with "cow savvy," and I'd been amused toward the end of the day when the younger calves were tired and slow and Ol' Paint had walked up behind them to boost them along with his nose.

What had probably been another day's work to Ruth and Walt had been a picnic to me. Anything after the visit with the Dryes would be an anticlimax. The cattle business has its drawbacks and headaches just like any other way of life, but there still seems to be an air of freedom and independence that clings to it. Certainly it's been regulated to some extent and maybe it will become more so. One rancher I met owns land that starts on the flat, rises gradually to higher country, then goes on to government-leased forest land in the high ponderosa pines. The government has a grand plan whereby the rancher is requested to rotate his stock on three quarters of the total pasture each year, leaving one quarter unused annually. At the end of four years, the entire range thus would have had a year's rest, all of which sounds feasible until you recall that a ranch is rarely one flat rectangle with the same weather conditions throughout. As the rancher in question put it, "How in hell do they expect me to rotate according to their plan when in December I have three inches of snow down at the home ranch and three feet of snow up in the pine country?"

Walt and I probably drove Ruth out of her mind with our constant return to the war years. We tried not to, but somehow we kept coming around to them in our conversation. Walt mentioned once that things he'd remembered had become so vague to him that he began to think they were imagined. I'd had similar thoughts and we were able to verify a number of happenings for each other.

We agreed that "Jeep" Luerez had indeed sat on a Japanese land mine to rest, and that when he'd had this carelessness pointed out to him he had crabwalked away not even daring to straighten up until he was well away from the gadget.

We also recalled the time when Billy Pratt had shared a deep, yet tiny, three-man foxhole with two friends, "King" Cole and me. Billy, a Montana cowboy, was the possessor of a rather large nose and was also an expert at cigarette rolling. We'd been pinned on a Luzon hillside for some days, subjected to heavy mortar fire, and were unable to smoke at night because of the glow of the cigarettes. We were out of cigarettes anyway, but we did have the remains of a can of Prince Albert pipe tobacco and some cigarette papers. Billy was elected to roll the last cigarette before dark; this was to be passed around the foxhole for the last few drags. Soon we heard Billy swear.

"I can't find the dam' cigarette papers," he complained, "an' they were right under my nose a minute ago."

"Hell, Billy," said Cole dryly, staring pointedly at his large nose, "they must be closer than that. The hole ain't that big."

The time came, as it had to, when a familiar green Rambler station wagon jolted down the ranch road hauling its two-horse trailer behind. The driver, Tom Atkinson, whom I had never met, was a friend of a friend. Walt and I stepped out of his back door as Tom emerged from the car and stretched.

"This is a hell of a long way to drive just to meet some stranger," he said as we shook hands all around.

It was indeed and I didn't envy him his long drive with the empty trailer; for some reason unknown to me they haul much more easily when they are loaded. But since we were so close to the Grand Canyon, it seemed logical to at least drive up and take a look.

I'd failed in my original objective of reaching the Grand Canyon by horse because of Sioux's stone-bruised hoof, but the real climax of my trek had been finding Walt. I could have turned straight home from his ranch with no regrets.

We said our goodbyes to Ruth and Walt after loading Sioux in the trailer, and I promised myself not to allow another twenty years to slide by before seeing them again. We pulled out of the ranch road headed toward Flagstaff, then cut north; and in a short time we entered the gates to the Grand Canyon National Park.

The glowing descriptions of the Grand Canyon are, I think, not overdone. Because of our excessive use of superlatives in everyday speech, language is no longer adequate to describe something of this nature. I'd expected the canyon to be big, yawning and colorful, but no photograph or description had really prepared me for the shock of approaching this monstrous cleft in the earth's surface.

Even Sioux was visibly impressed. I'd ridden her up from the camp area to complete the photographic record of our trip, and she'd casually gone along to within about fifteen feet of the brink. There she stopped short, threw up her head with a snap and scanned the vast sweep from one side to the other. Her ears flicked straight up, then slanted from right to left; throughout the entire photographic session with Tom Atkinson wielding my camera, she never once took her eyes from the edge. She was no more overwhelmed than Tom and I. Looking into the fathomless depths is somehow as ego shrinking as standing on a dark hill trying to visualize the universe on a starry night.

This was the first weekend of the tourist season and the camp area was full to overflowing. I'd been so spoiled by having national parks and forests all to myself that I felt suddenly and uncomfortably hemmed in. We had a long drive ahead — back through Texas to collect Conejo from her quiet aerie in the Davis Mountains — and it had been more than seven months since I'd seen my family. The itchy foot of the hobo had been scratched. . . .

One evening some months earlier I'd stood talking with a shriveled old man in an east Texas town. He'd asked all the questions that I'd come to expect as to daily mileage, horseshoeing, feed and destination. With each answer he'd shifted his chew of tobacco from one cheek to the other and several times he punctuated our talk with a brownish jet of tobacco

343

juice. When he had questioned me to his apparent satisfaction, the old man squinted solemnly at me for several wordless moments.

"Don't yew believe," he asked at length, his leathery poker face masking any trace of humor, "that it'd a bin a whole lot easier an' cheaper if you wuz to gone an' got yew one of them li'l bitty ol' auto-*mo*-biles?"

Momentarily stuck for a reply, I started to laugh, then told him that he was about right but that if I had, I wouldn't have met him.

The ancient, tobacco-stained mouth cracked wide into a toothless grin. He swung a playful paw at me and hobbled stiffly away, shaking his head.

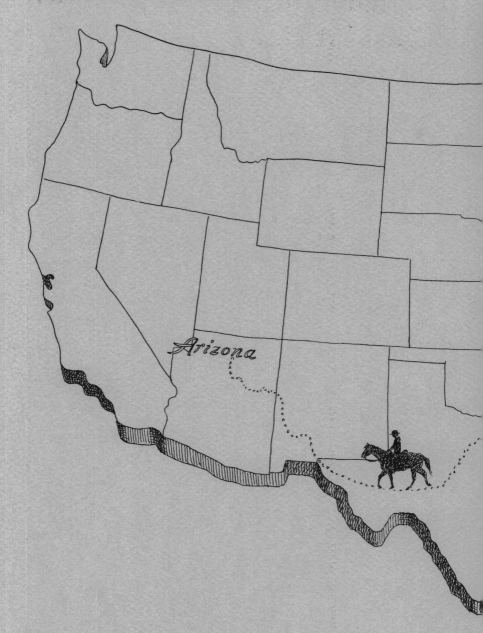

Arizona